FESTIVAL ICO...
THE CHRISTIA...

Dedicated

to the memory of my parents

Samuel Baggley
1900–1979

Edna Baggley
1905–1997

Festival Icons

FOR THE

Christian Year

JOHN BAGGLEY

MOWBRAY

By the same author:

Doors of Perception: Icons and Their Spiritual Significance
Mowbray, London (1987) and St Vladimir's Seminary Press, New York (1995)

Mowbray
A Cassell imprint
Wellington House
125 Strand
London WC2R 0BB

First published 2000

British Library Cataloguing in Publication Data
A catalogue record for this book is available from the British Library

ISBN 0-264-67487-1 (hardback)
       0-264-67488-X (paperback)

Designed and typeset by Kenneth Burnley, Wirral, Cheshire
Printed and bound in Great Britain by The Bath Press, Bath

Contents

CONTENTS

List of Plates

Acknowledgements

This book has had a long gestation period. The idea developed out of the experience of leading a number of retreats based on icons, and giving talks to groups who had expressed an interest in icons. During the past ten years several people have had a significant influence on the work that has eventually taken shape in this book, and I would like to express my gratitude to them. Jill Storer has stimulated further reading and research, and has generously shared her interest in the festival icons. During my time at St Mary's College, Oscott, Fr David McLoughlin encouraged me to persevere with the work and to seek publication. Ruth McCurry at Cassell was keen to take the work on and has been both encouraging and also tolerant of my difficulties in completing the work.

To Richard Temple I am indebted not only for the use of illustrations from the Temple Gallery, but for his friendship and his stimulus to my interest in the subject. Similarly, to Bishop Kallistos Ware I am indebted for permission to use texts which he and Mother Mary translated and published in *The Festal Menaion* and *The Lenten Triodion*, and for his interest in this undertaking. I must express my thanks to Fr Pachomius of the Holy Transfiguration Monastery, Brookline, for permission to use quotations from the Monastery's translation of texts in *The Pentecostarion*, and to Baron José de Vinck for permission to quote from his translation of texts published in *Byzantine Daily Worship*. I have been glad to have access to two unpublished research theses: Elizabeth Briere's Oxford University Ph.D. thesis on *Scripture in Hymnography – A Study in Some Feasts of the Orthodox Church* (1982), and Jill Storer's Birmingham University M. Litt. thesis on *The Anastasis in Byzantine Iconography* (1986). I am grateful to Ted Bazil of St Vladimir's Seminary Press for permission to use the illustration of Fr Gregory Kroug's icon of the *Anastasis*.

I am grateful to Monsignor Patrick McKinney, the former Rector of St Mary's College, Oscott, for permission to devote a lot of time to this work during my studies at Oscott, to Fr Timothy Ford for theological advice, and to Fr Simon Stephens for help with questions of colour. Three icon painters have each in different ways stimulated my interest and understanding: Mariamna Fortounatto, the Revd Brian Bessant, and Peter Murphy. A number of friends have read sections of the text at various stages in its development, and made valuable comments; these include Marney Cordingley, the Revd Anthony de Vere, Marie Lewis and Professor Richard Marks. In the latter stages of preparing the book for publication I have been particularly grateful to Mariamna Fortounatto and to Jill and Kenneth Storer for their generosity in undertaking a thorough examination of the text. Obviously, I accept responsibility for any errors that remain in the book. In addition to these specific acknowledgements, I am indebted to a large number of people whose interest and questions have been a stimulus to me over the years.

I am also grateful to the following for granting permission to reproduce illustrations in this book: The Temple Gallery, London (Plates 1, 3, 4, 5, 7, 9, 14, 15, 16, 18, 20, 21, 23, 24); State Russian Museum, St Petersburg and The Bridgeman Art Library, London (Plate 6); The Museum of Art, Novgorod, Russia and The Bridgeman Art Library, London (Plates 10 and 13); The Tretyakov Gallery, Moscow (Plate 11); The British Museum (Plate 12); The Mirozhsky Monastery, Pskov (Plate 17); Fr Andrew Tregubov and St Vladimir's Seminary Press, Crestwood, New York (Plate 19); The Tretyakov Gallery, Moscow and The Bridgeman Art Library, London (Plate 22).

A Note on Stylistic Conventions

Most biblical quotations are taken from the Revised Standard Version of the Bible; in other cases abbreviations indicate the source: AV for the Authorized Version, Knox for the 1946 translation by Monsignor Ronald Knox, NEB for the 1961 New English Bible, and NJB for the 1990 New Jerusalem Bible. The numbering of the Psalms is a difficulty: in the Orthodox Church and the Catholic Church the standard source is the Greek text of the Septuagint translation of the Old Testament, while Churches influenced by the Reformation have used the Hebrew text. I use the Hebrew numbering as in the RSV, with the Greek Psalm number in square brackets where there is a discrepancy.

The main biblical readings used at the Orthodox feasts are normally listed at the end of each chapter. It should be remembered, however, that these do not give the full impression of the Scripture applied to the feast, since many shorter texts also have a place and may be crucial to the significance of the feast.

Since there is a close relationship between icons and the texts of the feast, the terms 'liturgy' and 'liturgical' will occur frequently in this book. For the sake of clarity I have used the convention 'Divine Liturgy' to refer to the Eucharist, while 'liturgy' and 'liturgical' may refer to the full range of ritual observance, including services such as Mattins and Vespers.

The translations of the liturgical texts cited in this book have been drawn from different sources, and in using them I have retained the stylistic conventions of the translators. The 'Kontakion'* for each feast is normally cited and provides a summary particularly relevant to the icon of the feast. The Greek word 'hades' has the sense of the place of the dead, a place of waiting and loss rather than punishment, which does not carry the implications of torment associated with the English word 'hell'. In certain homilies and liturgical texts this concept of hades is personified, and his person is represented in some of the Resurrection icons. In my own writing I use 'hades' for the place or state of the departed, and '*Hades*' for the personification; it should be noted however that the translations of the liturgical texts do not follow the same convention, generally using 'Hades' for both the place and the personification, and in some cases the English term 'Hell' which may carry inappropriate associations.

Sources of quotations are given in the Notes on page 167, and an asterisk in the text (*) indicates that further information on a word can be found in the Glossary (page 174).

❧ 1 ❧

Introduction

You alone are made in the likeness of that nature which surpasses all understanding, the image of incorruptible beauty, the impression of true divinity, the receptacle of blessed life, seal of true light. You will become what he is by looking at him. By imitating him who shines within you, his gleam is reflected by your purity.[1]

❧ I ❧

This book is intended to provide an opportunity to look at icons as focal points for reflection on the Christian revelation and on aspects of Christian discipleship which have been handed on to us by the Orthodox tradition of iconography. I write as a Western Christian who has come to value the Orthodox tradition of iconography, and I assume that many of the people who will use this book will come from a non-Orthodox background.

In order to aid the process of prayer and reflection in relation to icons it will be useful to look at aspects of the liturgical, theological and spiritual background to the painting and use of icons in the Orthodox Churches. Icons do not exist in a vacuum, but in a religious culture that has evolved over nearly 2,000 years. For nearly half that time the Western Church has lived in varying degrees of separation from the Churches of the East. In East and West different theological, political and artistic traditions have evolved, which make it difficult to attune to the attitudes and faith of people from other parts of Christendom. In recent years much has happened to reduce the levels of antagonism between Christians of different traditions and to create an enriched mutual understanding. For many Western Christians this has involved exploring the theological heritage of the Eastern Churches which has its roots in the early centuries of Christianity, in the years before any fundamental schism occurred between East

1

and West. The period of the great Church Councils in the fourth and fifth centuries, through to the resolution of the Iconoclast Controversy* in the ninth century, was a particularly creative period in the East for the Church's theology and art. Renewed interest in the Eastern patristic tradition has helped many people to move beyond the historic divisions within Christendom. In this process icons have had a significant place, often providing the first step whereby Western Christians have begun to enter into the world of the Eastern Churches.

During the last hundred years there has been a gradual and persistent growth of interest in icons. Within many Western nations there has been a diaspora of Orthodox Christians from Russia since the 1917 Revolution. This has created a living presence of the Orthodox Church in places like France, Great Britain and the United States; the presence of Orthodoxy in the Western world has become a welcome force to be reckoned with, and its influence has been felt within the World Council of Churches. The movement of people from Russia, the Ukraine, Greece and Serbia, has brought Christians of the Orthodox tradition to other parts of the world. Among Orthodox Christians who have made a significant contribution to the wider Christian world we can give thanks for people like Fr Sergei Bulgakov with the St Sergius Institute in Paris, Nikolai Berdyaev, Vladimir Lossky, Fr Lev Gillet, Metropolitan Anthony Bloom, Fr John Meyendorf, Fr Alexander Schmemann, Nicholas and Militza Zernov, Bishop Kallistos Ware and Metropolitan John Zizioulas.

Since the latter years of the nineteenth century the process of cleaning and restoring Byzantine and medieval Russian icons has been taking place continuously. To see the significance of this work we need to remember that icons were never intended for museums, but for churches where the smoke of incense and candles soon found a resting-place on the surface of icons. The varnish on the icons helped in the process of building up a layer of dirt which within 50 years could transform the colours of a freshly painted icon into a dull and obscure image that soon needed repainting. Over the original icon, the repainting would take place, generally repeating the same image, but with variations of style and detail and according to the stylistic fashions of the later painter and his times. An icon might be repainted many times in the course of several hundred years.

Between the days of the great Byzantine and Russian icon painters and the present day there stand various episodes of history which saw serious changes in the whole practice of icon painting. In the Greek and Balkan areas after the fall of Constantinople the influence of Western religious art permeated via Venetian and Italian influences. In Russia changes were implemented through the Westernizing policies of Peter the Great (1672–1725) who regarded all things Western as desirable, whether they were knowledge about medicine and ship-building or traditions of art and religion. Under Peter and his successors the Orthodox Church in Russia was subjected to the latest Western fashions in art, with an almost total lack of discernment in the light of Orthodox theological principles. Although the timing was different, both in the Greek–Balkan area and in Russia the Orthodox Churches suffered an erosion of their authentic traditions of spirituality and iconography. The rediscovery during the last hundred years of the great Byzantine and medieval Russian traditions of iconography has had a major impact within and beyond the Orthodox Churches.

Within Orthodoxy painters and scholars like Leonid Ouspensky from the Russian tradition and Photios Kontaglou in Greece have undertaken a fresh articulation of the tradition of iconography both in theory and practice. The errors and confusions of some of the theory and practice during the seventeenth to nineteenth centuries have been recognized; renewed interest in the principles behind the use of icons that were formulated during the Iconoclast Controversy of the eighth and ninth centuries has brought greater appreciation of the theology of the icon; and the discovery of the pre-Renaissance Orthodox icons has brought about great changes in iconographic styles. For Orthodox and non-Orthodox Christians alike, the dissemination of good quality prints of some of the truly great icons has had a big impact. It has brought some of the world's greatest icons into our own homes – albeit in the form of modern reproductions. Some may decry the use of block-mounted prints for devotional purposes at home or in church, but there must be millions of people whose awareness of icons and the potential use of icons in prayer has been transformed by the availability of good quality prints. At the same time the work of contemporary icon painters has been inspired by the rediscovery of the great Orthodox heritage of iconography. A process of restoration has taken place in the living tradition of icon painting that is analogous to the process of restoring an ancient icon: layers of accretions have had to be removed before the glory of the authentic tradition could be revealed.

Another change has taken place in the way icons are actually seen. Early in the twentieth century Prince Eugene Trubetskoi (1863–1920) reiterated the simple fact that icons were meant to be seen. Trubetskoi recognized that icons were intended to be 'holy images' rather than 'holy things'. Icons had not only been overlaid through the process of repainting, but had also been covered with precious metal covers and jewels; the icon itself might be virtually unseen, or only small parts of a dark surface might be seen through an opening in the cover. The development of the metal cover (*oklad* in Russian) was originally due to the desire to embellish a holy object, particularly if it was regarded as a powerful wonder-working icon, and jewels might be added in gratitude for answers to prayer. But Trubetskoi saw that the end product of this process of embellishment was a holy object whose use had become far removed from the fundamental principles of iconography. Restoration work at the end of the nineteenth century began to open up the possibility of a renewed approach to icons, where the actual image was accorded its proper significance.

Prince Trubetskoi describes this changed approach:

The discovery of the icon is one of the major and at the same time one of the most paradoxical events in the history of Russian culture. Discovery is the word, for until quite recently everything in the icon was hidden from us – its lines, its colors, and above all the spiritual meaning of this unique art. Yet all of our Russian antiquity lived by that meaning.

We looked at the icon without seeing it. We knew it only as a dark blur in a rich gold setting. Then suddenly all the values were reversed: the setting [riza] that covered most of the icon turned out to be a late invention, dating from the end of the sixteenth century, and mainly a product of that pious bad taste that went with the decline of religious and esthetic feeling. At bottom, imprisoning the icon in metal was unconscious iconoclasm, a denial of the painting itself, for it meant that its brushwork and colors were considered unimportant from the esthetic and especially the religious points of view. And the richer the casing, the more clearly it signalled the obtuse lack of insight that could build an impenetrable wall between us and the icon . . .

At long last, the icon's beauty is revealed to the eye . . . An icon is beautiful only as the transparent expression of its spiritual content. Those who see only its outer shell are not much more advanced than the admirers of gold casings and dark spots.[2]

To many non-Orthodox Christians at that time the veneration of icons appeared indefensible: it was seen simply, as idolatry. Few people outside the Orthodox world were familiar with the theological rationale for the use of icons, and in Orthodox circles there was little intellectual understanding of the gap between theory and practice. The way views have changed can be illustrated by comparing the attitude of Anglican bishops to icons in 1888 with the more favourable view that has developed over the last hundred years. In 1888 a committee of the Anglican Lambeth Conference stated its position with regard to the Orthodox Church and its icons: 'It would be difficult for us to enter into more intimate relations with that Church as long as it retains the use of icons.'[3] Those Anglicans might be forgiven for their prejudice since their discussions took place before the process of icon restoration had begun to accomplish its work. A hundred years later, many Anglicans and other Christians regard icons as the accessible face of Orthodoxy – the way whereby they have been enabled to enter into the Orthodox tradition of liturgy, theology and spirituality.

II

It is obvious to anyone who is acquainted with icons that they are in some way connected with prayer. We hear them spoken of as an expression of the prayer of the Church, and the result of the icon painter's prayer; we hear about people praying in the presence of icons; we also hear or read about the place of icons in the Orthodox tradition of spirituality. Yet in spite of all this, for many people outside the Orthodox Church there seems to be a series of missing links that we would like to discover to help us to see how icons are related to prayer, and how we can make use of icons in our own praying. I hope that this book will help to create such links between the sacred tradition of Orthodox icons on the one hand, and on the other, people who feel they are on the threshold of this tradition.

For most Orthodox Christians, icons form a normal, taken-for-granted part of their heritage of Christianity. It is normal to find icons in churches; there they form a conspicuous part of the setting for the celebrations of the Divine Liturgy and are honoured with lights and incense. It is equally normal to find icons in the homes of Orthodox Christians; there they form a focal point for the place of prayer, and have traditionally occupied a commanding position in the main room of a house. Icons are given as presents at Baptism and Marriage. Children are taught to pray with their family at home and in church where icons form part of the environment of prayer. An Orthodox Christian on entering a church will make the sign of the Cross, and proceed to venerate or greet certain icons, making the sign of the Cross before each greeting. Candles are placed in front of icons, as a continuing sign of intercession or gratitude or love. To venerate an icon is to greet or honour the person or mystery represented in the icon. The greeting of icons of Christ, of the Mother of God, or of the saints is a realization of the Communion of Saints, and is closely linked with the greeting of one's fellow Christians in the flesh who are gathered together for the Divine Liturgy: all are part of the Mystical Body of Christ.

Sometimes icons seem to be treated as talismans – objects with inherent protective power. Some have a reputation as wonder-working icons, and have come to be associated with particular places and situations where divine intervention is believed to have taken place. There are stories of people being told by their priests to spend time sitting in front of icons, and to get on with their knitting as a way of channelling restless energy. And we hear of people remonstrating with icons in complaint, as well as returning to give thanks for obviously answered prayer. For Orthodox Christians, icons form a focal point for a wide variety of human experience in relation to the divine realm, and they have an unsophisticated immediacy which many Western people find hard to appreciate. The concern of non-Orthodox people to be able to see and study icons is very different from the attitude of most Orthodox Christians. Someone once told me, 'Orthodox people don't really *look* at icons'; the statement took me by surprise, but it contains more than a grain of truth.

For people of a non-Orthodox background the response to icons is very varied. On the whole the non-Orthodox are unfamiliar with icons as part of the setting for liturgical worship. Where icons are used in Western churches, they are likely to be few in number and to have a specific function as focal points for devotion, for example devotion to the Mother of God or a particular patron saint. In the Benedictine Church of the Multiplication of the Loaves at Tabgha on the northern shores of the Sea of Galilee, two large double-sided icons of Christ and the Mother of God are placed at the threshold of the sanctuary in a way that enables them to be used for private devotion and also to be focal points during the Eucharistic Liturgy. Many Western religious communities use in their chapels icons of the Transfiguration and the Holy Trinity as well as of Christ and the Mother of God in ways that relate well to the contemplative tradition of their worship. In Catholic and Anglican cathedrals and in parish churches icons and block-mounted prints of icons are finding a home, sometimes with little evidence of devotional significance; and in other places as major focal points for devotion. Generally speaking, it is rare to find Western Churches that use icons in anything like the developed schemes of Orthodox Churches. The major exceptions are the Greek Catholic and other Eastern Rite Churches, with the monastic community at Chevetogne in Belgium which seeks to hold together the spiritual, liturgical and iconographic traditions of Eastern and Western Rite Catholic Churches.

Many non-Orthodox Christians have experienced an intuitive response to particular icons, and from this have been led to explore further. Exhibitions of icons in museums and art galleries have caused pain to some Orthodox Christians, who see their holy icons treated as objects of art, valued for their price and their place in the history of art rather than as the object of prayer and veneration. Such exhibitions have, however, brought icons into the consciousness of many people who have later come to value them for their spiritual significance. Icons in art galleries do not receive the traditional Orthodox veneration, but they do possess a power to hold the attention of observers, Christian and non-Christian alike; the attitude of many visitors in the presence of icons in major exhibitions is one of attentiveness and respect, even if external devotional veneration is absent.

The sense of presence in great icons is also a reason why many Western Christians have reproductions of icons which they use in their praying. There is a recognition that something is given through these icons, that there is a sacramental quality in them. For many people there is a process of learning to live with icons, and allowing them to live with us. It may be rather a haphazard affair, and we may be hard pressed to explain why certain icons mean so much to us, but that does not invalidate the reality of the interaction that has taken place. If we live within a tradition which is different from the developed iconographic tradition of Orthodoxy, we shall inevitably feel as if we are picking up crumbs from the rich man's table.

There are three possible developments in our ways of praying with icons that seem to be worthy of comment, and I believe they are all closely connected.

First, we may discover that we have begun to pray with our eyes rather than with our minds or our lips. Perhaps some intuitive response has made this possible; on the other hand we may have begun to become familiar with the people and events represented in icons, familiar with the shapes and symbolic language of icons, so that we no longer need to rationalize and verbalize as we place ourselves before an icon. Visual attentiveness can allow a more receptive type of praying to unfold.

Second, Western people who make use of icons in their prayers may also be making use of the Jesus Prayer and growing in familiarity with the Orthodox tradition known as Prayer of the Heart, or 'hesychasm'★. In this process we become aware of the reality of prayer as something which takes place within the core of our being. This is not a simple matter of words, but a process in which the depths of our hearts are opened to the transforming presence of God. In the terminology of the Orthodox tradition, the intellect★ (nous) descends into the heart, and prayer takes place from the heart rather than from the head. Even though hesychasm involves going beyond images and what is visual, great icons have been created by people who have been nurtured within this tradition of Prayer of the Heart; these icons convey some of the fruits of the tradition, in particular attentiveness and inner stillness. In our noisy word-battering world, icons have the power to create a different climate of heart and soul.

Third, there is what I can only describe as a process of *interiorization*. While that word may appear clumsy, we may already be familiar with what it describes. In the Western Church devotions such as the Rosary and the Stations of the Cross have a prominent place in the devotion of many Christians. With the Rosary, certain key events associated with Christ and his Mother are grouped together for contemplative or intercessory prayer; the devotion enters into one's heart, mind and soul, and the Rosary becomes part of us. The Stations of the Cross involve attentiveness to the events and characters involved in the last hours of Christ's earthly life; regular use of the Stations of the Cross can bring together our reflections on Christ's suffering and work of redemption, our awareness of the world's present suffering, and our response to all this within the Church; the Stations of the Cross become an integral part of our praying and our awareness of the world around us.

Two other examples of this process of interiorization are worth considering.

Psalm 84 [83] celebrates the joy of going on pilgrimage to worship in the Temple at Jerusalem, and is a great declaration of trust and love for God. It includes the verse 'Blessed are those who find their strength in you, whose hearts are set on pilgrimage' (84:5 NJB; [83]). The pilgrimage journey to Jerusalem has become an inner reality, the heart is set on pilgrimage even when other tasks and concerns take up time and energy; the external physical journey with the crowds of pilgrims along the roads to the Holy City has shaped an interior awareness, an attentiveness and longing for God.

In her book on St Seraphim of Sarov, Valentine Zander describes how Seraphim was devoted to the Gospels and was moved by reports of those who had been on pilgrimage to the Holy Land. When Seraphim felt called to the 'desert' life of a hermit, and set out to live in the vast forest area near Sarov, he created various special places for his devotions:

So in his desert he chose places which reminded him of events in the life of our Lord and of his holy Mother. For instance, he would go and sing the Virgin's hymns and re-read the story of the Annunciation in a place which he called Nazareth; in a cave which he called Bethlehem he extolled the incarnation of God made Man. He also had his mountain of the Beatitudes, his Mount Tabor, and his Gethsemane. As for the joy of Easter, he relived it every day, constantly singing the hymns of the resurrection. Thus, faraway Palestine came very near and he lived at Jesus' feet as though in the Holy Land, 'watching in the interior Jerusalem of his heart', ceaselessly keeping the Name of Jesus on his lips.[4]

As we become familiar with many of the icons of the Orthodox Church, a similar process of interiorization takes place. We realize that our way of praying has changed, that the imagery of certain icons has become integrated into our consciousness, and that our perception has been transformed in the light of the revelation that is celebrated and transmitted through the icons.

III

This book is focused on the icons of Church Feasts: those icons associated with the major festivals of the Church throughout the course of the year. These feasts celebrate key events in connection with the Incarnation: events in the preparation for the Incarnation; the human birth of God the Son; Christ's Baptism and Transfiguration; the supreme events celebrated in Holy Week and Easter; the Ascension and Pentecost; and the Dormition of the Mother of God.

The icons of the Church Feasts occupy one whole tier of the iconostasis* (the icon-screen which marks the transition from the nave of the church to the sanctuary). In addition, a separate festival icon is placed on a stand in the church at the time of the feast, and this is venerated in the course of the liturgical celebrations. In some churches the iconography of the major feasts is also depicted on the vaults of the church. The order in which these icons will be considered does not follow the sequence of the feasts in the Church's calendar; in this book the chronology of the events celebrated has been the key principle on which the sequence has been planned. This follows the order found in the festival tier on the iconostasis, in the festival frescoes, and also in composite icons which display a selection of twelve Feasts.

Some people consider that the celebration of the Resurrection is not strictly speaking *within* the sequence of the Church's year, as Easter is the Feast of Feasts, and the celebration of the Resurrection illumines everything that precedes and succeeds it. Within the cycle of festival icons the Anastasis or Resurrection icon is not counted among the twelve main Feasts, although on the iconostasis it does appear among them. Around the supreme glory of the Resurrection the Orthodox Church gathers the

Great Feasts. The Feasts of the Mother of God include her Nativity, her Entry into the Temple, and her Dormition (literally, 'falling asleep'). The Feasts of Christ are the Annunciation, the Nativity, the Meeting of the Lord (Presentation in the Temple), the Theophany (Baptism), the Transfiguration, the Entry into Jerusalem, the Ascension, Pentecost and the Exaltation of the Holy Cross. In addition to these, other days and events have their own icons, notably the Resurrection of Lazarus, the Crucifixion, and other events of Holy Week; in some churches these may take the form of a 'Passion Cycle', or a composite icon with several scenes on one panel. These commemorations and their icons provide a strong liturgical basis for the celebration of the faith, and reflection on how that faith is to be lived out. Orthodox Christianity is set in a firm liturgical frame which allows God's work of revelation and redemption to be celebrated in a rhythmical sequence throughout the year. The Church Feasts tier on the iconostasis allows the sequence to be kept in sight at all times; thus each particular celebration is set in the context of the whole, and in this way the Church takes her children up into a cycle that leads us through the temporal sequence of our lives in the light of Divine mercy and love for humanity.

The liturgical texts used in the Orthodox Church contain frequent references to Adam and Eve. The distorted relationship between humanity and God created through the fall is explored through the relationship between God and Adam; Adam encompasses the whole human race. In the New Testament we find St Paul using the contrast between the first Adam and the second Adam – Adam representing the old, fallen humanity, and Christ the New Man bringing into existence a new humanity. In the second century St Irenaeus develops this theology further, making use of the parallel between Eve and Mary: Eve, the mother of all the living in the creation story, is balanced by Mary the Mother of Jesus and his new humanity in the story of redemption. In the liturgical hymns this way of exploring the personal implications of our creation and redemption is used extensively, and it finds expression also in the Easter icon where the full extent of Christ's redemptive work is expressed in the raising of Adam and Eve.

A number of quotations from the hymnody of the Feasts has been included in each chapter of this book. These quotations are worthy of deep reflection; they are part of a profound heritage of liturgical poetry, and take us into modes of expressing doctrinal truths that are unfamiliar to many Western Christians. The study of these texts is a major undertaking in its own right, and is not the direct concern of this book. But since the texts are so closely related to Scripture and the events celebrated in the Church Feasts, the icons cannot properly be considered without reference to the hymnody. The discussion of icons in relation to liturgical texts is not intended to refer exclusively to the icons reproduced in this book. The comments will be helpful to readers in praying with or reflecting upon other icons that they may be using. Readers may find it helpful also to be able to refer to the main Scripture readings used in the Orthodox Church at the great festivals.

The icons reproduced in this book represent works from the fourteenth to the twentieth centuries, and from Byzantine, Russian and Mediterranean areas. The broad spectrum of Orthodox iconography conveys a strong sense of consistent subject matter and form; this helps to ensure that icons are recognized for what they are: one would not easily confuse the resurrection of Lazarus with the Resurrection of Christ, or the Nativity of the Mother of God with the Nativity of Christ. Consistency of form is a quality that helps communication to take place through the icons. On the other hand significant changes in the way subject matter is expressed in icons do occur. The portrayal of Christ crucified, the celebration of the Resurrection of Christ, and the representation of the Holy Trinity in icons have changed a great deal over the centuries; there is an unmistakable freshness about many twelfth-century icons and frescoes which stems from contemporary interest in human emotions and psychology. Works within this tradition of church art can be seen from a period of about 1,500 years; some periods may be regarded as golden ages, while others are seen as times of decline, for the heritage of Orthodox iconography is not a static one. Within the tradition a consistent language of iconography transmits the Orthodox faith, and at the same time allows a variety of expression through different painters and theologians.

❦ 2 ❧

Barren Root and
Life-giving Branch

THE BIRTH OF THE MOTHER OF GOD (8TH SEPTEMBER)
AND HER ENTRY INTO THE TEMPLE (21ST NOVEMBER)

Today God who rests upon the spiritual thrones has made ready for Himself a holy throne upon earth. He who made firm the heavens in His wisdom has prepared a living heaven in His love for man. For from a barren root He has made a life-giving branch spring up for us, even His Mother. God of wonders and hope of the hopeless, glory be to Thee, O Lord.[1]

❦ I ❧

The Orthodox liturgical cycle begins in September, and the first major feast to be celebrated is the Birth of the Blessed Virgin Mary on 8th September. The full title of the feast is The Birth of our Most Holy Lady the Theotokos★. At a time when the cycle of the seasons in the northern hemisphere is taking us into autumn, and into the darkness and lifelessness of the winter period, the Church punctuates this barren period of the year with feasts that celebrate the life-giving work of God in the Incarnation. The celebration of the birth of Christ in the depth of the winter season is balanced by the two other feasts closely associated with the Incarnation, the Birth of the Theotokos on 8th September, and the Annunciation on 25th March. The external season of darkness and gloom is illuminated by celebrations of great light, joy and vitality.

The particular births that are celebrated during this period come as a crowning glory to the long series of births that have marked the various stages in God's work of revelation and redemption. The history of our salvation is intimately linked with the birth of specific people, births which have been seen as particularly providential, the result of divine activity. The story begins with Abraham: God's promise to him cannot be fulfilled until a son is born; the faith of Abraham and Sarah is severely tested by the apparent inability of Sarah to conceive; yet the promise is fulfilled with the birth of Isaac. The birth story of Moses is told in the Bible with great detail. It is a very human story of hardship, risk and intrigue, yet through it all God's providential care is seen, providing the one who will free his people from the burden of slavery in Egypt. Moreover, the work of Moses foreshadows the greater work of deliverance from sin and death that will be accomplished by Christ. Samuel is born in answer to the prayer of Hannah, and becomes a new prophet for the new epoch that is developing. There is no account in the Bible of the birth of the prophet Jeremiah, but in the midst of all the conflict created by his ministry he is sustained by the faith that it is God alone who has created him for this ministry, that he has been born for this. He is aware of the word of the Lord addressed to him: 'Before I formed you in the womb I knew you, and before you were born I consecrated you; I appointed you a prophet to the nations' (Jeremiah 1:5).

St Luke in his Gospel follows this long tradition of recognizing the providential work of God in the birth of those through whom the work of redemption and revelation is to be accomplished. We are told how the ageing couple Zechariah and Elizabeth came to be the parents of John the Baptist, the great forerunner of the Lord. For St Luke it is significant that both Zechariah and Elizabeth came from families with priestly responsibilities, and that the angelic annunciation to Zechariah took place while he was in the Temple fulfilling his duties of prayer and sacrifice. From this priestly setting is born the one who will be the last great prophet, the one who will prepare the way of the Lord in fulfilment of the prophecy of Isaiah. St Luke then goes on to tell of the angelic annunciation to Mary and the birth of Jesus – and to both of these we shall return in subsequent chapters.

About the birth of the Mother of God, the Bible is silent. Yet this birth is celebrated as a feast in the Orthodox Church, and icons for the feast are sometimes included in the festival range of the iconostasis. The traditions upon which the feast and its icons are based have come down to us in the second-century apocryphal *Book of James* (also known as *The Protevangelion*). We are told that Joachim, in spite of his wealth and riches, was burdened and embarrassed by guilt at being childless. Even the remembrance of God's gift of a son to Abraham did not ease Joachim's burden; he went off into the wilderness, fasting and praying for 40 days and nights, awaiting God's response to his prayers. At this absence of Joachim, Anna bewailed her childlessness and the loss of her husband; she went into her garden and prayed in her sadness: 'O God of our fathers, bless me, and hearken unto my prayer, as thou didst bless the womb of Sarah, and gavest her a son, even Isaac.'[2] She lamented her own barrenness in comparison with the teeming fertility of the earth, the waters, the birds of the air and the beasts of the earth. But the prayers of this grieving couple were already being answered, and an angel assures her that she will conceive a child who will be spoken of throughout the world. Anna's response is to promise the child as an offering to the Lord: 'As the Lord my God liveth, if I bring forth either male or female, I will bring it for a gift unto the Lord my God, and it shall be ministering unto him all the days of its life.'³ After his time in the wilderness Joachim returned to Anna, confident that his anguish would be ended, and that he would be able to approach the altar of God with a clear conscience. Joachim's offering in the Temple was acceptable and he returned to his house justified. In due time Anna's child was born and named Mary.

The poverty of barrenness was made good by the quickening power and will of God. The angelic message to Zechariah 'You will have joy and gladness, and many will rejoice' (Luke 1:14) could equally apply to Joachim and Anna. Here in this preparation for the Incarnation we can already see the transforming power of God that turns sorrow into joy (John 16:20). Here those who know their need of God are blessed and used as instruments in the drama of salvation. Joachim and Anna, in spite of their material prosperity, epitomize the poor in spirit; through hardship and emptiness they learn to trust in the providence of God. 'My soul magnifies the Lord, and my spirit rejoices in God my Saviour, for he has regarded the low estate of his handmaiden . . . He has filled the hungry with good things, and the rich he has sent empty away' (Luke 1:46–48, 53). These words from the Magnificat sum up the response of Mary herself to her vocation, and equally the pattern of faithful response to God on the part of many before her who in their barrenness and nothingness found themselves filled from the generosity and goodness of God. The pattern is repeated time and time again in the history of the Church.

The lives of the saints frequently present us with men and women who are conscious of their own brokenness and frailty but become great instruments of God's mercy and grace. Many icons of popular Orthodox saints show scenes from their lives, starting with the birth that marks the beginning of a life that will manifest the holiness and love of God, and be a sign of the new life in Christ that we are all called to share. The particular births that are celebrated in the Church's liturgy and icons seem to point us on to the birth 'of water and the Spirit' (John 3:5) which is required if we are to see the Kingdom of God, and to the new life in the Spirit which is the fruit of being born 'anew' or 'from above' (John 3:7). The dynamics of the Kingdom of God require that we become as little children if we are to enter into the life of the Kingdom (Matthew 18:3, Mark 10:15). In icons of the Nativity of the Lord the sacramental aspect of our entry into life in Christ may be hinted at with the washing of the Christ-Child by the midwives at a bowl that looks very much like a font. (See the Christmas icon in **Plate 6**.)

Throughout the cycle of the Church Feasts there is a sense of purpose and accomplishment concerning the destiny which is being set before us. The destiny of life in the Kingdom is not simply revealed at the end of the sequence. Since that goal is already known, it is the very motive of our celebration. Knowledge of the full significance of the birth of the Mother of God is assumed as the Church celebrates her birth. And the same is true in the icons of all the feasts: the full doctrinal significance of what is celebrated is expressed in the icons. The icons and the liturgical texts complement each other, and together with Holy Scripture express the faith of the Church. 'We are God's children now; it does not yet appear what we shall be, but we know that when he appears we shall be like him, for we shall see him as he is' (1 John 3:2). 'We all, with unveiled face, reflecting the glory of the Lord, are being changed into his likeness from one degree of glory to another' (2 Corinthians 3:18). Such is the goal of the journey, and in the light of that destiny we may now retrace our steps to consider the icon of the Birth of the Mother of God.

⤝ II ⤞

The sixteenth-century Russian icon of the Birth of the Mother of God in **Plate 1** shows Anna sitting up on her bed, having given birth to the Mother of God; she wears a dark greyish-blue undergarment, and a vermilion outer garment. Three attendants approach Anna from the right; beneath the figure of Anna we see two midwives preparing to wash the infant Mary, while at the right side of the icon we see Anna again, together with Joachim, holding the child; Joachim wears a dark blue undergarment and a mantle shimmering with light red, vermilion and pale blue colours. In some icons Joachim is also shown gazing attentively at Anna from one of the buildings in the upper section. In this icon the architectural features in the upper section have prussian-blue roofs and are linked with a rich vermilion cloth, one of the devices used to indicate that the event set forth in the icon is taking place indoors. In the lower part some delightful birds drink at the well in the centre, and feed around it in a dark earth-green field; they add to the liveliness of the icon, and seem to make the point that Anna no longer needs to compare her former barrenness with the teeming fertility of birds and animals. The following lines from the Akathistos Hymn* are worth bearing in mind. Although this hymn does not form part of the liturgical texts for this feast, these extracts give us examples of some of the imagery that is used in connection with the Mother of God, and express the sense of joy that is associated with her whole life, a joy that is eloquently expressed in this icon.

> Hail, for through thee joy shall shine forth: . . .
> Hail, for through thee the creation is made new:
> Hail, for through thee the Creator becomes a newborn child.
> Hail, heavenly ladder by which God came down:
> Hail, bridge leading men from earth to heaven.[4]
>
> From thee, the field untilled, has grown the divine Ear of corn.
> Hail, living table that hast held the Bread of Life; hail, Lady,
> never-failing spring of the living water.[5]

Hail, spring that maketh the River with many streams to flow.
Hail, for thou dost prefigure the baptismal font:
Hail, for thou takest away the filth of sin.
Hail, water washing clean the conscience.
Hail, cup wherein is mixed the wine of mighty joy.[6]

The composition of this icon is one of tranquillity and harmony, with rich, joyful colours. The icon takes us into the joy of the parents at the birth of their child; our attention moves gently from one group of figures to another, as if to enter into their sense of wonder at the fulfilment of God's promises in this birth, while the deceptively simple scene with the birds and the well moves us to reflect upon the wider significance of this birth of the one who is to become the Mother of God.

The liturgical texts for the Feast are full of the sense of joy that Anna's barrenness has come to an end, and that the birth of the Theotokos foreshadows the Incarnation itself. All the titles lavished on Mary in this Feast are linked with her role as Mother of the Incarnate God; they are also drawn from the complex fabric of the Old Testament tradition, thereby linking together Old and New Covenants, and showing the Incarnation to be the fulfilment of God's preparatory work and revelation in the Old Testament period. The reiterated 'Today' shows how the Feast makes present the reality of what is being celebrated; from the vantage point of the birth of the Mother of God the drama of salvation is manifested. The following extracts from the liturgical texts express the sense of joy that permeates this Feast.

> She is the fountain of life that gushes forth from the flinty rock; [Exodus 17:6] She is the Bush [Exodus 3:2] springing from barren ground and burning with the immaterial fire that cleanses and enlightens our souls.[7]

> Today the barren gates are opened and the virgin Door of God comes forth. Today grace begins to bear its first fruits, making manifest to the world the Mother of God, through whom things on earth are joined with heaven, for the salvation of our souls.[8]

> The Joy of all the world has shone forth upon us, the far-famed Virgin sprung from righteous Joachim and Ann. On account of her exceeding goodness she is become the living Temple of God, and is in truth acknowledged as the only Theotokos. At her prayers, O Christ our God, send down peace upon the world and on our souls great mercy.[9]

> Today let Ann, barren and childless, clap her hands with joy. Let all things put on their bright array . . . No more shall women bear children in sorrow: for joy has put forth its flower, and the Life of men has come to dwell in the world. No more

are the gifts of Joachim turned away: for the lament of Ann is changed to joy. 'Let all the chosen of Israel rejoice with me', she says: 'for behold, the Lord has given me the living Pavilion of His divine glory, unto the joy and gladness of us all and the salvation of our souls.'[10]

Today the Bridge of Life is born. Through her mortal men, fallen into hell, find their way up again, and they glorify in song Christ the Giver of life.[11]

Ann's barrenness was transformed, thereby destroying the world's barrenness in good things; and this wonder plainly foreshadowed Christ's coming to dwell with mortal men. He has brought us from not being into being: His praises do we sing and we exalt Him above all for ever.[12]

The last quotation brings together the transformation of Anna's barrenness and the ending of 'the world's barrenness in good things'. The life-giving power of God transforms the fallen humanity that dwells 'in the shadow of death' into the renewed life and joy of God's Kingdom. In celebrating the Feast and in contemplating the icon we are taken from death into life, 'from not being into being'. 'For from a barren root He has made a life-giving branch spring up for us, even His Mother. God of wonders and hope of the hopeless, glory be to Thee, O Lord.'

The Feast was known in the East by the eighth century, and was referred to in Rome by Pope Sergius in the late seventh century. It was only in the eleventh century that the Feast was generally observed in the West.

✎ III ✎

Closely linked with the Feast of the Birth of the Mother of God is the Feast of the Entry of the Most Holy Theotokos into the Temple (21st November). Here again we are dealing with a tradition of the Church that is expressed in the apocryphal *Book of James* and in the liturgy of the Church.

And the child became three years old, and Ioachim said: Call for the daughters of the Hebrews that are undefiled, and let them take every one a lamp, and let them be burning, that the child turn not backward and her heart be taken captive away from the temple of the Lord. And they did so until they were gone up into the temple of the Lord.

And the priest received her and kissed her and blessed her and said: The Lord hath magnified thy name among all generations: in thee in the latter days shall the Lord make manifest his redemption unto the children of Israel. And he made her to sit upon the third step of the altar. And the Lord put grace upon her and she danced with her feet and all the house of Israel loved her. And her parents gat them down marvelling, and praising the Lord God because the child was not turned away backward. And Mary was in the temple of the Lord as a dove that is nurtured: and she received food from the hand of an angel.[13]

It is generally recognized that this tradition cannot be accepted as being literally and historically true. But we should not overlook the New Testament evidence of the relationship between Mary and Elizabeth, the wife of Zechariah the priest (Luke 1:36, 39ff), and the possibility that he may have had some part to play in the upbringing of Mary; nor should we discard the possibility that there may be some truth in the tradition that young maidens lived in the Temple precincts and were used to spin and weave the purple silk for the Temple veil. However, it is the spiritual significance of this tradition that we find explored in the liturgical texts. They make great play on the imagery of the Temple and dwelling-place of God: the Temple in Jerusalem is but a shadow of the Theotokos as the dwelling-place of God in the Incarnation. Rich and lavish imagery is used in this celebration of the preparation of the young child Mary for her vocation as the Mother of God. She enters the Jerusalem Temple in preparation to become the Temple of the Living God; she will be nourished by the bread of angels as a sign of the grace that is preparing her for the fulfilment of her vocation. To some Western Christians the language of this devotion may seem excessive and even misplaced, but for the Orthodox it is entirely appropriate to the magnitude of the mystery that is being honoured.

The Kontakion of the Feast sums up what is being celebrated:

The all-pure Temple of the Saviour, the precious Bridal Chamber and Virgin, the sacred treasure of the glory of God, is led today into the house of the Lord, and with her she brings the grace of the divine Spirit. Of her God's angels sing in praise: 'She is indeed the heavenly Tabernacle'.[14]

The tradition that we have seen in the *Book of James* is expressed in the hymns:

Having received the fruit of the promise come from the Lord, today in the temple Joachim and Ann offered the Mother of God as an acceptable sacrifice; and Zacharias the great High Priest received her with his blessing.

Into the holy places the Holy of Holies is fittingly brought to dwell, as a sacrifice acceptable to God. The virgins adorned with virtues go before her carrying torches, and offer her to God as a most sacred Vessel.

Let the gate of the temple wherein God dwells be opened: for Joachim brings within today in glory the Temple and Throne of the King of all, and he consecrates as an offering to God her whom the Lord has chosen to be his Mother.[15]

The contrast between the tender years of the Virgin and her spiritual maturity is stressed:

> Three years old in the flesh and many years old in spirit, more spacious than the heavens and higher than the powers above, let the Bride of God be praised in song.[16]

> A child in the flesh but perfect in soul, the holy Ark enters into the house of God, there to feed upon divine grace.[17]

Within the Holy of Holies, the Theotokos is nourished by heavenly food:

> The living Bridal Chamber of God the Word receives bread from the hands of a divine angel, as she dwells in the Holy of Holies.[18]

The spiritual significance of this tradition is explored in a rather different way by St Gregory Palamas (1296–1359). He regarded the entry of the Mother of God into the Temple as a symbol of the ascent of the soul to God, and he saw her preparation for her vocation as being accomplished through holy stillness, through the inner silence which can create the depth of heart that enables us to respond to God with great love. She acquired the ability to 'be still and know' God, to possess a fullness of love and awareness through silence that enabled her to listen to and receive the Word of God at the Annunciation (Luke 1:38). Her ability to keep 'all these things, pondering them in her heart' (Luke 2:19) was not a sudden development but had its roots deep in the formation of her soul and personality from an early age. St Gregory Palamas, the great defender of the hesychast tradition of prayer in the fourteenth century, saw Mary as being in the same spiritual tradition that he did so much to defend and develop.[19] Hesychasm, or Prayer of the Heart, is a discipline of attentiveness to God through silence and inner stillness, which had its roots in early Christian monasticism; this spiritual tradition bore fruit in many areas of Orthodox life, and particularly in Byzantium in the fourteenth century and in Russia in the fifteenth century. The significance of St Gregory Palamas is so great that he is commemorated on the second Sunday of Lent (see Chapter 8).

The historical origins of the Feast appear to be linked with the dedication of the Basilica of St Mary the New in Jerusalem on 21st November 543; by the late seventh century it was celebrated throughout Jerusalem, and in Constantinople by the early eighth century. The observance of the Feast spread in the West during the Middle Ages; it was suppressed and then reinstated during the sixteenth century, and has survived recent revisions of the Roman Calendar, albeit in a rather attenuated form.

In **Plate 2a** we have a twelfth-century fresco of the Entry of the Mother of God into the Temple from the Church of St Nicholas of the Roof, Kakopetria, Cyprus.

On the left, Zacharias the Priest welcomes the young Theotokos whose parents have brought her into the Temple accompanied by a procession of young girls carrying lamps or candles. The girls stand in the background on the right. In the centre stand Joachim and Anna; their left hands point forward towards Zacharias welcoming their child into the Temple, but their eyes and faces indicate a concern to return home without causing their child to be distracted from the new setting into which she has just been introduced. In the background, curtains have been drawn aside for the family group to enter into the Temple. Many icons of the Entry of the Mother of God into the Temple include another figure of the Virgin high up in the Holy of Holies where she is being fed by an angel, symbolizing the spiritual nourishment she received in the Temple.

≼ IV ≽

In both the Birth of the Theotokos and her Entry into the Temple we can contemplate the work of God in preparing for the Incarnation. The Church's tradition in these two Feasts takes us into the faith and trust of the faithful of the Old Covenant; this faith and waiting upon God are exemplified in Joachim and Anna, and will be exemplified again in Simeon and Anna who greet the Lord as he is presented in the Temple. For Joachim and Anna, their child is held on trust, not as a private possession, and their fidelity involves them in handing over the child to the Temple priests in order that her vocation may be appropriately nurtured and developed. These traditions point us to the spiritual growth of the Theotokos, and to the spiritual potential that needs to be awakened and developed in all children. In these traditions we find none of the twentieth-century fashion of leaving children to make up their minds about religious and spiritual matters when they are old enough. The spiritual nurture and nourishment of children in the tradition of the faith is the obvious pattern for the faithful poor in spirit of the Old Testament, and likewise for the faithful of Orthodoxy.

The language used in these and other celebrations of the Mother of God draws on imagery that is rooted in the Old Testament Scriptures. In Isaiah the barren wilderness which can be so suddenly changed by a downpour of rain becomes a symbol of transformation into fertility and new life (Isaiah 41:18–19). The Orthodox liturgical texts speak of the barren root bringing forth a life-giving branch. The same imagery is used to express the blessing of fertility, new life and hope. The mystery of the Incarnation and the place of Mary in this mystery is expressed in the titles that are used of her in the texts already quoted. These titles and symbols applied to Mary affirm the mystery of the Incarnation – the wonder of God's self-giving and love in the union of God the Son with God's human creation in the person of Jesus Christ. These symbols are drawn from the Old Testament and bear witness to the fulfilment of that tradition in the Incarnation. The veritable galaxy of imagery that is used in relation to Mary demonstrates the richness of the imagery developed in the Old Testament, and the wonder of its fulfilment in the Incarnation.

The images mentioned in the quotations from the Festal Menaion are worthy of prolonged reflection: the Mother of God is the 'life-giving branch' that has sprung up from the barren root; 'the fountain of life that gushes forth from the flinty rock'; 'the Bush springing from the barren ground'; 'the Virgin Door of God'; 'the living Temple of God'; 'the living Pavilion of His divine glory'; 'the Bridge of Life'; 'the Tabernacle of God, the most holy Mountain'; 'the Temple and Throne of the King of all'; 'the living Bridal Chamber of God the Word'; 'His hallowed Tabernacle, the living Ark, that contained the Word who cannot be contained'; 'the living Temple of the holy glory of Christ our God'. And to add to these images of the Mother of God, when we come to the celebration of the Annunciation she is referred to as 'the Living City of Christ the King'.

★   ★   ★

The main Scripture readings for the Birth of the Mother of God are:

> *At Great Vespers:* Genesis 28:10–17; Ezekiel 43:27–44:4; Proverbs 9:1–11.
> *At Mattins:* Luke 1:39–49, 56.
> *At the Divine Liturgy:* Philippians 2:5–11; Luke 10:38–42, 11:27–28.

The main Scripture readings for the Entry of the Mother of God into the Temple are:

> *At Great Vespers:* Exodus 40:1–5, 9–10, 16, 34–35; 1 Kings 7:51, 8:1, 3–4, 6–7, 9–11; Ezekiel 43:27–44:4.
> *At Mattins:* Luke 1:39–49, 56.
> *At the Divine Liturgy:* Hebrews 9:1–7; Luke 10:38–42, 11:27–28.

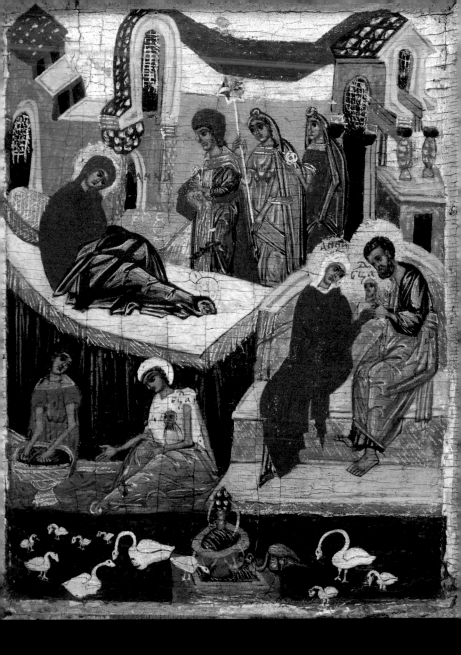

Plate 1: *The Birth of the Mother of God*, panel icon, Russian, sixteenth century

Plate 2a: *The Entry of the Mother of God into the Temple*, fre[sco,] [St N]icholas of the Roof, Kakopetria, Cyprus, twelfth cent[ury]

Plate 2b: *The Nativity of Christ*, fresco, Panagia
Phorbiotissa, Asinou, Cyprus, c. 1350

Plate 3: *The Annunciation*, panel icon, the Balkans,
seventeenth century

Plate 4: *The Annunciation*, upper section of a pair of Royal Doors, Rostov-Suzdal area, Russia, sixteenth century

Plate 5: *The Annunciation*, upper section of a pair of Royal Doors, Rostov-Suzdal area, Russia, sixteenth century

Plate 6: *The Nativity of Christ*, Russian icon, tempera on panel, Russian School, sixteenth century

Plate 7: *The Meeting of the Lord*, panel icon, Novgorod, Russia, c. 1470

Plate 8a: *The Meeting of the Lord*, fresco, Panagia Phorbiotissa,
Asinou, Cyprus, c. 1350

Plate 8b: *The Raising of Lazarus*, fresco, Panagia Phorbiotissa,
Asinou, Cyprus, 1105–6

3

The Living City of Christ the King

THE ANNUNCIATION OF THE MOST HOLY THEOTOKOS AND EVER-VIRGIN MARY (25TH MARCH)

Having reached the city of Nazareth, Gabriel now salutes thee, the living City of Christ the King, and he cries aloud to thee: Hail, thou who art blessed and full of divine grace: thou shalt hold in thy womb God made flesh, and through thee in His compassion He shall call back mankind to its ancient state. Blessed is the divine and immortal fruit of thy womb, who through thee grants the world great mercy.[1]

I

In both Eastern and Western Churches, all sorts of artists have responded with great devotion and creativity to the mystery of the Annunciation. Poetry, drama, painting and sculpture have all been used to explore the significance of this great event in the history of our redemption. The Gospel account as we have it from St Luke is dramatic and moving, and permeated by theological reflection. Those who wrote the liturgical texts for the Feast positively relish exploring the implications of the Incarnation, and the ways in which the Virgin's response fulfils the various prefigurations of the Incarnation given in the Old Testament. Similarly, the range of icons of the Annunciation is enormous, for the Annunciation is represented frequently, on the walls or pillars of an Orthodox church, on the iconostasis in the Church Feasts series of icons, on the Royal Doors leading through the iconostasis, as well as in icons provided for veneration in church on the day of the Feast. The mystery of the Annunciation is so central to the faith that it has inevitably been explored and represented in a great variety of ways.

In the previous chapter we have seen how the liturgical texts make use of Old Testament imagery in speaking of the Mother of God. When we come to the Annunciation we find a huge range of images and symbols brought into use. This way of using Scripture was for many centuries one of the chief methods of conveying the significance of the revelation given through Christ: what was given in the past, in the Old Testament, was fulfilled in the New Testament; only in the fullness of the revelation given through Christ can the significance of earlier revelation be understood. This method of interpretation in relation to the Mother of God is made explicit in a text where the Archangel says to Mary, 'It is thou who art prefigured by the utterances and dark sayings of the prophets and by the symbols of the Law.'[2] These utterances and symbols have a place at the Feast of the Annunciation because they illuminate the doctrine clarified at the Council of Ephesus (431) concerning the role of the Virgin as Theotokos, Mother of God. The following quotations show how this rich imagery is used to elucidate the significance of the Incarnation:

> Revealing to thee the pre-eternal counsel, Gabriel came and stood before thee, O Maid; and greeting thee, he said: 'Hail, thou earth that has not been sown; hail, thou burning bush that remains unconsumed; hail, thou unsearchable depth; hail, thou bridge that leads to heaven, and ladder raised on high that Jacob saw; hail, thou divine jar of manna; hail, thou deliverance from the curse; hail, thou restoration of Adam, the Lord is with thee'.[3]

> Hail, O Theotokos, deliverance from the curse of Adam. Hail, holy Mother of God; hail, living Bush. Hail, Lamp; hail, Throne; hail, Ladder and Gate. Hail, divine Chariot; hail, swift Cloud. Hail Temple; hail, Vessel of gold. Hail, Mountain; hail, Tabernacle and Table. Hail, thou release of Eve.[4] (cf Genesis 3:15–17; Exodus 3:4, 25:31; Genesis 28:12, 17; Ezekiel 44:2; Isaiah 19:1; Exodus 16:33; Daniel 2:34–35; Exodus 26:1, 25:23)

Throughout the celebration of the Annunciation Adam and Eve are kept much in mind; they were deceived and led astray, and the consequences spread to all humanity. Mary, faced with the Archangel, is afraid lest she be deceived and led astray like Eve; she questions the messenger vigorously, and receives reassurance:

> Mary said to the Angel: 'Strange is thy speech and strange thine appearance, strange thy sayings and thy disclosures. I am a Maid who knows not wedlock, lead me not astray. Thou sayest that I shall conceive Him who remains uncircumscribed: and how shall my womb contain Him whom the wide spaces of the heavens cannot contain?' 'O Virgin, let the tent of Abraham that once contained God teach thee: for it prefigured thy womb, which now receives the Godhead.'[5] (cf Genesis 18:1–16)

> 'I am filled with joy at thy words, yet am afraid: I fear lest thou deceive me, as Eve was deceived, and lead me far from God. Yet lo, thou criest out: O all ye works of the Lord, bless ye the Lord.'[6]

The mystery of the Incarnation is honoured in the liturgical celebration, in hymns of praise, and with canticles involving a lavish poetic embellishment of the angelic greeting. The event of the Annunciation is never left to stand on its own.

Just as for St Luke the event has profound theological implications, so for the Church there is a continuous exploring and relishing of the implications of our humanity being taken by God the Son in the womb of the Virgin Mary, to be redeemed, perfected, and raised to glory. The Virgin's 'Yes' to God reverses the sin of Eve, and begins to reverse the consequences of the fall. Time and again we are reminded that whereas the serpent's deception beguiled Eve, kindled human pride and led to the fall, the Archangel's message of the redeeming love and humility of God leads to the Virgin's obedience and the accomplishment of God's work of redemption through the Incarnation. The fruit of Eve's deception is the curse, especially in relation to the pain of childbearing, whereas the fruit of Mary's obedience is joy, with the conception of the Child who is both God and man. The Archangel's greeting is often rendered as 'Rejoice!' in the hymnody of the Feast, for it is more than a simple greeting; Mary is to rejoice because of her vocation, and what is to be accomplished through her; and joy will be the hallmark of the renewed humanity that is brought to life through the self-giving and humility of God's human birth. 'Now God becomes man, that he may make Adam God.'[7] What greater statement of the doctrine of theosis★ – the taking up of human life into union with God – could there be?

> Today there come glad tidings of joy: it is the feast of the Virgin. Things below are joined to things above. Adam is renewed, and Eve set free from her ancient sorrow; and the Tabernacle of the human nature which the Lord took upon Himself, making divine the substance He assumed, is consecrated as a Temple of God. O mystery! The manner of his emptying is unknown, the fashion of his conceiving is ineffable. An angel ministers at the wonder; a virgin womb receives the Son. The Holy Spirit is sent down; the Father on high gives his consent; and so the covenant is brought to pass by common counsel. In Him and through Him are we saved, and together with Gabriel let us cry aloud unto the Virgin: 'Hail, thou who art full of grace: the Lord is with thee. From thee has Christ our God and our Salvation taken human nature, raising it up unto Himself. Pray to Him that our souls may be saved.'[8]

⊰ **II** ⊱

In Jerusalem by the fifth century the celebration of the Annunciation was regarded as the occasion when the Fathers of the Church who had upheld the doctrine of the Incarnation should be honoured. In Constantinople during the sixth century, because of the growing significance of the commemoration of the Mother of God, the celebration of the Annunciation was taken out of the immediate Christmas period and given a feast in its own right: 25th March, nine months before Christmas, became the date for celebrating the Annunciation. The truth of the Incarnation of the second Person of the Trinity, and the identity of God the Word with the Child conceived in the womb of Mary, had been at the heart of the issues faced at the Council of Ephesus, so it is appropriate that the texts for this Feast are concerned with the significance of the title 'Mother of God'; the scriptural texts which draw our attention to the role of Mary are used to defend, illustrate and enhance the significance of the Incarnation. It is important to see this Feast as a dogmatic celebration, and the Scriptures, hymns and icons connected with it as having a teaching function.

The earliest existing image of the Annunciation seems to be a third-century one in the catacomb of Priscilla in Rome; the theme becomes widespread in the Byzantine Orthodox world, and as the iconography develops, details such as a ray of light descending on Mary and the dove hovering above her as a symbol of the Holy Spirit become familiar. In some of the later fresco scenes of the Life of the Virgin two Annunciation scenes are depicted, in accordance with details from the apocryphal *Book of James*: first Mary is at the well and hears a voice calling her highly-favoured and blessed among women; seeing no one, Mary moves away in fear, and is then approached by the angel as she is working on the veil for the Temple, and the dialogue that is recounted is much in keeping with St Luke's Gospel. The majority of the Annunciation images involve, however, only one meeting of Gabriel and the Virgin, and present the scene as we have it from St Luke; this is particularly true of panel icons of this subject. The ways in which the scene is depicted have been influenced by the heritage of rhetoric that became part of the Christian preaching tradition from the fourth century onwards. In particular it has been claimed that elaborate descriptions of the season of spring found their way into the metaphors and imagery used in homilies on the Annunciation, and that this can be detected in the iconography of the feast.[9] Springtime and ideas of renewal naturally become associated, and the springtime feast of the Annunciation, celebrated as the beginning of God's work of re-creation and new life, enables details such as trees, flowers and birds to become readily absorbed into the iconography.

Some Orthodox churches have the Annunciation set before us in two separate images – with the Archangel on the left, and the Mother of God on the right. This is usually the case with the representation of the Annunciation in the upper levels of the church building on the walls or pillars on each side of the sanctuary area, and also on the royal doors at the centre of the iconostasis. In this case the Annunciation is often at the top of the doors (see **Plates 4 and 5**), above the four figures of the evangelists, or else it occupies the whole of the two doors, the evangelists then being depicted on the adjacent pillars of the iconostasis; a third possibility involves the Annunciation at the top of the doors, two of the Church Fathers associated with the Divine Liturgy on the doors, and the Evangelists on the pillars of the iconostasis. This conspicuous placing of the figures of Gabriel and the Theotokos over the sanctuary area and on the royal doors shows how fundamental the mystery of the Annunciation and the Incarnation are for Orthodox Christians and their worship. The Divine Liturgy is celebrated as a meeting of the human and the divine; there is a living dynamic in the Divine Liturgy as participants enter into the mystery that has been revealed in Christ. The transcendent Godhead has raised us into the divine life; we are already partakers of the divine nature (2 Peter 1:4) and already we share in the life of the Kingdom. All of this is a consequence of Mary's response to God at the Annunciation.

In some Russian representations of the Annunciation at the top of the royal doors, the various forms of perspective which are used can be quite bewildering (see **Plates 4 and 5**). We seem to be looking down at one figure and up at another, and the architectural features can appear bizarre. (This is also true of architectural features in other icons.) It is as if every possible technique has been employed to make it clear that the Annunciation is the most amazing event in human history and that it defies normal forms of representation. This is an event in which the world's values are thrown aside and the very different values of the Kingdom of God have to be recognized as one comes before God in the Divine Liturgy. After all, it is God's humility that has conquered Adam's pride. 'He has put down the mighty from their thrones, and exalted those of low degree; he has filled the hungry with good things, and the rich he has sent empty away' (Luke 1:52–53). The normal power structures of this world do not apply as we approach the Divine Liturgy, and we are soon reminded of this when the Beatitudes are read:

> Blessed are the poor in spirit, for theirs in the kingdom of heaven. Blessed are those who mourn . . . , blessed are the meek . . . , blessed are those who hunger and thirst for righteousness . . . , blessed are the merciful . . . , blessed are the pure in heart . . . , blessed are the peacemakers . . . , blessed are those who are persecuted for righteousness sake, for theirs is the kingdom of heaven. (Matthew 5:2–10)

She who is hailed in the liturgy of this Feast as 'The Living City of Christ the King' is honoured as an example of this blessedness, an embodiment of the values of the Kingdom, a living presence where the Kingdom can be seen. All generations call her blessed because of her openness to God, her willingness to co-operate with the purposes of God, her willingness to receive the greatest possible gift. Our approach in worship has to be shaped by the Annunciation: it must be inspired by a spirit of willing collaboration as we receive the gift of Christ, a willingness to seek and do his will: 'Let it be to me according to your word' (Luke 1:38). Beneath the Annunciation icon on the royal doors or adjacent to them are the figures of the four Evangelists. The Gospel record has to be heard and lived; it can only be entered into in the spirit of the Annunciation, in response to the Holy Spirit; it is not an intellectual assent that is required but a turning of heart and mind and will, a new beginning in Christ. In the Divine Liturgy we find that Word, Sacrament and Icon belong together as means of grace, instruments through which human life is transfigured and brought to share in the glory of the Kingdom.

Other icons of the Annunciation consist of a single panel (**Plate 3**) which forms part of the Church Feasts tier on the iconostasis, or is the festal icon to be venerated in church during the Feast. Some single-panel icons can be relatively simple in composition, consisting basically of the two figures of Gabriel and Mary, while others can be very complex compositions. The twelfth-century Ustyug Annunciation in the Tretyakov Gallery in Moscow is a very simple and dignified composition. It is often reproduced in prints, postcards and books about icons, which helps to make it a reasonably familiar image.[10] However, such reproductions can be very misleading, for the icon is over seven feet high, and whereas we may be used to looking at prints, the impact of seeing the actual icon is hard to imagine. One is simply faced with the Annunciation. The two silent, restrained and monumental figures stand there, the Archangel and the Mother of God, bringing us into that moment and that creative relationship through which God enters into human life to renew and transfigure his creation. The silent figures seem to have such dynamic power as to be almost overwhelming, and yet to be waiting with immense patience for some response of love and obedience from those who behold the icon. The figure of Christ depicted within the Virgin's breast reminds us of the great mystery of the faith: 'Christ in you, the hope of glory' (Colossians 1:27).

In many icons we see the eyes of both the Archangel and the Theotokos raised to heaven. This detail expresses the concern of both that the will of God should be done, that both the bearer and the recipient of the message should co-operate willingly in fulfilling the divine purpose. This gaze may also reflect the dialogue in the liturgical canticles where both Gabriel and Mary cry, 'O all ye works of the Lord, bless ye the Lord',[11] a sign of their steadfast purpose in serving God. Both are concerned that the whole of creation should glorify God, and the Archangel's desire for this is evidence to Mary that she is not being deceived.

Most icons of the Annunciation include architectural details indicating the place where the Annunciation took place. These features often have more in keeping with buildings that might be encountered in our own dream world than with any recognizable edifice in the external world. This seems to be one of the techniques used in icons, which indicate that the significance of what is represented extends beyond the historical dimension, and is able to make connection with our own interior world. The significance of the event goes beyond the particular time and place. The Annunciation to the Virgin is celebrated as a specific event in history, but our celebration of the Feast opens us also to an annunciation, to new possibilities, to the reality of the divine presence seeking to enter in to this particular person, this community, this particular state of affairs. Because of the Annunciation and the Incarnation, humanity has been taken into the Godhead, and in celebrating this we cannot simply regard annunciation as one event of the past.

One detail in the Annunciation icons is worthy of further reflection. According to the *Book of James*, Mary had been assigned the task of preparing the purple and scarlet material to be used in making a veil for the Jerusalem Temple:

> Now there was a council of the priests, and they said: Let us make a veil for the temple of the Lord. And the priest said: Call unto me pure virgins of the tribe of David. And the officers departed and sought and found seven virgins. And the priests called to mind the child Mary, that she was of the tribe of David and was undefiled before God: and the officers went and fetched her. And they brought them into the temple of the Lord, and the priest said: Cast me lots, which of you shall weave the gold and the undefiled (the white) and the fine linen and the silk and the hyachinthine, and the scarlet and the true purple. And the lot of the true purple and the scarlet fell unto Mary, and she took them and went unto her house.[12]

It may be appropriate to speculate on the significance of this veil: perhaps it is implied that this is to be the veil for the Holy of Holies, the veil which would be rent in two at the time of Christ's death, rending the barrier between the human and the Divine in the new dispensation. In some icons Mary is shown holding the yarn; in others it is shewn falling to the ground as she lets go and attends to the appearance and message of the Archangel. Work on the veil for the Temple is allowed to fall aside as Mary attends to the higher vocation announced by Gabriel. The task of needlework that is being accomplished for the Jerusalem Temple is laid aside at the moment when Mary is called upon to fulfil her vocation to be the Temple of God, to be the 'Living Pavilion of the glory'.[13] From this moment she will be the Theotokos, the God-Bearer, the one through whom the Second Adam will be born. She is to prepare not only furnishings for the Jerusalem Temple, but the very flesh and humanity of him whose presence heralds a New Creation. She becomes the 'Living City of Christ the King'.

The process of letting go is a vital part of human living and dying. It is not only a matter of letting go of bad habits and attitudes, of laying aside our sins. It is also a matter of letting go even of good things when the time is ripe for us to receive something better. If we are forever holding on to our possessions, our selves, our achievements, our ways of living and working that have been shaped over the years – if we are forever holding on, we will never be able to receive fresh gifts from the hand of God. So often we are driven by acquisitiveness: success in the eyes of the world depends on acquiring things, accumulating wealth, status, reputation, power and influence. If our lives are so trained to be acquisitive, we will not easily let go in self-giving and generosity, and we will hardly be able to welcome gifts of God when they are presented to us. In sending out his disciples on a mission, Jesus told them that their equipment for the mission was 'no gold, nor silver, nor copper in your belts, no bag for your journey, nor two tunics, nor sandals nor a staff' (Matthew 10:9–10). The mission is to be accomplished through the absence of those very things about which we are so often most acquisitive. We may have to let go of what matters most to us if we are to become servants of the Kingdom. And at the Annunciation itself, tradition shows us Mary letting go of a task that could well have become obsessive and all-consuming: religious needlework, human activity for a religious purpose. Mary's vocation is to receive: to receive and welcome him 'who cannot be contained', but 'empties Himself, takes flesh, and is fashioned as a creature'.[14]

The letting go that may be required of us in our response to God may need to take place at a deep interior level. There may be all sorts of anxieties and attitudes to be surrendered that have been formed over the years. Negative influences that have been interiorized and have shaped our very being may need to go, and so may the frenetic acting-out of a work ethic. The compulsion to be busy in good works can almost reach the proportions that St Paul warns against: 'If I give away all I have, and if I deliver my body to be burned, but have not love, I gain nothing' (1 Corinthians 13:3). Many who would disclaim any enthusiasm to give their bodies to be burned may well be consumed by the good causes they adopt. And for all of us there is the ultimate letting-go to be faced in our dying and death. So much time and energy goes into the prevention or postponement of death that death in the twentieth century has come to be seen as the ultimate failure of the medical profession rather than the final handing over of life to the One from whom it was received as a gift.

For Mary, the Annunciation, with the letting-go and the receiving that it involved, also prepared the way to Calvary. Her obedience took her into the heart of the pain and suffering that would be brought into focus in the death of her Son. At Compline of Good Friday, these words form part of the lament of the Mother of God:

> 'Where, O my Son and God, are the good tidings of the Annunciation that Gabriel brought me? He called Thee King and God and Son of the Most High; and now, O my sweet Light, I behold Thee naked, wounded, lifeless'.[15]

The Feast of the Annunciation, 25th March, sometimes falls in Holy Week, and even on Good Friday, Holy Saturday or Easter Sunday. In the Western Church when this conjunction of dates occurs, the Annunciation is celebrated after the Octave of Easter. In the Eastern Churches the conjunction of dates is accepted, and they generally get on with a double celebration. It is hard for Western Christians to imagine going through all that would be involved in such a double celebration, but the Orthodox Church seems to relish the conjunction and the paradoxes involved. The self-emptying and self-giving love of God are exemplified in both the Annunciation and the Crucifixion: in the one, the love and the gift of love in the person of Christ are welcomed and cherished by the young Theotokos; in the other, the redemption of the world is accomplished in a way that appears to be utter failure, and the Theotokos stands by her Son in loving attentiveness at the divine self-emptying. And if the conjunction of Feasts falls on Easter Day, what greater celebration of joy could there be?

◁ III ▷

Plate 3 shows a seventeenth-century panel icon of the Annunciation from the Balkans. It presents us with the mystery of the Annunciation in great simplicity. The Virgin stands on a pedestal in front of a seat; her left hand holds the yarn and her right hand is raised in a gesture of co-operative acceptance of the Archangel's message. The Archangel approaches the Virgin with his wings and right hand outstretched, and the left hand holding his staff. The gaze of the Archangel is towards the Theotokos, while her eyes and her posture express an inward contemplation of the message. 'Rejoice!' and 'Let it be' seem to sum up the message of the icon. In the background are two buildings linked at the lower level by two walls and at the upper level by a vermilion-scarlet cloth flecked with gold. A reddish-crimson colour is used for the outer garments of both Gabriel and the Mother of God, with darker shading on the latter's; their undergarments are in dark blue-green. The stance of the Archangel is similar to that in a famous fourteenth-century Constantinopolitan icon at Ohrid, only without the much more dramatic sense of urgency represented in the Ohrid icon, conveyed particularly by the downward sweep of the Archangel's left wing.

Plates 4 and 5 show a sixteenth-century presentation of the Annunciation on the upper section of the Royal Doors from the iconostasis of a church in the Rostov-Suzdal area of Russia. St Basil and St John Chrysostom, the two Fathers of the Church who are the presumed authors of the two main Orthodox versions of the Divine Liturgy, occupy the main two panels of the Royal Doors, beneath the Archangel on the left and the Mother of God on the right. The familiar features of buildings linked by a vermilion cloth are there in both panels. On the left we seem to be looking down on the scene as Gabriel approaches the Virgin. On the right the architectural details and the raised seat of the Virgin ensure that we look up to the Mother of God, who is 'Greater in honour than the cherubim, and past compare more glorious than the seraphim . . . who without corruption hast borne the Word of God'.[16] The position of the Archangel's left wing, right arm and feet emphasize his descent from the heavenly realms to this world; above Gabriel the diagonal lines of the buildings draw our attention down towards the Mother of God. Above the Virgin the segment of a circle represents the divine realm, from which three rays emerge; the blue used for the divine realm is echoed in the undergarment and wings of the Archangel, on the buildings behind the Virgin, and on her undergarment;

elsewhere in the two panels vermilion is used a great deal, and the reddish-brown colour of the Virgin's maphorion is probably created by the use of vermilion over-laid with blue.

In her left hand the Mother of God holds the scarlet yarn, while the other end of the yarn falls free as her right hand is raised in a gesture of acceptance in response to Gabriel's message. The posture of the Mother of God expresses willing co-operation with God's plan of salvation. In this image we see little of the questioning and testing that forms part of the Virgin's response in much of the hymnody of the Feast; here the stress seems to be on the willingness of Mary's response, the welcome which she gives to the Incarnate Son, and the whole mystery of God coming to dwell among us as a man. The outer edge of this top-right panel, the upper levels of the three buildings, and the slightly fanned, near-vertical lines on the buildings draw our attention in towards the Virgin; the curve of her body echoes the curve of the edge of the panel. Everything in these two panels draws us into the mystery of the Annunciation and the Incarnation, and in the Divine Liturgy it is through these doors that Christ comes to be with his people in the holy gifts. The mystery of the Annunciation set before us on the Royal Doors is vitally linked to the mystery of Christ's presence in the Divine Liturgy. The past event made present in the icons becomes part of the reality that is celebrated in the Eucharistic Liturgy as we enter into the fore-taste of the Heavenly Banquet in the Marriage Supper of the Lamb.

★　　　★　　　★

The main Scripture readings for the Feast of the Annunciation are:

At Great Vespers: Genesis 28:10–17; Ezekiel 43:27–44:4; Proverbs 9:1–11.
At Mattins: Luke 1:39–49, 56.
At the Divine Liturgy: Hebrews 2:11–18; Luke 1:24–38.
At Great Vespers: Exodus 3:1–8; Proverbs 8:22–30.

The Paradise that is Within the Cave

THE NATIVITY ACCORDING TO THE FLESH OF OUR LORD AND GOD AND SAVIOUR JESUS CHRIST (25TH DECEMBER)

> Bethlehem has opened Eden: come, and let us see. We have found joy in secret: come, and let us take possession of the paradise that is within the cave. There the unwatered Root has appeared, from which forgiveness flowers forth: there is found the undug Well, whence David longed to drink of old (2 Samuel 23:15). There the Virgin has borne a Babe, and made the thirst of Adam and David to cease straightway, Therefore let us hasten to this place where now is born a young Child, the pre-eternal God.[1]

The Feast of Christmas on 25th December developed in the West at the beginning of the fourth century. The Christian celebration of the birth of the Sun of Righteousness (cf Malachi 4:2) soon spread from Rome and was well established in the Eastern empire by the late fourth century, although it was not until the sixth century that the Feast was fully accepted in Palestine. This celebration of the Nativity of the Lord owes much to the fact that major theological questions about the divinity of Christ had been resolved at the Council of Nicaea★ in 325, and the liturgical texts strongly emphasize Christ's divinity. In the historical event of Christ's birth the Lord's humanity is quite obvious, but the Feast is not only about a human birth; it is about the human birth of the second Person of the Holy Trinity and the implications of the Incarnation for the salvation of the world. There is a constant interplay in the texts between the visible details of the event and the invisible reality of what is taking place as God the Son, the eternal Word, takes flesh in the womb of the Virgin Mary and is born at Bethlehem.

In the Orthodox Church, the celebration of the Lord's birth takes place after a long period of preparation. There is a fast of 40 days, similar to the preparation for Easter. On the second Sunday before Christmas there is a commemoration of the forefathers of Christ, the human ancestors of the Incarnate Son, and on the last Sunday before Christmas there is a commemoration of all the righteous men and women whose lives were pleasing to God from the beginning of human life to the time up to Joseph who was betrothed to the Mother of God. These commemorations help to place the Incarnation and Feast of the Nativity of Christ in the wide context of God's purposes throughout history. On 20th December the Forefeast of the Nativity begins, and on Christmas Eve services which form the final preparation for the Feast, known as the Royal Hours, date from the time when the Byzantine Emperor was present for these services. Christmas itself commemorates the birth of Christ, the visit of the shepherds and the Adoration of the Magi; the Gospel reading at the Divine Liturgy is Matthew's account of the Magi's visit to pay homage to Christ. Thus the details that we shall see in the Christmas icon accurately reflect the scriptural content of the Feast: the homage of the Magi is an integral part of the Christmas celebration, and not a separate commemoration on 6th January as in Western liturgical practice. After Christmas the Mother of God is commemorated on 26th December, and on the first Sunday after the Feast there is the commemoration of 'Joseph the Betrothed', David the royal ancestor of Christ, and James the 'Brother of God' – an interesting collection of people who in various ways can literally be described as having been 'close' to Jesus. During the ten days after Christmas there is no fasting, as the sense of joy at the birth of the Saviour permeates this period.

The Nativity Feast takes place in the northern hemisphere in the depths of winter darkness. The placing of the celebration of the Incarnation in the darkest time of the year makes possible the gathering together of all the rich symbolism of light and darkness around the birth of Christ. Texts such as Isaiah 9:2, Luke 1:78–79 and John 1:1–14 are not actually used in the liturgical celebration of this Feast, but the imagery of those biblical texts permeates the hymnody of the Feast: 'The light shines in the darkness, and the darkness has not overcome it' (John 1:5). Here we have the juxtaposition of light and darkness, not as two opposing absolutes, but as contrasting elements which are not destined to co-exist for ever. The darkness is dispersed by the power of the light, but until the final victory of the light we live in a world where we still experience the polarities and conflicts of light and darkness; we recognize the need for illumination, and we welcome the Son of God who comes as Light to a darkened world:

He has come in the flesh to enlighten those in peril of darkness.[2]

Today Adam has been recalled from error and from the dark deceiving of the adversary, for Christ is made flesh as man from a Virgin; and renewing Adam, he has removed the curse that came from the virgin Eve.[3]

The peril, ignorance and deception of the darkness have been replaced by the enlightenment and knowledge brought by Christ, and the light of truth that shows up the deceptions of the darkness. The Adam and Eve who turned their backs on God and hid themselves from the presence of the Lord are called back from the exile of error and darkness:

> Foreseeing thy coming from the Virgin, Habakkuk cried out marvelling: O Deliverer, Thou art come incarnate from Teman, to call back Adam from his exile.[4]

Here we find a theme that will recur with greater force and prominence as we move towards the climax of the work of redemption in the Crucifixion and Resurrection of Christ. He comes to call back Adam, to bring the humanity that is living 'in darkness and in the shadow of death' (Luke 1:79) into the light and glory of the Trinitarian life and Kingdom. The birth, life, ministry, death and resurrection of Christ can all be seen as embodying the call to Adam, the call to humanity to turn to face the glory that is being revealed. 'And the Word became flesh and dwelt among us, full of grace and truth; we have beheld his glory, glory as of the only Son from the Father' (John 1:14).

In the texts associated with the Forefeast of the Nativity there is great urgency in the way we are encouraged to make our way to Bethlehem, to go there in company with the Magi, to see the mystery of the Incarnation, to worship and adore. We are urged to behold the self-emptying love of the Son of God, and with the Magi to discover the true enlightenment:

> Let us celebrate, O ye people, the Forefeast of the Nativity of Christ, and raising our minds on high let us go in spirit to Bethlehem; and let us look upon the great mystery in the cave. For Eden is opened once again, when from a pure Virgin God comes forth, perfect in His divinity as in His manhood.[5]

> A star shewed plainly to the Magi
> The Word that was before the sun,
>   and who has come to make transgressions cease.
> They saw Thee wrapped in swaddling clothes,
>   within a poor and lowly cave,
> Who sharest all our sufferings,
> And in joy they gazed upon Thee,
>   who art at once both man and Lord.[6]

'In joy they gazed upon Thee, who art both man and Lord.' This phrase holds together the historical birth and the theological truth of the event celebrated at Christmas. The Scripture readings for the Feast (listed at the end of this chapter) likewise relate to the event and its theological significance. In particular they make the point that this birth is a fulfilment of prophecy, as God himself comes in the flesh to his people to bring salvation and enlightenment, reversing the sin of Adam, and opening the way to true theosis. The hymnody of the Feast relishes the paradox of the Incarnation – God the creator, uncontainable and unapproachable, yet made flesh, contained in the womb of the Virgin and born in the darkness of the cave. Hence, 'Bethlehem has opened Eden', and 'the paradise that is within the cave' is there as a gift of God to his people. In a similar way the icons of the Nativity invite us to gaze upon him who is both Man and Lord. The icons form part of the liturgical celebration of the Feast, and help us to focus our attention and our prayers on the mystery of the Light shining in the darkness, the Word made flesh and dwelling among us, the God 'who cannot be contained . . . now . . . made poor in the wealth of His tender mercies', for 'the Master of all has come to live with his servants':

> The holy sayings of the Prophets (Isaiah 7:14; Micah 5:2) have been fulfilled in the city of Bethlehem within a cave. The whole creation is made rich: let it rejoice and be of good cheer. The Master of all has come to live with his servants, and from the bondage of the enemy He delivers us who were made subject to corruption (Romans 8:20–21). In swaddling clothes and lying in a manger, He is made manifest a young Child, the pre-eternal God.[7]

The mystery of the Incarnation which unites God and man, and brings together heaven and earth, is seen as drawing a joyful response from the whole creation, as the created order welcomes and seeks to co-operate with the self-emptying love of God:

> What shall we offer Thee, O Christ, who for our sakes hast appeared on earth as man? Every creature made by Thee offers Thee thanks. The angels offer Thee a hymn; the heavens a star; the Magi, gifts; the shepherds, their wonder; the earth, its cave; the wilderness, the manger: and we offer Thee a Virgin Mother. O pre-eternal God, have mercy upon us.[8]

The sixteenth-century icon illustrated in **Plate 6** is an impressive example of a Nativity icon and includes most of the details one would expect to find in an icon for this festival. The whole icon has a colourful and joyful appearance appropriate for the celebration of the events whereby 'the whole creation is made rich'. The three saints on the top edge of this icon are St Eudoxia, St John Climacus and St Juliana; the people who commissioned the icon may well have been named after these saints, who were popular in Novgorod; but they have, of course, no integral place in the icon itself. Some of the details in the Nativity icon derive from the apocryphal *Book of James* (mid-second century). There we are told how on the journey through the desert Mary was about to give birth, and Joseph found a cave in which to leave Mary with his sons while he went off in search of a Hebrew midwife in the Bethlehem region.[9]

At the upper edge of the icon is a segment of a circle representing the divine realm, and from it comes a ray of light which descends to the star shining above the darkness of the cave where the infant Christ rests in the manger. The threefold ray of light radiating from the star implies the revelation of the whole Trinity in the Incarnation, and this feature will be seen again in the icon of Christ's Baptism, where the threefold ray of light spreads out over Christ in the waters of the Jordan. Two angels are shown praising and glorifying God; another bends low announcing the good tidings to a shepherd, who responds joyfully. Opposite the shepherd three Magi approach the cave; here they are shown as men of different ages. The Magi and the Shepherds are often regarded as representing different types of humanity and their response to God: the Shepherds stand for those whose response to God is direct, an intuitive response to the revelation; the Magi stand for those whose path to God is through long and arduous study and philosophical enquiry. Together, the two types are united around the revelation given in the Christ. At the centre of the icon are the cave, the manger and the Virgin reclining on a mattress; this central section is obviously at the heart of the Christmas celebration:

> The Great King comes in haste to enter a small cave, that He may make me great who had grown small, and that, as transcendent God, by His poverty without measure He may enrich me who had grown poor.[10] (cf 2 Corinthians 8:9)

> Thou hast shone forth from a Virgin, O Christ, Thou spiritual Sun of Righteousness. And a star showed Thee, whom nothing can contain, contained within a cave. Thou hast led Magi to worship Thee, and joining them we magnify Thee: O Giver of life, glory to Thee.[11]

The star serves to reveal the Christ who might otherwise not be recognized in such a humble setting. The ox and ass are shown adoring the incarnate Lord, in fulfilment of Isaiah 1:3, 'the ox knows its owner, and the ass its master's crib; but Israel does not know, my people does not understand', showing that the incarnate God comes to fulfil the plan prepared long before. These animals are the first witnesses to the Incarnation; they are always shown in the earliest known depictions of Christ in the manger, even when many of the other details are absent. 'The angels offer Thee a hymn; the heavens, a star; the Magi, gifts; the shepherds, their wonder; the earth, its cave; the wilderness, the manger: and we offer Thee a Virgin Mother.'[12] The earth offers its cave – the dark place from which 'the life-giving light', the 'Spiritual Sun of Righteousness' will shine forth upon the world. The symbolism is very powerful: the earth that takes part in the rejoicing at the Incarnation, that takes part in the great cosmic offering to welcome the Saviour, is spoken of as offering its cave. In some icons (for example, the one in the grotto of the Nativity at Bethlehem) the earth is personified, and carrying a cave makes its way to Bethlehem! It is as if the liturgical texts and the icon are acknowledging our need to offer the darkness of our ignorance to God as the first step towards receiving the gifts of grace. The cave is offered and becomes the place where the Word made flesh will dwell among us (John 1:14), the place of darkness where the true Light that enlightens everyone (John 1:9) will shine with great brilliance. This symbolism can be explored in a great many ways: the dark cave as representing the dark, hidden unconscious side of our nature, the 'shadow' side of reality; the cave as a place of death and burial, and the Holy Birth in the cave as a foreshadowing of the saving death that will be accepted by Christ as he enters more and more completely into the depths of the world's darkness; the cave also as a place of new life, the 'tomb and womb' paradox; yet again there is the darkness of the mystery of God, the essence which forever remains beyond our understanding (cf Chapter 7). It is best not to attempt to explain the depth and complexity of the symbolism; it is something that has to be seen and heard as it makes itself known; it has to become part of a language by which we discern both the things of God and the depths of our own being. We place ourselves on the threshold of God's revelation as we look at and listen to what the holy icons are offering to us. The earth offers its cave, and we must continue to offer up our ignorance, our darkness, and our need of illumination.

The wilderness offers a manger. Here the imagery and symbolism refers to the story of the children of Israel in the wilderness being nourished by the manna given by God (cf Exodus 16). Now the empty wilderness offers the manger to welcome him who is the True Bread from heaven, who comes to be born at Bethlehem, the 'House of Bread', and who continues to give himself as the Bread of Life in the Liturgy of the Eucharist.

> I am the bread of life. Your fathers ate the manna in the wilderness, and they died. This is the bread which comes down from heaven, that a man may eat of it and not die. I am the living bread which came down from heaven; if any one eats of this bread, he will live for ever; and the bread which I shall give for the life of the world is my flesh. (John 6:48–51)

Again, in some icons (including the one in the grotto of the Nativity) we see a personification of the wilderness, carrying the manger towards the cave of the Nativity. The manger forms a link with the altar of sacrifice and communion, with the Lamb of God whose death brings life to his people. The swaddling clothes likewise form a link between birth and death, for they remind us of the burial garments of Lazarus (see **Plates 13 and 8b**) and of Christ himself in icons of the entombment. Thus in the Nativity icon we have a powerful conjunction of the themes of birth and death: the Son of God is born into a world where the full extent of his self-giving love will only be seen as he accepts the death of the Cross. The divine kenosis★ or self-emptying that we celebrate in the Incarnation at Christmas will take Christ on to Calvary and into Hades before the fullness of his redemptive work can be completed (see Philippians 2:5–8). St Ephraim the Syrian (c. 306–373) in one of his homilies expresses dramatically the view that the Lord needed to take human flesh in order to be able to get into Hades to release the dead:

> And because Death was not able to devour Him without the body, nor Sheol to swallow Him up without the flesh, He came unto the Virgin, that from thence He might obtain that which should bear Him to Sheol . . . With the body then that [was] from the Virgin, He entered Sheol and plundered its storehouses and emptied its treasures.[13]

'We offer Thee a Virgin Mother.' Mary is seen as humanity's offering to God – an offering of the one prepared by God to be the 'living City of Christ the King' and the 'Bridal Chamber made by God'.[14] Some of the background details of the Nativity icon actually reflect some of the liturgical titles given to the Virgin on the basis of Old Testament typology, such as 'holy mountain', 'height of holiness' and 'original rock'. The Virgin is shown reclining on a mattress, having truly given birth to the incarnate Son. On her mantle and shoulders are the three stars which came to symbolize her virginity before, during and after the birth of her Son. Her posture and gaze are directed towards Joseph who has had no direct involvement in the birth that has taken place, and is traditionally shown seated apart in a thoughtful, even anxious pose, still failing to comprehend the mystery of the Incarnation. Many texts for the Forefeast of the Nativity concentrate on the doubts and the dilemma of Joseph:

> Joseph spoke thus to the Virgin: 'What is this doing, O Mary, that I see in thee? I fail to understand and am amazed, and my mind is struck with dismay. Go from my sight, therefore, with all speed. What is this doing, O Mary, that I see in thee? Instead of honour, thou hast brought me shame; instead of gladness, sorrow; instead of praise, reproof. No further shall I bear the reproach of men. I received thee from the priests of the temple, as one blameless before the Lord. And what is this that I now see?'[15]

> O Virgin, when Joseph went up to Bethlehem wounded by sorrow, thou didst cry to him: 'Why art thou downcast and troubled, seeing me great with child? Why art thou wholly ignorant of the fearful mystery that comes to pass in me? Henceforth, cast every fear aside and understand this strange marvel: for in my womb God now descends upon earth for mercy's sake, and He has taken flesh. Thou shalt see Him according to His good pleasure, when He is born; and filled with joy thou shalt worship Him as Thy Creator. Him the angels praise without ceasing in song and glorify with the Father and the Holy Spirit.'[16]

The gaze of Mary towards the troubled and downcast Joseph is one that suggests compassion for all who cannot understand or are tempted to deny the mystery of the Incarnation. The person facing Joseph is sometimes interpreted as the devil in disguise, tempting Joseph; alternatively he may be seen as one of the prophets helping Joseph to understand the mystery. At the bottom-right of the icon we see the midwives preparing to give the incarnate Son his first bath; in some icons one of the midwives is seen testing the temperature of the water. The rocky surface of the landscape seems to be illuminated from the heavenly realm, and the many fruit-bearing bushes help to reinforce the significance of Christmas as a celebration of re-creation.

The structure and balance of this icon demonstrate the Incarnation as the union of heaven and earth, the coming together of God and humanity in the person of Christ. The cry of the prophet, 'O that thou wouldst rend the heavens and come down' (Isaiah 64:1), has been answered by God in the Gospel: 'And the angel said to her, "The Holy Spirit will come upon you, and the power of the Most High will overshadow you; therefore the child to be born will be called holy, the Son of God"' (Luke 1:35). Around this fundamental divine act are gathered with the angels the Magi and the shepherds to whom the revelation was mysteriously made known. At the lowest level of the icon are placed Joseph with his doubts and temptations, and the midwives performing their practical tasks for the incarnate Child; this latter detail is adopted from other birth scenes that were common in the Greek world, such as the birth of Alexander, and is used in the icon to reinforce the truth that a real birth has taken place. Within this lowest part of the icon, however, two important theological elements may be implied. First is the gift of faith, for Joseph remained the faithful spouse of the Virgin and guardian of her Son, in spite of the doubts and questions that are explored in the texts. Secondly, the washing undertaken by the midwives affirms the humanity of Christ, and may also suggest a reference to the Christian Baptism of infants: in the Orthodox tradition one of the roles of the godmother is to test the temperature of the water before the baptism takes place. In Baptism we are initiated into the faith and sacramental life of the Church; we come to share the mystery of the divine life which has been opened to us.

> Come, let us greatly rejoice in the Lord as we tell of this present mystery. The middle wall of partition has been destroyed; the flaming sword turns back, the cherubim withdraw from the tree of life, and I partake of the delight of Paradise from which I was cast out through disobedience. For the express Image of the Father (Hebrews 1:3), the Imprint of His eternity, takes the form of a servant, and without undergoing change He comes forth from a Mother who knew not wedlock. For what He was, He has remained, true God: and what He was not, He has taken upon Himself, becoming man through love for mankind. Unto Him let us cry aloud: God born of a Virgin, have mercy upon us.[17]

In **Plate 2b** we have a fresco of the Nativity (c. 1350) from the Church of the Panagia Phorbiotissa at Asinou in Cyprus. There are some obvious points of contrast with the icon in **Plate 6**. In the Asinou fresco the Virgin is shown seated in the cave rather than lying down as usual; this posture is used here to stress the painless nature of the Nativity and the divine origin of the child. The manger has something of the appearance of an altar; and the approach of the Magi bearing their gifts to lay before the Lamb of God and join with the angels in glorifying God suggests a liturgical dimension. This in turn reflects the view that the Magi – star worshippers – are led by a star to abandon star worship, and to worship instead the Incarnate Son of God.

The Kontakion for the Feast is a concise summary of what we hear in the liturgical texts and see in the icons:

> Today the Virgin gives birth to Him who is above all being, and the earth offers a cave to Him whom no man can approach. Angels with shepherds give glory, and Magi journey with a star. For unto us is born a young Child, the pre-eternal God.[18]

★　　★　　★

The main Scripture readings for the feast are as follows:

> *At Vespers:* Genesis 1:1–13; Numbers 24:2–3, 5–9, 17–18; Micah 4:6–7, 5:1–3; Isaiah 11:1–10; Baruch 3:3–4:4; Daniel 2:31–36, 44–45; Isaiah 9:6–7, 7:10–16, 8:1–4, 9–10; Hebrews 1:1–12; Luke 2:1–20.
> *At Mattins:* Matthew 1:18–25.
> *At the Divine Liturgy:* Galatians 4:4–7; Matthew 2:1–12.

5

Simeon Was Amazed

The Meeting of Our Lord and God and Saviour Jesus Christ
(The Presentation of Christ in the Temple) (2nd February)

Simeon was amazed when he beheld incarnate the Word that is without beginning, carried by the Virgin as on the throne of the cherubim, the Cause of all
being, Himself become a babe; and he cried aloud to Him: 'The whole world
has been filled with Thy praise.'[1]

I

The events that form the subject of this Feast are recounted in St Luke's Gospel
(2:22–38). Christ is brought into the Temple by Mary and Joseph in fulfilment of the
requirements of the Law, and in the Temple they are greeted by Simeon and Anna.
Simeon is described by St Luke as 'righteous and devout, looking for the consola-
tion of Israel, and the Holy Spirit was upon him. And it had been revealed to him by
the Holy Spirit that he should not see death before he had seen the Lord's Christ'
(Luke 2:25–26) (Simeon is often assumed to have been a priest, but this is not stated
in Luke's Gospel). Anna is described as a prophetess, and she in her old age 'gave
thanks to God, and spoke of him to all who were looking for the redemption of
Jerusalem' (Luke 2:38). In this event the Law, the spirit of prophecy and the Temple rituals all come together and are used to express the significance of the
Christ-child. In the meeting with Simeon, Christ is welcomed as 'a light for revelation to the Gentiles, and for glory to thy people Israel' (Luke2:32). Simeon prophesies
that the child will precipitate the reversal of the fortunes of many in Israel, and be a
sign that evokes conflict, as the innermost workings of the human heart are laid bare;
a sword will pierce the soul of Mary also (Luke 2:34–35). St Luke's narrative echoes
the story of the young Samuel being dedicated to the Lord by his mother Hannah in
the sanctuary at Shiloh (1 Samuel 1:24–28), and also echoes the prophecy of Malachi
(3:1–2) about the Lord coming to his Temple. As we shall see later, the developed

celebration of these events in the Feast of the Meeting of the Lord places them in an even richer theological context, with a heightened sense of paradox and the use of other Old Testament imagery to stress the marvel of the Incarnation and the dramatic response of Simeon.

The earliest homilies associated with the Meeting of the Lord come from a time before the associated feast was observed on the fortieth day after Christmas. The Gospel text may well have been read during the Christmas season or else at a commemoration of the Circumcision of Christ, and could have been the occasion for these homilies. By the late fourth century a feast on the fortieth day after Christmas was observed in Jerusalem, and from these seems to have spread to other Churches. The emphasis of the Feast is on the Incarnation, particularly on the meeting of the Incarnate God and faithful Simeon, who represents the old dispensation and awaits the fulfilment of prophecy; after seeing the fulfilment of the promise Simeon departs from the scene, ready (according to some of the hymns) to spread the news of the Incarnation to the dead.

Some homilies from the sixth to the ninth centuries make great use of hyperbole, exaggerating certain elements in the story with dramatic effect to heighten awareness of the significance of the meeting between the Lord and Simeon. One anonymous example from the sixth century describes the vigour and hope with which Simeon approaches the Temple:

> The old man Symeon, having stripped off the weakness of age, and having put on the vigour of hope, hurried before the law to receive the provider of the law . . . He was full of yearning; he was full of hope; he was full of joy . . . The Holy Spirit proclaimed the glad tidings, and before Symeon reached the temple he was excited by the eyes of understanding, and had rejoiced as if he already had what he desired . . . And most swiftly travelling raised from the ground on his steps he reaches the long-holy shrine and . . . spreads out his holy arms before the temple's Lord.[2]

According to George of Nicomedia in the ninth century, Simeon invokes the assistance of the Spirit to get him to the Temple for this momentous Meeting:

> Give your hand to old age, O Paraclete. For my body is now weary, and is too tired to walk. Lift me up, O omnipotent and untiring force, lift me up in my weakness and old age, and carry me off quickly to these events. For should I wish to use my own feet for walking, I will certainly delay on the road, and those events will pass and I will not see them.

The answered invocation means that Simeon 'does not use his own feet in the service of the mystery, but the Holy Spirit becomes his chariot and brings him to the temple like a person with wings and like another airborne Habakkuk'. According to this same homilist the Mother of God is not fully aware of the wondrous way in which Simeon has arrived at the Temple. 'But then, when she saw the divine baby leaping in her arms and striving to jump out into his hands, she more quickly recognized the force of the mystery, and gave over the child to the outstretched hands of the old man.'[3] Even though the most extravagant elements from the imaginative minds of the homilists do not find a permanent place in the liturgical usage of the Orthodox Churches, in some hymns and icons one can sometimes detect the influence of this heritage of rhetoric in the running steps of Simeon, his flowing garments and outstretched hands, and the Child's movement towards the old man.

II

The account of Isaiah's vision of God in the Temple where the prophet is overcome by the sense of his own sin and unworthiness is read at Great Vespers.

> Then flew one of the seraphim to me, having in his hand a burning coal which he had taken with tongs from the altar. And he touched my mouth, and said, 'Behold, this has touched your lips; your guilt is taken away, and your sin forgiven.' (Isaiah 6:6–7)

This text comes to be seen in the light of the Incarnation as a foreshadowing of the Incarnation itself: the burning coal which takes away guilt and brings forgiveness is a symbol of the Incarnate Son, and the tongs with which the seraph brings the coal from the heavenly altar to the prophet are a symbol of the Virgin through whom the Incarnation takes place. In the context of the Meeting of the Lord, the typological interpretation is apt: the seraph with the tongs and the coal of fire are effective in purifying the prophet Isaiah and preparing him for his ministry as a prophet, and so much more does the approach of the Virgin Mother bearing in her arms the Incarnate fire of divinity prepare Simeon for his departure to proclaim to Adam and Eve the good news of the Incarnation and the mystery of grace.

The great range of imagery and understanding that is to be found in the hymnody for this feast is worth exploring before we look at the icon.

Details of the Gospel narrative are taken up by the hymn-writers, and frequently used to incorporate more developed theological understanding. Much is made of the paradox that the God who is higher than the cherubim and the seraphim humbles himself to be carried in the arms of the Theotokos and the old man Simeon (and the same sort of paradox is explored in the texts for Palm Sunday):

The Ancient of Days, a young child in the flesh, was brought to the temple by His Mother the Virgin, fulfilling the ordinance of His own Law.[4]

He who is borne on high by the cherubim and praised in hymns by the seraphim, is brought today according to the Law into the holy temple and rests in the arms of the Elder as on a throne.[5]

The reality and wonder of the Incarnation permeates the whole feast:

O God, who wast before all things began, of Thine own will Thou hast become man and art carried, a child forty days old, into the temple.[6]

Not parted in Thy divinity from the bosom of the Father, Thou wast made flesh according to Thy good pleasure; and upheld in the arms of the ever-Virgin Thou hast been committed to the hands of Simeon, the receiver of God, O Thou who upholdest the whole world with Thine hand.[7]

The imagery drawn from Isaiah 6 has a conspicuous place in the hymnody; the symbol of fire for the presence of God is a key element in the symbolic language of Patristic and Orthodox theology:

Christ the coal of fire, whom Isaiah foresaw, now rests in the arms of the Theotokos as in a pair of tongs, and He is given to the Elder. In fear and joy Simeon held the Master in his arms, and asked for his release from life, singing the praises of the Mother of God.[8]

The Elder bent down and reverently touched the footprints of the Mother of God who knew not wedlock, and he said: 'O pure Lady, thou dost carry Fire. I am afraid to take God as a babe in my arms . . .'[9]

Mary, thou art the mystic Tongs, who hast conceived in thy womb Christ the live Coal.[10]

The paradox that the Law-giver becomes subject to the Law in his humanity is a conspicuous theme at this Feast. We are left in no doubt of the significance of the Old Testament Law, its place in the providence of God, and its fulfilment in the New Covenant accomplished through Christ. The Incarnation involves God the Son becoming human within the particular religious and cultural circumstances of the people of Israel.

Today He who once gave the Law to Moses on Sinai submits Himself to the ordinances of the Law, in His compassion becoming for our sakes as we are. Now the God of purity as a holy child has opened a pure womb, and as God He is brought as an offering to Himself, setting us free from the curse of the Law and granting light to our souls.[11]

The theophany experienced by Moses on Sinai at the giving of the Law is a point of comparison with the reception of the Law-giver himself as a babe in the arms of Simeon.

Today Simeon the Elder enters the temple rejoicing in spirit, to receive in his arms Him who gave the Law to Moses and who Himself fulfils the Law. For Moses was counted worthy to see God through darkness and sounds not clear (Exodus 19:16–20); and with his face covered (Exodus 34:29–33) he rebuked the unbelieving hearts of the Hebrews. But Simeon carried the pre-eternal Word of the Father in bodily form, and he revealed the Light of the Gentiles, the Cross and the Resurrection; and Ann was proved to be a prophetess, preaching the Saviour and Deliverer of Israel.[12]

The Jerusalem Temple naturally has a place in these hymns. The Temple is the place where the Meeting occurs, and where various elements of the holy converge. This is the earthly site where the place and the people that are temples of God come together:

Today the holy Mother who is higher than any temple, has come into the temple, disclosing to the world the Maker of the world and Giver of the Law.[13]

The holy Virgin offered in the Holy Place Him who is Holy, giving Him to the minister in holy things. And Simeon with exceeding joy received Him in his outstretched arms . . . and he cried out: 'O Master, now lettest Thou Thy servant depart in peace according to Thy word, O Lord.'[14]

The influence of some of the homilies mentioned above can be seen in a few places in the hymnody where the renewed vigour of the old man and the work of the Spirit in bringing him to the Temple are mentioned:

Ye hands of Simeon, weakened by age, be strong, (Isaiah 35:3) and ye, the feeble legs of the Elder, run straight to meet Christ.[15]

The Elder brought to the temple by the Spirit, took in his arms the Master of the Law and cried: 'Now let me depart in peace . . . from the bond of the flesh according to Thy word . . .'[16]

Simeon's awe in welcoming in the incarnate Word and Lover of mankind is appropriately expressed:

> Beholding Thee as a babe, O Word begotten of the Father before all ages, Simeon the venerable cried aloud: 'I am distraught by fear at holding Thee, O Master, in my arms. But now, I pray Thee, lettest Thou Thy servant depart in peace, for Thou art compassionate.'[17]

The joy of the meeting brings to an end Simeon's years of waiting for the fulfilment of the hope of Israel:

> Simeon, having now been granted the fulfilment of the prophecies concerning himself, blesses the Virgin and Theotokos Mary, and foretells in figures the Passion of her Son. From Him he begs release, crying aloud: 'Now let me depart, O Master, as Thou hast before promised to me: for I have seen Thee the pre-eternal Light, the Lord and Saviour of the people that bear the name of Christ.'[18]

The way in which Simeon's release is interpreted may seem unusual to people outside the Orthodox tradition, for his departure is not simply to the blessedness of the world to come, but on a mission to share the good news of the Incarnation with Adam, and announce to the dead the restoration of humanity to the glory of the Father's presence. Thus our attention is moved towards the fully accomplished work of Christ at Easter, and in the words of the hymn we can already say, 'Now let the gate of heaven be opened.'

> Now let the gate of heaven be opened: for God the Word, begotten timelessly of the Father, has taken flesh and is born of a Virgin. He desires in His goodness to call back mortal nature and to set it at the right hand of the Father.[19]

> 'I depart', cried Simeon, 'to declare the good tidings to Adam abiding in hell and to Eve' . . . 'To deliver our kind formed from dust, God will go down even unto hell; He will give freedom to all the captives and sight to the blind, and will grant the dumb to cry aloud: O God of our fathers, blessed art Thou.'[20]

> 'Thou hast committed to me the exceeding joy of Thy salvation, O Christ', cried Simeon. 'Take Thy servant, who is weary of the shadow, and make him a new preacher of the mystery of grace . . .'[21]

The Song of Simeon (Luke 2:29–32), which has a place in the worshipping life of the Church in both East and West, provides the theme that Christ comes as both a Light for the Gentiles and as the Glory of Israel; this is developed in the hymnody for the Feast:

> As a light to lighten the Gentiles, hast Thou made Thyself manifest, O Lord: the Sun of Righteousness seated upon a swift cloud (Isaiah 19.1), Thou hast fulfilled the shadow of the Law and shown forth the beginning of the new Grace.[22]

Simeon's prophecy that a sword would pierce the soul of the Mother of God is, rather surprisingly, not developed very fully, but it is mentioned, and linked with Mary's place at the Cross of her Son:

> 'And a sword shall pierce thy heart, O All-Pure Virgin', (Luke 2:35) Simeon foretold to the Theotokos, 'when thou shalt see thy Son upon the Cross to whom we cry aloud: O God of our fathers, blessed art Thou.'[23]

≪ III ≫

Plate 7 shows an icon from Novgorod painted about 1470. It is an icon with considerable simplicity of form and composition. We seem to look from various angles at the architecture in the background representing the Temple; the altar and other details of the Temple have the appearance of ecclesiastical buildings, perhaps implying the emergence of the Christian Church; the clear forms which are involved do not create any sense of confusion or fussiness. Simeon is not a priest, nor is he dressed as one, but he is placed on a step near the altar, and has received the Christ-child into his covered hands; he bows over the child in his arms, and towards the group on the left led by the Mother of God. The hands of the Mother of God are still covered and stretched out towards Simeon and her Son. Behind her another female figure represents the prophetess Anna, and behind her comes Joseph holding in his veiled hands the two birds to be offered in sacrifice.

The undergarments of all the figures in the icon are in a greyish-green colour which is used also on the roofs and the background wall in the icon; for the outer garments a variety of colours are used, gold ochre for Joseph, vermilion for Anna, a warm sepia for the Mother of God, and a brownish-red for Simeon. The three figures on the left form a united group, as if the Mother of God is leading them in homage to the Incarnate Son in the arms of the old Simeon. The fact that the hands of three of the figures in the icon are covered, a traditional way of expressing reverence for holy things, adds to the sense of restraint and liturgical movement in this icon. The pigeons or doves in the hands of Joseph, brought to be offered in accordance with the Law, already seem unnecessary, as the Live Coal of the Incarnate Godhead has been brought into the Temple by the Theotokos in fulfilment of prophecy, and has been welcomed with joy in the arms of Simeon.

Our attention naturally comes to rest at Simeon's welcome of the One who fulfils the purposes of God and the promises made to Simeon. The sense of stillness and dignity takes one into an attitude of reverence at the mystery of this Meeting of the Lord with those who have waited for his coming. As we ponder on this mystery, so it will permeate our hearts and souls and enable them to become living temples of God where the Lord is present and welcomed at the core of our being.

Plate 8a shows the fresco of the Meeting from the church of the Panagia Phorbiotissa at Asinou in Cyprus, painted about 1350. Here on the left we have the Mother of God with the Christ-child in her arms, and behind her Joseph carrying the two pigeons. Simeon's posture would seem to indicate that he has arrived at great speed, as described in the homilies mentioned earlier; he seems to be balancing on his toes, as he leans forward with his covered hands and arms outstretched, eager to receive the Christ-child; the gaze of Simeon is met by that of the Mother of God, and of the Child; he is in his Mother's arms, clinging to her and looking nervously at Simeon. The elongated thumb and first finger of the right hand of the Mother of God could be interpreted as indicating the tongs imagery taken up from Isaiah by homilists and hymnographers. Anna stands behind Simeon, pointing to heaven with her right hand, and in her left holding a scroll with the inscription 'This Child has made heaven and earth secure'. The altar cover is of sumptuous material, and the baldachino with lamps has a cross at the top. The Asinou fresco does not have the stillness and hieratic quality of the Novgorod icon, but with its lively homeliness it certainly conveys the meaning of the Feast.

★   ★   ★

The main Scripture readings appointed for the Feast are as follows:

> *At Great Vespers:* extracts from Exodus 12:15–13:16; Leviticus 12 and Numbers 8; Isaiah 6:1–12, 19:1, 3–5, 12, 16, 19–21.
> *At Mattins:* Luke 2:25–32.
> *At the Divine Liturgy:* Hebrews 7:7–17; Luke 2:22–40.

≪ 6 ≫

A Wonderful Restoration by Fire and Spirit and Water

THE HOLY THEOPHANY OF OUR LORD AND GOD AND SAVIOUR
JESUS CHRIST (THE BAPTISM OF THE LORD) (6TH JANUARY)

O Creator, who art the New Adam, Thou makest new those born on earth, and Thou bringest to pass a strange regeneration and a wonderful restoration by fire and Spirit and water.[1]

≪ I ≫

In the early centuries of the Church's life a celebration of the 'Theophany'★ or 'Epiphany' (literally 'manifestation of God' and 'revelation') took place on 6th January. This celebration of the revelation of God in Christ focused on various events that we read about early in the Gospels. These were celebrated from the point of view that in them God had made himself known to the world, had 'appeared' and 'revealed' himself in ways that were definitive and unique. The events that were the focus of the Feast were the Birth of Christ, the visit of the Magi to worship Christ, and the Baptism of Christ. Strange though it may seem to us, the celebration of these events in a chronological sequence of separate commemorations was a later practice, and led to changes in the direction and content of the feasts. The Feast on 6th January in the West came to be known as the Epiphany, with its focus on the visit of the Magi and the revelation of Christ to these men who personified the Gentile, non-Jewish world; in the East, the Feast has continued to be known as the Theophany or the Epiphany, and from the fourth century onwards the primary focus has been the Baptism of Christ, an event in which the Holy Trinity is revealed, Christ is baptized, and the origins of Christian Baptism are discerned. St John Chrysostom (c. 347–407) comments on the appropriateness of the title for this Feast: 'It is not the day when Christ was born that should be called Epiphany, but the day when he was baptized. Not through his birth did he become known to all, but through his Baptism. Before the day of his Baptism he was not known to the people.'[2]

In the early part of the fourth century the Church answered the fundamental questions about the divinity of Christ which had been raised by Arius, a priest in Alexandria (c. 250–c. 336). He had denied that Christ was co-eternal with the Father, so various questions followed from that denial: In what sense can we speak of Jesus as divine? If he is a divine being, does that mean he 'is' God? Or is he some created spiritual being, higher than man and the angels, who became man? If he 'is not' God, how is human redemption achieved? And equally, if he is not truly man, how can human redemption be achieved? The Church's answer at the Council of Nicaea in 325 was that in Jesus we have the second Person of the Trinity, God the Son, Incarnate – one Person of the Trinity taking human flesh and blood, becoming as we are in all respects except for sin. As we continue to affirm in the Creed: Christ is

> the only Son of God, eternally begotten of the Father, God from God, Light from Light, true God from true God, begotten, not made, of one Being with the Father. For us men and for our salvation he came down from heaven: by the power of the Holy Spirit he became incarnate from the Virgin Mary, and was made man.

The teaching of Arius was condemned as heresy, and although it took many years for 'Arianism' to be overcome, the fourth century saw a great burgeoning of the Church's liturgical life in the light of the decisions reached at Nicaea. The celebration of the Lord's birth as a separate feast began about this time in the West; the practice spread to the East, and was vigorously promoted by St John Chrysostom. In the Orthodox Church the celebration of the Theophany has a similar liturgical structure to that of Christmas: the Feast is preceded by a Forefeast, and followed by the Synaxis of the Forerunner and eight days of Afterfeast; the liturgical texts for both feasts are greatly influenced by the doctrinal decisions made at Nicaea. Both feasts reverberate with the faith that Christ is the Son of God Incarnate, that he is truly God and truly Man; and that God and man are united in the person of Jesus Christ by an act of the most amazing divine humility and self-giving, for the sake of our salvation.

The Forefeast of the Theophany on 5th January is a fast day, and the liturgical observances include the Royal Hours (cf page 32). On both the Forefeast and the Feast itself, the Great Blessing of the Waters takes place; normally this takes place in church on 5th January and out of doors on 6th January. The first blessing is of water for the sacrament of Baptism and for other uses in the Church's life, and takes place at the font or at a large vessel of water in the centre of the church. The second blessing is of the waters that form part of our everyday life and environment such as rivers and the sea. This liturgical act is best seen as an extension of what Christ did at the Jordan: Christ, present in his Church, continues to bless the waters that we may enter into the renewed life of his creation and the new life of the baptized within his Church. During the blessing of the waters the priest immerses the Cross three times in the waters, symbolizing Christ's immersion in the Jordan and our own immersion in the waters of Baptism. This action, its symbolism and the liturgical texts for the Feast not only associate the events that occurred at the Jordan with the rite of Christian Baptism; they also bring together elements in the whole drama of redemption, for Christ's descent into the waters of the Jordan foreshadows his death and descent into Hades and his glorious resurrection from the dead. And our baptism is a baptism into Christ's death: 'For you have died, and your life is hid with Christ in God' (Colossians 3:3). Throughout this Feast, and others as well, our attention is drawn to the details of the event that is celebrated and also to its wider significance in the work of salvation. To use an analogy from landscape painting, it is as if our attention oscillates between foreground detail and the wider background of the canvas.

⋟ II ⋞

When we look at the liturgical texts associated with the Feast of the Theophany, it is obvious that the event of the Lord's Baptism is celebrated in a distinctive theological context. Apart from the details recorded in the Bible, there is great emphasis on Christ's coming 'in the form of a servant' to his Baptism 'to fulfill all righteousness' (Philippians 2:7; Matthew 3:15); on his coming 'to save Adam the first-formed man';[3] on the significance of the Jordan and its water; and on the cleansing and enlightenment that are accomplished through Christ's Baptism at the hand of John. All these themes are present in the first group of quotations below which reiterate and develop the details of the biblical narrative:

> [Christ to John:] 'Only baptize Me in silence and in expectation of all that shall come from this My baptism. For this cause shalt thou have such honour as belongs not to the angels, and I shall make thee greater than all the prophets. Not one of them saw Me openly, but only in figures and shades and dreams, while thou hast seen Me standing of Mine own will before thee. For I am come to save Adam the first-formed man.'[4]

> Thus spake the Lord to John: 'O Prophet, come and baptize Me who created thee, for I enlighten all men by grace and cleanse them. Touch My divine head and doubt not. O Prophet, suffer it to be so now: for I have come to fulfill all righteousness. Be in no doubt at all: for I am in haste to slay the enemy hidden in the waters, the prince of darkness, that I may now deliver the world from his snares, granting eternal life in my love for mankind.'[5]

> The streams of the Jordan received Thee who art the fountain, and the Comforter descended in the form of a dove. He who bowed the heavens, bowed His head, and the clay cried aloud to Him that formed him: 'Why dost Thou com-

mand of me what lies beyond my power? For I have need to be baptized of Thee.'
O sinless Christ, glory to Thee.[6]

A distinctive feature of these Orthodox liturgical texts is their use of paradox, and in the next group of quotations we see how the hymn-writers revel in the use of imagery to heighten this sense of paradox, as we celebrate the Invisible being made visible, the River of joy being baptized in the stream of the Jordan, the Master being baptized by the servant, and the immaterial fire of Christ's divinity being wrapped in the waters of the Jordan:

> The River of joy is baptized in the stream: He dries up the fount of evil and pours forth divine remission.[7]

> Jesus Christ comes forth to drown the rivers of sin in the streams of Jordan, granting enlightenment to all.[8]

> How shall the streams of the river receive Thee, the unbearable fire that now approaches? How shall the angels of heaven look upon this stripping? How shall John stretch out his hand upon Thee, O Word of God who wast before all things began and who hast fashioned him from earth.[9]

> The waters saw Thee, O God, and were afraid. The Jordan turned back, seeing the fire of the Godhead descending bodily and entering its stream. The Jordan turned back, beholding the Holy Spirit coming down in the form of a dove and flying about Thee. The Jordan turned back, seeing the Invisible made visible, the Creator made flesh, the Master in the form of a servant. The Jordan turned back, and the mountains skipped, looking upon God in the flesh . . .[10]

> The Lord, King of the ages, in the streams of the Jordan formed Adam anew, who was fallen into corruption, and He broke in pieces the heads of the dragons that were hidden there; for He has been glorified.[11]

> That which was revealed to Moses in the bush
> We see accomplished here in strange manner.
> The Virgin bore Fire within her, yet was not consumed,
> And the streams of Jordan suffered no harm when they received Him.[12]

The remaining quotations from the texts for the Feast have been selected to emphasize various aspects of the theology represented in the hymns, some of which have been touched on above.

1. The material creation is seen as ministering to Christ at his Baptism as it did at his Nativity; this text extends the ideas expressed in the Kontakion for Christ's Nativity which was quoted in Chapter 4 (page 39).

> O Lord, wishing to fulfil that which Thou hast appointed from eternity, Thou hast received from all the creation ministers at this Thy mystery: Gabriel from among the angels, the Virgin from among men, the Star from among the heavens, and Jordan from among the waters; and in the stream Thou hast washed away the transgression of the world.[13]

2. As in the Christmas liturgy there is a great stress on the humility and self-emptying of the Son of God in taking our humanity, coming to human birth and to his baptism, and following this path through to his death, descent into Hades, and resurrection from the dead. The influence of Philippians 2:5–11 is obvious: 'Have this mind among yourselves, which is yours in Christ Jesus, who, though he was in the form of God, did not count equality with God a thing to be grasped, but emptied himself, taking the form of a servant, being born in the likeness of men . . .' As we have seen in earlier chapters this kenotic imagery and its paradoxes pervades a great deal of the Orthodox hymns for the feasts.

> That Thou mightest fill all things with Thy glory, Thou hast emptied Thine own self, even unto the form of a servant. And now as a servant Thou dost bow down Thy head beneath the hand of the servant, granting me restoration and cleansing.[14]

> Let us sing together the praises of Him who is beyond all understanding, who was in flesh made poor and came to baptism, working thereby our restoration, for He is God rich in mercy . . .[15]

3. Christ comes to his Baptism as the Second Adam, the prototype and representative of renewed humanity, and he comes bearing our sinful humanity down into the waters of the Jordan, and raising it up cleansed and renewed. The Christian celebrating this Feast is at one with Adam in participating in the fruits of Christ's work of redemption: 'Thou hast clothed Thyself in Adam, and all the posterity of Adam Thou makest new again.' In the following quotations the figure of Adam is prominent, representing humanity as both needing and receiving God's loving-kindness.

> When the Lord descended today into the waters of the Jordan, He cried aloud to John: 'Be not afraid to baptize me: for I am come to save Adam the first-formed man.'[16]

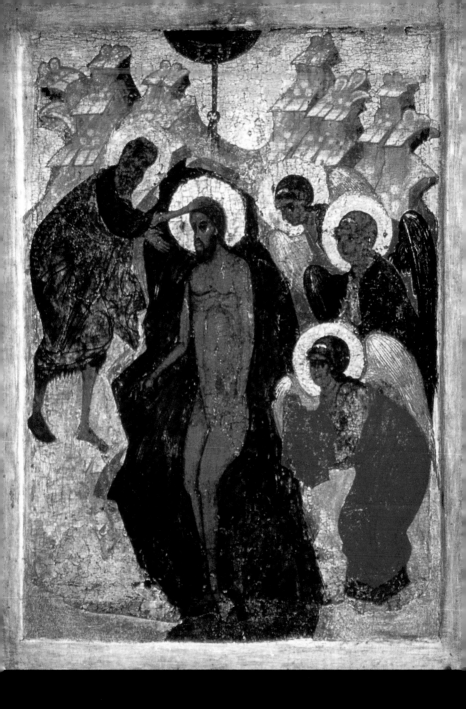

Plate 9: *The Baptism of Christ*, panel icon, Russian,
sixteenth century

Plate 10: *The Transfiguration of Our Lord*, tempera on panel, Russian icon from the Holy Theotokos Dormition Church on the Volotovo field near Novgorod, Novgorod School, fifteenth century

Plate 11: *The Transfiguration of Christ*, panel icon, by Theophanes the Greek, early fifteenth century

Plate 12: *The Triumph of Orthodoxy*, panel icon, Byzantine, probably Constantinople, c. 1400

Plate 13: *The Raising of Lazarus*, Russian icon, tempera on panel, Novgorod School, Russia, fifteenth century

Plate 14: *The Entry into Jerusalem*, panel icon, Russian,
early sixteenth century

Plate 15: *The Crucifixion*, northern Greece,
eighteenth century

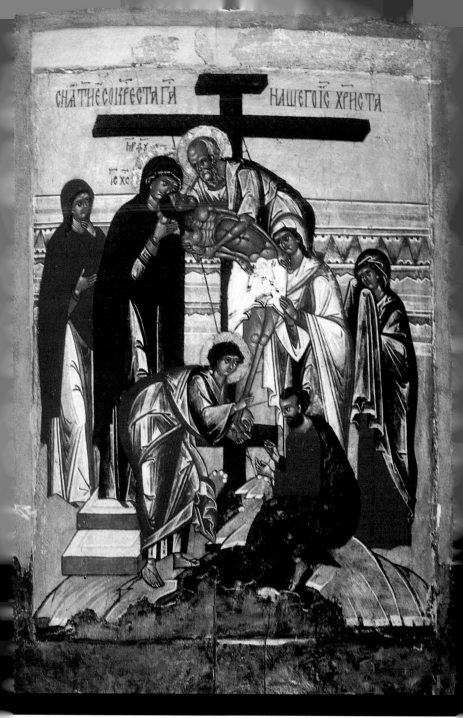

СНА ТИЕ СОКРЕСТА ГА НАШЕГОІС ХРИСТА

Plate 16: *The Descent from the Cross*, panel icon, Novgorod School, Russia, late fifteenth or early sixteenth century

Plate 17: *The Lamentation over the Dead Christ*, detail of fresco, Cathedral of the Transfiguration of Our Saviour, Mirozhsky Monastery, Pskov, Russia, twelfth century

Plate 18: *The Resurrection*, panel icon, Russian,
fifteenth century

Plate 19: *The Resurrection*, wall painting by Fr Gregory Kroug,
The Skete of the Holy Spirit, Mesnil-St-Denis, near Paris, twentieth century

Plate 20: *Mid-Pentecost,* panel icon, Novgorod School, Russia,
fifteenth century

Plate 21: *The Ascension*, panel icon, Russian,
seventeenth century

Plate 22: *The Holy Trinity*, 1420s, tempera on panel, by Andrei Rublev (c. 1370–1430)

Plate 23: *The Descent of the Holy Spirit*, panel icon, Cretan,
sixteenth century

Plate 24: *The Dormition of the Mother of God*, panel icon, Russian, sixteenth century

Beyond all thought and without measure is Thy poverty, O Word of God! I know that, for my sake who am fallen, Thou hast clothed Thyself in Adam, and all the posterity of Adam Thou makest new again.[17]

> The Maker saw in the obscurity of sin, in bonds that knew no escape,
> The man whom He had formed with His own hand.
> Raising him up, He laid him on His shoulders,
> And now in abundant floods He washes him clean
> From the ancient shame of Adam's sinfulness.[18]

4. In coming to the Jordan for Baptism Christ cleanses and sanctifies the waters themselves, so that water, a key element of the material creation, can become the instrument of renewal, healing and sanctification through the ministry of his Church. The symbolism of forces of evil residing in the waters is prominent in these texts, and is used to affirm the triumph of Christ over the evils that threaten and seduce humanity.

> Of old the prince of this world was named king also of all that was in the waters; but by Thy cleansing he is choked and destroyed, as Legion in the lake. With Thy mighty arm Thou has granted freedom, O Saviour, to Thy creation, which he had enslaved.[19]

> Christ now comes in haste to the waters, to crush the heads of the dragons . . . (cf Psalm 74:13[73])[20]

> O marvellous gifts! O divine grace and forbearance past speech! For behold, the Fashioner and Master now wears my nature in the Jordan, yet without sin; He cleanses me through water, enlightens me through fire, and makes me perfect through the divine Spirit.[21]

5. In keeping with the whole theme of Theophany, the manifestation of God, the hymns celebrate the fact that at the Baptism of Christ the Trinity is made manifest, and also that Christ's divinity is revealed by the Spirit:

> The Trinity, Our God, today has made Itself indivisibly manifest to us. For the Father in a loud voice bore clear witness to His Son; the Spirit in the form of a dove came down from the sky; while the Son bent His immaculate head before the Forerunner, and by receiving baptism He delivered us from bondage, in His love for mankind.[22]

> When Thou, O Lord, wast baptized in the Jordan, the worship of the Trinity was made manifest.[23]

6. The imagery of light and illumination is common:

> Being Himself the Bestower of light, Jesus needs not to be baptized, but in the
> flesh He descends into the streams of Jordan, wishing to give light to those in
> darkness. Let us go eagerly in faith to meet Him.[24]

> Today the creation is enlightened. Today all nature is glad, things of heaven and
> things upon earth . . . The grace of God that brings salvation to all men has
> appeared, shining upon the faithful and granting them great mercy.[25]

7. The Feast of the Theophany celebrates not only Christ's Baptism but also its consequences for the Church. Our life in Christ, the sonship we share, and the
enlightenment we receive are all linked to Christian Baptism. This sacrament takes
us into the heritage that stems from Christ's work of redemption which was finally
achieved through his death and Resurrection, but is already signified in his Baptism.

> Christ comes to grant through baptism deliverance to all the faithful. For thereby
> He cleanses fallen Adam and lifts him up, putting to shame the tyrant who had
> laid him low; He opens the heavens, brings down the divine Spirit, and grants
> man a share of incorruption.[26]

> One is the grace of the Father, Son, and Spirit, making perfect those who in faith
> desire the gift of divine baptism and receive the power of adoption unto sonship,
> that so they may cry aloud: O God, blessed art Thou.[27]

8. At the Great Blessing of the Waters it is clear that Christ who has already blessed
the waters at his Baptism is the one who is now invoked to bless the particular waters
that are the object of the Church's attention:

> Today the waters of the Jordan are transformed into healing by the coming of the
> Lord. Today the whole creation is watered by mystical streams. Today the trans-
> gressions of men are washed away by the waters of the Jordan. Today Paradise has
> been opened to men and the Sun of Righteousness shines down upon us.[28]

⫷ III ⫸

The composition of the icon for the Theophany developed between the third and
sixth centuries and has remained remarkably consistent over the centuries. In the
sixteenth-century Russian icon in **Plate 9** the background consists of mountainous
rocky peaks; the dark central area representing the waters of the Jordan, looks very

much like the mouth of a cave, and is reminiscent of a similar feature in the Nativity and Anastasis (Easter) icons; Christ is portrayed standing naked in the Jordan, in a way that recalls some of the hymns: 'O compassionate Saviour, putting on the nakedness of Adam as a garment of glory, Thou makest ready to stand naked in the flesh in the river Jordan.'[29] Christ's right hand is raised to bless the waters; on the left St John the Baptist (known as 'St John the Forerunner' in the Orthodox tradition) places his right hand on the head of Christ and with his left points to the One he is baptizing. On the right three angels attend on this mystery, showing the participation of the heavenly host at the Baptism of him who is both God and man; their hands are covered in the traditional manner of veneration; the clothes they are holding are sometimes interpreted as the Lord's garments. At the top of the icon we see the dark-blue segment of a circle representing the divine realm, and from that segment comes a dark ray; in a small circle between the divine realm and the head of Christ the dove is represented, and beneath this figure the dark ray divides into three; the Trinitarian nature of the Theophany is made clear in the icon. The whole scene is very concisely expressed in one of the hymns for the Feast:

> A strange wonder it was to see the Maker of heaven and earth stand naked in the river, and as a servant receive baptism from a servant for our salvation. The choirs of angels were filled with amazement, fear and joy. Joining with them, we worship Thee: O Lord, save us.[30]

In some icons the scene is embellished with further details. Sometimes we see the gates of heaven shown open against the background of the divine realm at the top of the icon. Some icons incorporate additional small scenes of the Baptist preaching and baptizing, and in some cases putting an axe to the root of a tree (Matthew 3:10; Luke 3:9); there may be a larger number of angels. Fishes are sometimes shown in the water around Christ, and also dragons, in accordance with the imagery in the hymns derived from Psalm 74:13 [73]: 'Thou didst divide the sea by thy might; thou didst break the heads of the dragons on the waters.' 'Thou, our God, hast appeared on earth and dwelt among men, Thou hast sanctified the streams of Jordan, sending down from on high the most Holy Spirit, and Thou hast broken the heads of the dragons hidden therein.'[31] Frequently we see a male and a female figure in the water – personifications of the Jordan and the sea. The place of these figures in the icon is linked to Old Testament events which were seen to prefigure the Baptism, namely the turning back of the Jordan by Elisha to create a path across the river, and the crossing of the Red Sea in the account of the Exodus from Egypt; both events being brought together in Psalm 114:3 [113], 'The sea looked and fled, Jordan turned back.' These images help to interpret Christ's Baptism as opening a path to new life, and the placing of the figure of Christ against the waters that evoke the symbolism of both death and life reminds us that the path to new life is through his death. The story of the flood (Genesis 6–9) is one of the Old Testament events which came to be seen as prefiguring Baptism; it involved destruction and a new beginning, God's judgement and mercy, and was used by early Christian teachers in their exposition of the significance of Baptism (cf 1 Peter 3:18–22). In the icon, as in the Scriptures, the waters of the Jordan and the presence of the Dove as a symbol of the Spirit recall the story of the flood and its significance for Christian theology.

In the icon the strong vertical line formed by the body of Christ and the ray descending from the heavenly realm create a powerful axial symmetry around which the other figures are grouped. This vertical axis is to the left of the centre of the icon; St John is placed to the left of Christ at a higher position in the icon, thereby emphasizing the humility of Christ who comes as the Servant of God to be baptized by a servant; the broader right section of the icon is occupied by the three angels. The outer curved edge of the Baptist's figure, the disposition of the angels bowing before Christ, and the bottom edge of the waters seem to be contained within a circle; it is as if there is an unseen mandorla within which all the figures in the icon are contained. This use of form within the icon reinforces the truth that this event is being celebrated as the Theophany – the manifestation of God through the Incarnate Son whose love takes him to the waters of Baptism, not out of need for forgiveness, but in order to provide a way for the children of Adam to find their way to become children of God through the waters of the new rite of Christian Baptism which Christ institutes.

☜ IV ☞

The texts and the icons for this Feast present us with a great mystery in the Lord's Baptism at the hands of John. The hymn-writers explore the mystery using all the theological resources they can muster. Scripture, the doctrine of the Church and its spiritual traditions all nourish the thought and imagination of the hymn-writers. In contrast, the icon painters seem to be more constrained; the form of the icon for the Feast was developed at an early stage, and whereas the traditions of poetry and hymnody in the Church had an elaborate development, icon painting, especially after the iconoclast period, was under much stricter control. Because of the dangers of misunderstanding and idolatry that had been addressed by the Church during the iconoclast period, the continuing use of icons after their restoration in 843 was, at least in theory, under the guidance of the bishops, and was closely related to the preservation of Orthodox doctrine.

The icon of the Baptism of Christ is reminiscent of four other festival icons, and some reflection on these links is worthwhile. As already suggested, the way in which the Jordan river is depicted brings to mind the cave in the Christmas icon and in the Raising of Lazarus, and the underworld in the Anastasis icon. God the Son descends to earth, descends into the waters of the Jordan, calls Lazarus from the grave, and descends to Hades. In icons of the Theophany and the Ascension the gates of heaven may be shown wide open; heaven, open at the Baptism for the Spirit to descend, is again open at the Ascension for Christ to enter in, bearing our humanity. As Christ's descent into the Jordan carried our sinful humanity through the waters of cleansing and redemption, and his Ascension carried humanity up to the throne of God, so in a similar way the Church is called to be present in this world amid the life of the old Adam, while at the same time rejoicing that it is already united to the New Adam and the glory of heaven.

A fourth icon which comes to mind has more conceptual parallels: the Meeting of the Lord. As the Christ-child is received by the old man Simeon we see the Incarnate Son being welcomed as the fulfilment of the Old Testament; so at the Jordan we see a meeting of Christ with John who is the last and greatest of the prophets of the old dispensation (Matthew 11:11–15; Luke 16:16). Both icons represent the coming together of the human and the Divine, and the fulfilment of hopes and expectations kindled in earlier generations. The Gospel accounts of the Baptism and its consequences, and the liturgical texts for the Feast are all written in the light of what were, historically speaking, subsequent developments; with hindsight we are able to explore the implications of these various meetings which are important points in the unfolding of Christ's life and ministry. The mystery of the meetings in the Gospel story, especially in these events which the Church has raised to the level of feasts, can shape our expectations and prepare our hearts to be responsive to God in the circumstances of our own daily life.

★ ★ ★

The main biblical readings for the Feast are as follows:

> *At Vespers:* Genesis 1:1–13; Exodus 14:15–18, 21–23, 27–29, 15:22–16:1; Joshua 3:7–8, 15–17; 2 Kings 2:6–14, 5:9–14; Isaiah 1:16–20; Genesis 32:1–10; Exodus 2:5–10; Judges 6:36–40; 1 Kings 18: 30–39; 2 Kings 2:19–22; Isaiah 49:8–15; 1 Corinthians 9:19–27; Luke 3:1–18.
>
> *At the Great Blessing of the Waters:* Isaiah 35:1–10, 55:1–13, 12:3–6; 1 Corinthians 10:1–4; Mark 1:9–11.
>
> *At Mattins:* Mark 1:9–11.
>
> *At the Divine Liturgy:* Titus 2:11–14, 3:4–7; Mark 3:13–17.

The Timeless Light and Brightness of the Father

THE TRANSFIGURATION OF OUR LORD AND GOD AND
SAVIOUR JESUS CHRIST (6TH AUGUST)

Before Thy precious Cross and Thy Passion, taking with Thee those among Thy holy disciples that Thou hadst specially chosen, Thou hast gone up, O Master, into Mount Tabor, wishing to show them Thy glory. And when they saw Thee transfigured and shining more brightly than the sun, falling upon their faces, they were smitten with wonder at Thy power, and cried aloud: O Christ, Thou art the timeless Light and Brightness of the Father (Hebrews 1:3), yet of Thine own will without changing Thou art manifest in the flesh.[1]

I

With the Transfiguration of Christ we come to a mysterious event that is central to Christ's earthly ministry; it is an event which directs our attention to his divinity shining through his humanity, and forward through the mystery of the Cross to the glory of the Resurrection and the Last Day. The Transfiguration is also 'a mirror in which the Christian mystery is seen in its unity'[2]: in the Transfiguration we see that we are called to share in the divine life, to find our final end in union with Christ in God, and to realize the possibility of the vision of God.

The origins of this Feast are rather obscure. It is possible that the Feast may derive from the dedication of three basilicas on Mount Tabor, the 'high mountain' where, according to tradition, the Transfiguration occurred. By the early eighth century the Feast was observed in Constantinople, and seems to have been derived from the Church in Jerusalem. The theological significance of this event was appreciated long before the Feast became widely established, for the Transfiguration was the subject of homilies by St John Chrysostom, St Cyril of Alexandria (378–444), and St Andrew of Crete (c. 660–740); similarly this theme was depicted in Church art before the Feast became widely observed; at San Apollinare in Classe (Ravenna) there is a sixth-century symbolical representation of the Transfiguration in the apse of the church, and from the same period in the apse of the main church in St Katherine's Monastery on Mount Sinai we have a fully developed presentation of the scene as given in the Synoptic Gospels. In the West the Transfiguration has long been commemorated on the second Sunday of Lent, but the separate observance of the Feast on 6th August was recognized only in 1457, in spite of attempts by Cluny to propagate the Feast in the twelfth century.

In contrast to the uncertainty of the origins of the Feast, its theological significance for the Eastern Churches is very great indeed, and was given great impetus in the fourteenth century by the triumph of hesychasm. As we shall see, the Feast acts as a focal point for many important strands of Orthodox theology. The reductionist attitude of some modern biblical scholars who deny that the event ever occurred or see it as a displaced post-Resurrection story could not be further away from mainstream Orthodox theology. For the Orthodox, the Transfiguration (Greek: *metamorphosis*) is a revealing of the glory of Christ and a manifestation of his divinity. The icon shows Christ present in this world with the glory of God. There is also an eschatological dimension to the event and its Feast, for 'Christ was transformed not without purpose but to show us the future transformation of nature and the coming second advent . . . bringing salvation'.[3]

The Transfiguration of Christ occupies a key place in the first three Gospels (Matthew 17:1–8; Mark 9:2–8; Luke 9:28–36). Jesus took the apostles Peter, John and James with him up a high mountain, and while they were on the mountain Jesus was transfigured in the sight of his apostles; his face shone like the sun and his garments became glistening white. Moses and Elijah appeared with Christ, talking to him; according to St Luke their conversation was about the departure Jesus was to accomplish at Jerusalem. St Luke also stresses that although the apostles were heavy with sleep they 'kept awake, and they saw his glory, and the two men who stood with him' (Luke 9:32). Peter declared how good it was for them to be there, and expressed the desire to make three booths for Moses, Elijah and Christ. (Peter's mention of the booths could imply the time of the Feast of Tabernacles when the Jews would be camping out in the fields for the grape harvest; this Feast had acquired other associations in the course of its history, including the memory of the wanderings in the wilderness, and a looking forward to the fullness of time.)

While Peter was still speaking, the three apostles were overshadowed by a bright cloud, and a voice from the cloud said, 'This is my beloved Son, with whom I am well pleased; listen to him.' After this Jesus only was present with the apostles. According to St Matthew and St Mark, on the way down from the mountain Jesus instructed the three 'to tell no one what they had seen until the Son of man should have risen from the dead'. From this event onwards, the Gospel narrative is marked with the shadow of the Cross, as Jesus reiterates the teaching that his ministry will reach its climax with his death and Resurrection in Jerusalem. Even as he accompanies the disciples down from the Mount of Transfiguration Jesus teaches that the Son of Man is destined to suffer and be treated with contempt. The link between the Transfiguration and the Passion of Christ is stressed in the Kontakion for the Feast:

> Thou wast transfigured upon the mountain, and Thy disciples beheld Thy glory, O Christ our God, as far as they were able so to do: that when they saw Thee crucified, they might know that Thy suffering was voluntary, and might proclaim unto the world that Thou art truly the Brightness of the Father (cf Hebrews 1:3).[4]

II

Before considering the liturgical texts and icons for the Feast, it may be helpful to consider three themes that are closely related to the Transfiguration in Orthodox theology, namely the *vision* of God, the *glory* of God, and the *divine energies*.

The phrase the *vision of God* succinctly expresses the goal of the human longing for God. In the book of Genesis, we see how mankind is made to be in the image and likeness of God. Adam and Eve then disobey God, and hide from him, unable to face the presence of the One who comes in search of his human image; they turn away from God, and lose the vision of God and the intimate friendship with God for which they have been created. Yet as the biblical story unfolds it is clear that God's concern for mankind is never in doubt, and that people still have a yearning for the One who is the source of life and blessing. The gulf between the Creator and creature is not forgotten, and neither is the fact that sin has marred the relationship; but the relationship between God and his human creation has not been completely severed; the God who clothed Adam and Eve before they were excluded from the Garden of Eden continues to love those whom he has brought into existence.

The story of Moses includes several episodes that become focal points for reflection on the development of the relationship between God and his people. When Moses encounters God at the burning bush on Mount Sinai (Horeb), he is told to keep his distance and remove his shoes, because he is on holy ground; a sense of awe is there at this manifestation of God: 'Moses hid his face, for he was afraid to look at God' (Exodus 3:6). At the giving of the tables of the Law, Moses' ascent to the summit of Mount Sinai is seen as a movement towards God, and the imagery of the mountain top, the cloud and fire are part of the language used in articulating the human encounter with God: 'Now the appearance of the glory of the Lord was like a devouring fire on the top of the mountain in the sight of the people of Israel. And Moses entered the cloud and went up on the mountain. And Moses was on the mountain forty days and forty nights' (Exodus 24:17–18). 'Moses drew near to the thick darkness where God was' (Exodus 20:21).

In Exodus 33 we find the paradox of intimacy and distance, knowledge and ignorance, presence and transcendence. Moses in the Tent of Meeting seeks guidance from the Lord for his work as leader of the people of Israel; he is told, 'My presence will go with you, and I will give you rest' (v. 14); but Moses wants more, and asks to see the glory of God. To this request comes the reply, 'You cannot see my face; for man cannot see me and live' (v. 20). As this incident unfolds we see a distinction between what Moses does see and what he is unable to see: 'And the Lord said, "Behold, there is a place by me where you shall stand upon the rock; and while my glory passes by I will put you in a cleft of the rock, and I will cover you with my hand until I have passed by; then I will take away my hand, and you shall see my back; but my face shall not be seen"' (vv. 21–23). The mystery remains, and Moses is not able to see God face to face. But the Israelites are aware of the effect of Moses' time in the presence of God, for the face of Moses shines 'because he had been talking with God', shines with a brightness so great that his face had to be veiled (Exodus 34:29–35). Here we have an early example in the Scriptures of the human face transfigured because of close contact with God; it is an experience that is repeated in the lives of many saints. Much of what we see in the life of Moses we see also in the lives of other Old Testament prophets, such as Elijah (1 Kings 19) and Isaiah (Isaiah 6), so it is not surprising that these Old Testament episodes become 'types'* which help to interpret later events, and which find greater significance in the light of the subsequent developments.

St Gregory of Nyssa used the life of Moses[5] as a starting point and framework for his exposition of Christian ascetical theology, and from Gregory derives a whole tradition of apophatic theology which uses the imagery of darkness to articulate the Christian experience of living with the mystery of God's presence. The theophanies involving Moses and Elijah are included in the Scripture readings at Vespers for the Feast of the Transfiguration.

In the New Testament also we find the same paradoxes of intimacy and distance, knowledge and ignorance, presence and transcendence, but there is a fundamental difference: through the Incarnation of the Word, things have become possible which were impossible before: we have been called 'to his own glory and excellence' and 'become partakers of the divine nature' (2 Peter 1:3, 4). The mystery of God's being is still something which is not open to ordinary human sight, for 'No one has ever seen God', even though 'the only Son who is in the bosom of the Father . . . has made him known' (John 1:18). But Jesus does promise a vision of God: 'Blessed are the pure in heart, for they shall see God' (Matthew 5:8); St Paul looks forward to the fullness of revelation: 'Now we see in a mirror dimly, but then face to face' (1 Corinthians 13:12); and St John holds out the promise that the servants of God 'shall see his face, and his name shall be on their foreheads' (Revelation 22:4). It is clearly expressed in many of the hymns for the Feast that the Transfiguration is for the three apostles a vision of God in the person of the Incarnate Son; it is a vision which prepares them to face the mystery of the Cross; and it is also a foretaste of the

Resurrection and Christ's Second Coming in glory. Looking forward to the vision of God becomes an integral part of Christian spirituality because of what has been opened up to us through the Incarnation: because of the union that is already established between God and humanity through Christ we live in the hope of its fulfilment in the vision of God the glory of heaven.

The second theme to be considered is the *glory* of God. In the Bible this phrase is one way of talking about a visible manifestation of the invisible God, a way of describing an experience of the tangible presence of the God who is at the same time holy and transcendent. Thus, the glory of God is experienced in the created order of the world: 'The heavens are telling the glory of God; and the firmament proclaims his handiwork' (Psalm 19:1 [18]); the creation which God has declared to be good and beautiful (Genesis 1:31) is capable of mediating the presence of the Creator. In the course of the history of the people of Israel a variety of expressions were used to defend the transcendence of God and at the same time to speak of his presence with his people. References to the angel of the Lord, the Word of the Lord, the name of God, as well as the glory of God, recur throughout the Old Testament as expressions of the presence and activity of God, while at the same time safeguarding against an anthropomorphic or a pantheistic concept of God.

The Hebrew word *kabod* (glory) expressed an idea of weightiness; people could gain this quality through riches and wealth, through a large family and plentiful livestock, and through righteousness and love. God's *kabod* is perceived through his works, including historical events and the vindication of divine judgement. The priestly tradition of the Old Testament stresses the association of the glory of God with the pillar of cloud and the fire that led the people through the wilderness, with the Tabernacle, with Mount Sinai, with the Tent of Meeting, and then with the Temple in Jerusalem. In all these instances the glory of God signifies the reality of God's presence. With Ezekiel the glory seems to be spoken of more as a specific entity which can be present or absent from the Temple, and is also closely associated with 'a likeness as it were of a human form' (Ezekiel 1:26). With Daniel and 1 Enoch the figure of the Son of Man is developed in ways that are linked to the glory of God, and the expectation of final judgement.

In the New Testament the Greek word *doxa* is taken over from the Septuagint (the second-century BC Greek translation of the Hebrew Scriptures) as an equivalent to the Hebrew *kabod*, and tends to be associated with light and vision when the glory of Christ or the glory of God is made manifest. The use of the word 'glory' is conspicuous in St John's Gospel from the beginning: 'And the Word became flesh and dwelt among us, full of grace and truth; we have beheld his glory, glory as of the only Son from the Father' (1:14). The signs that are mentioned by St John are signs of glory; thus after the miracle at Cana we read: 'This, the first of his signs, Jesus did at Cana in Galilee, and manifested his glory; and his disciples believed in him' (2:11). Much later, on the eve of the Passion, when Judas has gone from the upper room

into the night, Jesus says: 'Now is the Son of man glorified, and in him God is glorified' (13:31); and the climax of the Lord's High Priestly prayer is in terms of glory:
'Father, I desire that they also, whom thou hast given me, may be with me where I
am, to behold my glory which thou hast given me in thy love for me before the foundation of the world' (17:24). The theme of glory and its manifestation in Christ is so
ubiquitous in St John's Gospel that it could be described as a gospel of transfiguration. It is in the person of Christ that the divine glory is revealed; even though St John
does not mention the event of the Transfiguration itself, some see John 1:14 as an
allusion to that event, and the Knox translation may support this view: 'and we had
sight of his glory'.[6]

The imagery of transfiguration is also extended by St John to the life of the
Church: 'Beloved, we are God's children now; it does not yet appear what we shall
be, but we know that when he appears we shall be like him, for we shall see him as
he is' (1 John 3:2). And in a similar way St Paul links the tradition of the radiant face
of Moses to the transformation of the lives of Christians: 'And we all, with unveiled
face, beholding the glory of the Lord, are being changed into his likeness from one
degree of glory to another; for this comes from the Lord who is the Spirit' (2 Corinthians 3:18), and he can say this because of what has been revealed in Christ: 'For it is
the God who said, "Let light shine out of darkness", who has shone in our hearts to
give the light of the knowledge of the glory of God in the face of Christ' (2 Corinthians 4:6). We can see how the language of glory is closely linked to the language of
transformation in the New Testament, and this is particularly conspicuous in the
Transfiguration itself; in fact St Luke actually says 'they saw his glory' (9:32), an expression very reminiscent of John 1:14.

We come now to the concept of the *divine energies*. The question of the transcendence and immanence of God has been touched on already in this chapter, but
we need to remember that in the Eastern theological tradition from the fourth century onwards there has been a particular way of articulating this issue which since the
Reformation has become largely unfamiliar to Western Christians. A distinction is
made between the *essence* of God and the *energies* of God. According to St Basil the
Great (c. 329–379), 'We know the essence through the energy. No one has ever seen
the essence of God, but we believe in the essence because we experience the energy.'[7]
The essence of God is his otherness and transcendence, his inner life and being which
will always remain hidden from us; the energies of God are the ways in which God
makes himself known to his creation, the ways in which he is present to his created
world; the energies should not be thought of as separate 'things' that God uses, or as
something that is an emanation from God; rather the energies are *God himself* mani-
festing himself to his created beings, and through these energies human beings come
to know and participate in the life of God as far as is possible for created beings to do
so. This distinction between the divine essence and energies forms part of the theological resources by which Orthodox theologians defend the transcendence of God

and the reality of God's communication of himself to his creation, and particularly the reality of theosis, the participation of human beings in the divine life as a result of the Incarnation and the grace of God received through the Holy Spirit within the life of the Church.

This distinction may also help us to appreciate the complementary aspects of two different traditions of spirituality and theology. First, there is the *apophatic*, negative tradition with its insistence on the unknowability of God; this unknowability is not due to any inadequacy of revelation but to the finite nature of the creature who cannot comprehend the infinity of the Creator; hence in this tradition there is great stress on the divine darkness, particularly in the West, and human ignorance of the divine essence. In the West this tradition is represented in works such as *The Cloud of Unknowing*.[8] Second, there is the *kataphatic*, positive tradition with its emphasis on what has been revealed, the light of God's truth, and the human experience that God is knowable through the divine energies. It is worth noting that in Orthodox iconography, the mandorla representing the divine presence is usually darker at the centre and increasingly lighter in colour in the outer circles – holding together the concept of the unknowable essence of God and the reality of God's knowability through the divine energies. (See **Plates 10, 11, 18 and 19**.)

During the fourteenth century these theological distinctions became a matter of serious controversy as a traditional Orthodox spiritual practice came under attack. The attack was headed by Barlaam of Calabria who objected to some of the practices and claims of the hesychast monks on Mount Athos. The defence of this tradition was largely the work of St Gregory Palamas (c. 1296–1359) who was for many years a monk on Athos and later became Archbishop of Thessalonika. In Gregory's defence of this tradition he turned to the Transfiguration as an important demonstration of his theology. On Tabor the energies of God were seen in the uncreated light that was perceptible to the apostles, while the essence remained hidden; this light was neither an ordinary sensible light nor a metaphorical light of the intellect, but a manifestation of the divine splendour which the apostles were able to behold as a result of the work of the Spirit. Gregory stressed that 'God is called Light, not according to his Essence, but according to his energy'.[9] The teaching of St Gregory Palamas was vindicated at the local Councils of Constantinople in 1341, 1347 and 1351. In the wake of this vindication, the influence of the hesychast tradition increased throughout the Orthodox world; its influence on Orthodox art can be detected in icons and frescoes, particularly icons of the Transfiguration where the brilliance of Christ's mandorla and the rays falling on the apostles are greatly enhanced.

These three themes of the vision of God, the glory of God and the energies of God permeate the theology of the Transfiguration as we shall see in the texts quoted in the next section of this chapter.

III

1. Many texts reiterate the details of the narrative in the Synoptic Gospels, often with theological comments added:

> Thou wast transfigured upon the mountain, O Christ our God, showing Thy glory to Thy disciples as far as they were able to bear it.[10]

> Enlightening the disciples that were with Thee, O Christ our Benefactor, Thou hast shown them upon the holy mountain the hidden and blinding light of Thy nature and of Thy divine beauty beneath the flesh; and they, understanding that Thy glory could not be borne, loudly cried out, 'Holy art Thou'. For Thou art He whom no man may approach, yet wast Thou seen in the flesh by the world, O Thou who alone lovest mankind.[11]

> Moses who saw God and Elijah who rode in the chariot of fire, passing across the heavens unconsumed, beheld Thee in the cloud at Thy transfiguration, O Christ, and they testified that Thou art the maker and the fulfilment of the Law and the prophets. With them, count us also worthy of Thy light, O master, that we may sing Thy praises unto all ages.[12]

2. Great emphasis is laid on the fact that both the divinity and the perfect humanity of Christ are manifested at the Transfiguration:

> He who once spoke through symbols to Moses on Mount Sinai, saying, 'I am He who is', was transfigured today upon Mount Tabor before the disciples; and in His own person he showed them the nature of man, arrayed in the original beauty of the Image. Calling Moses and Elijah to be witnesses of this exceeding grace, He made them sharers in His joy, foretelling His decease through the Cross and His saving Resurrection.[13]

> Being complete God, Thou hast become complete man, bringing together manhood and the complete Godhead in Thy Person which Moses and Elijah saw on Mount Tabor in the two natures.[14]

> On Tabor the ministers of the Word looked upon strange and marvellous wonders, and hearing the voice of the Father, they cried out: 'This is the imprint of the archetype, even our Saviour.'
>   O unchanged image of the One Who Is, O Seal that cannot be removed or altered, Son and Word, Wisdom and Arm (1 Corinthians 1:24 and Isaiah 53:1),

Right Hand (Exodus 15:6) and Strength of the Most High, Thee do we sing with the Father and the Spirit.[15]

3. The links between Christ's Transfiguration and his suffering and Crucifixion, and the strengthening of the faith of the disciples, have already been illustrated in a quotation on page 60. Further quotations illustrate the same point:

> Before Thy Crucifixion O Lord, the mountain became as heaven and a cloud spread itself out to form a tabernacle. When Thou wast transfigured and the Father testified unto Thee, Peter, James and John were there, who were to be present with Thee also at the time of Thy betrayal: that, having beheld Thy wonders, they should not be afraid before Thy suffering. Grant in Thy great mercy that we too may be counted worthy to venerate these Thy sufferings in peace.[16]

At Mattins of the Transfiguration, at the end of each Canticle a Katavasia from the Exaltation of the Holy Cross is sung, for at the Feast of the Transfiguration the Church begins its preparation to celebrate the Feast of the Exaltation of the Holy Cross (14th September). Two examples of such a Katavasia now follow:

> O thrice-blessed Tree, on which Christ the King and Lord was stretched! Through thee the beguiler fell, who tempted mankind with the tree. He was caught in the trap set by God, who was crucified upon thee in the flesh, granting peace unto our souls.[17]

> O Theotokos, thou art a mystical Paradise, who untilled hast brought forth Christ. He has planted upon earth the life-giving Tree of the Cross: therefore at its exaltation on this day, we worship Him and Thee do we magnify.[18]

4. Christ's Transfiguration looks forward not only to the Cross, but through the Crucifixion to the Resurrection.

> Prefiguring, O Christ our God, Thy Resurrection, Thou hast taken with Thee in Thy ascent upon Mount Tabor Thy three disciples, Peter, James and John. When Thou wast transfigured, O Saviour, Mount Tabor was covered with light. Thy disciples, O Word, cast themselves down upon the ground, unable to gaze upon the Form that none may see. The angels ministered in fear and trembling, the heavens shook and the earth quaked, as they beheld upon earth the Lord of glory.[19]

5. Christ's Transfiguration is a foretaste also of our resurrection at Christ's Second Coming:

Thou wast transfigured upon Mount Tabor, showing the exchange mortal men
will make with Thy glory at Thy second and fearful coming, O Saviour.[20]

6. The Transfiguration is seen as a theophany, a manifestation of the Holy Trinity:
of the Son in the person of Jesus; the Spirit in the bright, overshadowing cloud; and
the Father in the voice from the cloud. There is thus a link between the Feasts of
Christ's Baptism and his Transfiguration, for both involve the activity and manifestation of the Trinity.

> Today on Tabor in the manifestation of Thy Light, O Word, Thou unaltered
> Light from the Light of the unbegotten Father, we have seen the Father as Light
> and the Spirit as Light, guiding with light the whole creation.[21]

7. The greatest emphasis is laid on the divine light manifested on Mount Tabor:

> The shining cloud of the Transfiguration has taken the place of the darkness of
> the Law. Moses and Elijah were counted worthy of this glory brighter than light
> and, taken up within it, they said unto God: 'Thou art our God, the King of the
> ages.'[22]

> The sun which makes the earth bright sets once more; but Christ has shone as
> lightning with glory upon the mountain and has filled the world with light.[23]

> As they gazed upon Thy glory, O Master, they were struck with wonder at Thy
> blinding brightness. Do Thou who hast then shone upon them with Thy light,
> give light now to our souls.[24]

The following quotation accords well with the scene depicted in most icons of
the Transfiguration:

> On Mount Tabor, O Lord, Thou hast shown today the glory of Thy divine form
> unto Thy chosen disciples, Peter, James and John. For they looked upon Thy
> garments that gleamed as the light and at Thy face that shone more than the sun;
> and unable to endure the vision of Thy brightness which none can bear, they fell
> to the earth, completely powerless to lift up their gaze. For they heard a voice
> that testified from above: 'This is my beloved Son, who has come into the world
> to save mankind.'[25]

8. The following texts show how the themes transfiguration, transformation, and
enlightenment relate to the restoration of human life that has been accomplished in
Christ:

O Christ our God, who wast transfigured in glory on Mount Tabor, showing to Thy disciples the splendour of Thy Godhead, do Thou enlighten us also with the light of Thy knowledge and guide us in the path of Thy commandments, for Thou alone art good and lovest man.[26]

Thou, O Christ, with invisible hands hast fashioned man in Thine image; and Thou hast now displayed the original beauty in this same human body formed by Thee, revealing it, not as in an image, but as Thou art in thine own self according to Thine essence, being both God and man.[27]

Today Christ on Mount Tabor has changed the darkened nature of Adam, and filling it with brightness He has made it godlike.[28]

⤖ IV ⤖

The icon in **Plate 10** comes from the Church Feasts tier in the Church of the Dormition-in-Volotovo Field, Novgorod, and has been dated to the last quarter of the fifteenth century. It contains all the elements that one would expect to see in a Transfiguration icon, without the additional elements which sometimes augment the basic composition. Compared with the sixth-century mosaic in St Katherine's Monastery, which has already been mentioned, this icon differs mainly in the disposition of the figures within the available space, the different design of the mandorla, and the addition within the icon of the mountains and foliage; the fundamental elements are the same in the two images, in spite of the fact that the icon was created some 900 years later than the mosaic.

In this icon the brilliant white figure of Christ stands within a circular mandorla on the central mountain peak, his right hand raised in blessing, his left hand holding the scroll; the halo is inscribed with a cross and *Ho on* ('The One Who Is') in Greek script, and the Greek letters IC XC indicate the name Jesus Christ. The mandorla consists of four concentric circles ranging from dark blue in the centre to a very light blue-green on the outer circle; rays of gold radiate across the second and third circles. Elijah and Moses stand at the top of separate mountain peaks to the left and right of Christ; they bow towards Christ, their right hands raised in a gesture of intercession towards him. St John Chrysostom gives three possible explanations for the presence of Moses and Elijah at the Transfiguration: they represent the law and the prophets; they both experienced visions of God – Moses on Mount Sinai and Elijah on Mount Carmel; they represent the living and the dead – Elijah, the living, because he was taken up into heaven by the chariot of fire, and Moses, the dead, because he did experience death. From the upper section of the icon, beneath the figure of Christ, three shafts of light indicating the Trinitarian nature of the theophany extend the mandorla down to the three apostles, and they reel at the impact of the vision. On the left, St James falls over backwards with his hands over his eyes. In the centre St John has fallen prostrate; a sandal has fallen from his right foot, a detail which possibly creates an allusion to the removal of Moses' sandals at his vision of the Burning Bush; John steadies himself with his left hand while partially covering his eyes with his right hand. On the right St Peter, kneeling, steadies himself with his left hand, and raises his right hand towards Christ in a gesture expressing his desire to build three booths to accommodate Christ, Moses and Elijah (Matthew 17:4). The garments of the apostles are in such a state of disarray as to indicate the dramatic impact the vision has had on them.

There is a strong geometrical structure to this icon. The figure of Christ is central in the upper section, and his dominant position within the circular mandorla establishes him as the visual and theological centre of the icon. Elijah and Moses are closely linked to Christ by their symmetrical positions in the upper section, and by their inclusion within the outer sections of the mandorla. The three figures in the upper part of the icon are balanced by the three apostles in the lower section. Whereas the circular design of the mandorla includes Elijah and Moses in the divine glory, the placing of the apostles towards the base of an equilateral triangle beneath the mandorla seems to stress their terror and incomprehension at the vision they have beheld, 'for they were exceedingly afraid' (Mark 9:6), and 'they fell on their faces, and were filled with awe' (Matthew 17:6). The dominantly green colour within the equilateral triangle helps to separate the apostles with their earth-bound perspective from the manifestation of the divine Son in his transfigured glory. The rock surfaces of the whole of the landscape – both the ochre-coloured rocks beneath Moses and Elijah, and the darker areas beneath the feet of Christ – are illuminated by the radiance of Christ; this helps to give cohesion to the whole icon, which might otherwise have appeared as an assembly of geometrical segments. These illumined rocks and the highlights on the apostles' garments help to convey the sense that even in spite of their shock and amazement the apostles have been overshadowed by the cloud, been touched by the divine glory and have to some degree experienced a transfiguration, though it is beyond their human comprehension.

The abundance of plants in this icon is reminiscent of the landscape in the Nativity icon (see **Plate 6**), and in the same way helps to create a sense of vitality, and the life-giving consequences of the Incarnation for the whole of creation.

In **Plate 11** we have another Russian icon, from the early fifteenth century, and painted by Theophanes the Greek for the Cathedral of the Transfiguration in Perslavl. In the upper section three figures are placed at the top of mountain peaks which are more precipitous than in the Novgorod icon: Christ is in the centre, Elijah on the left, and Moses on the right. Elijah bows towards the central figure of Christ; his left hand is brought to rest on the upper-right arm, and his right hand is stretched out towards Christ with the fingertips just touching the outer edge of the mandorla. Moses similarly bows towards Christ, holding the tablets of the Law, which slightly overlap the edge of the mandorla. Behind the heads of Elijah and Moses are two small scenes showing them being escorted by angels as they come on clouds to be with Christ on Mount Tabor; these scenes are a rather late development and are not typical of a Transfiguration icon. The standing figure of Christ slightly echoes the posture of Elijah and Moses, and conveys a sense of gentleness; Christ's right hand is raised in blessing; his left hand holds a scroll; a gold, cross-inscribed halo surrounds his head. The figure of Christ is placed against a flash of brilliant white shaped like a double arrow; this detail is sometimes shown as a star, and is generally taken to signify the 'bright cloud' mentioned in the Gospels; this in turn is superimposed on the circular mandorla which is light blue in the outer sections, shading into dark green in the centre; gold rays emanate from the centre; bronze-brown lines delineate the folds in the garments of Christ and reinforce the arrow-shaped flashes of white light. From behind the figure of Christ three dark-blue rays indicating the Trinitarian theophany spread out to the heads of the apostles in the lower part of the icon.

In the lower section of the icon, as in the Novgorod painting, the apostles are shown to be overcome by the brilliance of the vision of the transfigured Christ. On the left St Peter seems to have raised himself from the ground and gazes firmly at his Lord; Peter's left hand is raised to indicate that he is speaking to Christ. St John in the centre kneels low on the ground and faces the lower-left corner of the icon; his right hand is stretched out on the ground, while his left hand supports his head. On the right St James is bent over towards the right edge of the icon, covering his eyes with his left hand. Light from Christ's glory on the summit of Mount Tabor is reflected from the bodies of the disoriented apostles and from the rocks.

In the outer sections of the central area of the icon two small scenes give this icon a narrative content which is not typical. On the left Christ leads the three apostles up the high mountain (Matthew 17:1; Mark 9:2; Luke 9:28), and on the right he leads them back down the mountain after the Transfiguration (Matthew 17:9; Mark 9:9), instructing them to tell no one of the vision 'until the Son of Man is raised from the dead'. Theophanes' inclusion of these two scenes from the Gospel narrative augments the central presentation of the fact of the Transfiguration.

The arrangement of the different elements in this work by Theophanes conveys an impression quite different from that created by the Novgorod icon. The broader shape of the rectangular panel makes it possible to place Elijah and Moses at a greater distance from Christ, and thus allow more of the upper section of the icon to be used for the mandorla, the double arrow-shaped bright cloud, and the brilliant figure of Christ. The lower two-thirds of the panel are painted in dark tones, in sharp contrast to the brilliance of the transfigured Christ; even the highlights in the lower section are less brilliant than those in the upper section, and the light blue reflected light on the apostles seems very gentle in comparison with the dazzling luminosity of Christ. The small scale of the two groups of people on either side in the central level of the icon, and the precipitous nature of the landscape, together seem to increase the sense of distance between the Transfigured Christ and the disoriented apostles.

The brilliance of the way in which Christ is presented in this icon may reflect the increased interest during the fourteenth and fifteenth centuries in the nature of the light seen by the apostles on Mount Tabor. This light was no ordinary light, but was a manifestation of the divine energies in such a way that the apostles were able to perceive the divine glory of Christ. As the liturgical texts reiterate, this vision of Christ's glory was to prepare them to face the mystery of the Cross, and to recognize that Christ's suffering was voluntary. This vision also points forward to the Kingdom in all its fullness, when the whole creation is transfigured and filled with light.

> Thou wast transfigured, and hast made the nature that had grown dark in Adam to shine again as lightning, transforming it into the glory and splendour of Thine own divinity. Therefore we cry aloud unto Thee: O Lord and Creator of all things, glory to Thee.[29]

★　　　★　　　★

The main Scripture readings for the Feast are:

At Great Vespers: Exodus 24:12–18, 33:11–23, 34:4–6, 8. 1 Kings 19:3–9, 11–13, 15–16.
At Mattins: Luke 9:28–36.
At the Divine Liturgy: 2 Peter 1:10–19; Matthew 17:1–9.

8

To Call Back Adam

THE ORTHODOX OBSERVANCE OF GREAT LENT

Blessed art Thou that comest to call back Adam.[1]

I

While considering the Transfiguration of the Lord in the previous chapter, our attention inevitably moved on towards the Passion and death of Christ, and to the Resurrection. This chapter looks at the spiritual transformation that takes place in the Church's life during Lent, and our attention will be largely on the liturgical texts for Great Lent. The icon for the Sunday of Orthodoxy will be considered in detail, but the significance of this chapter is as a preparation for the events and icons associated with the Paschal Mystery, namely icons for Lazarus Saturday, Palm Sunday, Good Friday and Easter.

The phrase 'Great Lent' is used in the Orthodox Church to distinguish this pre-Easter period of fasting from the other *Lenten* observances which precede the Feasts of Christmas, St Peter and St Paul, and the Dormition of the Mother of God. By the second century the Saturday and possibly the Friday before Easter were days of fasting in preparation for the Paschal Feast; this had become expanded in many areas by the middle of the third century to include the whole week before Easter. At a later stage further liturgical observances marked the particular stages in the drama of the Passion and Resurrection, and became what we now refer to as Holy Week or Great Week. A period of prayer and fasting observed by catechumens in preparation for Baptism at Easter and by penitents seeking reconciliation also contributed to the development of Great Lent. Holy Week was certainly well established by the time of the Council of Nicaea (325). The pre-Easter fast for penitents and catechumens developed significantly after the Peace of the Church★ which resulted from Constantine's Edict of Milan in 313; the large numbers of people who were seeking

Baptism and the issues raised by post-baptismal sin meant that during the fourth century the Church's life and discipline had to be developed to cope with a radically new state of affairs. By the end of the fourth century the pattern of Lent, Holy Week and Easter was well established, but there were considerable variations in the details of how the duration of Lent was calculated – Rome, Jerusalem and Constantinople all having a different system. The significance of the 40 days of Lent was not simply a matter of external discipline for catechumens and penitents; it was primarily a spiritual discipline which Christians came to observe in solidarity with those preparing for Baptism and those seeking reconciliation; but this practice was then associated with participating in the Lord's own period of fasting and prayer between his Baptism and the beginning of his public ministry. Moreover, other biblical traditions contributed to the 40-day observance of Lent: the 40 years spent in the wilderness by the people of Israel between their exodus from Egypt at the Passover and their entry into the Promised Land; the 40 days spent by Moses on Mount Sinai; and the 40 days spent by Elijah on Mount Horeb.

The present variations in the calculation of the Lenten observance between the Western Catholic tradition and the Eastern Orthodox tradition need to be explained. In the West, the 40 days fast includes Holy Week, but does not include the Sundays in Lent; hence, it consists of the six weeks excluding the Sundays, plus the four days from Ash Wednesday to the Saturday before the first Sunday in Lent. In the East, however, Holy Week is not regarded as part of the Lenten 40 days, but the Saturdays and Sundays of Lent are. Two days form a link between the 40 days of Lent and Holy Week: the Saturday of Lazarus and Palm Sunday. Thus Lent in the West begins on Ash Wednesday, before the first Sunday in Lent, and ends on Holy Saturday; in the East it begins on the Monday before the first Sunday of Lent, but ends on the Friday before the Saturday of Lazarus. However, that is not the end of story, for in the East there is also a pre-Lenten period of four Sundays, including a week of partial fasting before Lent itself begins, and various other commemorations form an important part of the whole preparation for the celebration of the Paschal Mystery.

The relevant parts of the Orthodox calendar are set out below, including the Epistles and Gospels for the Divine Liturgy on the days mentioned.

Pre-Lenten period

The Sunday of the Publican and the Pharisee: 2 Timothy 3:10–15; Luke 18:10–14.
The Sunday of the Prodigal Son: 1 Corinthians 6:12–20; Luke 15:11–32.
The Saturday of the Dead: 1 Thessalonians 4:13–17; John 5:24–30.
The Sunday of the Last Judgement: 1 Corinthians 8:8–9:2; Matthew 25:31–46. (The last day on which meat is eaten before Easter; hence this week is often known as 'Cheese Week'.)
The Sunday of Forgiveness: Romans 13:11–14:4; Matthew 6:14–21. (The commemoration of the casting out of Adam from Paradise.)

Lent

Monday to Friday of the week before the first Sunday of Lent.

The Saturday before the first Sunday of Lent; the commemoration of St Theodore the Recruit: 2 Timothy 2:1–10; John 15:17–16:2.

The First Sunday in Lent (The Sunday of Orthodoxy): Hebrews 11:24–26, 32–40; John 1:43–51.

The Second Sunday in Lent: Hebrews 1:10–2:3; John 10: 9–16. (St Gregory Palamas: Hebrews 7:26–8:2; John 10:9–16).

The Third Sunday in Lent (The Adoration of the Precious and Life-Giving Cross): Hebrews 4:14–5:6; Mark 8:43–9:1.

The Fourth Sunday in Lent: Hebrews 6:13–20; Mark 9:17–31. (Our Holy Father, St John of the Ladder: Ephesians 5:9–19; Matthew 4:25 – 5:12).

Thursday in the Fifth Week (The Great Canon).

Saturday in the Fifth Week (The Akathistos Hymn).

The Fifth Sunday in Lent: Hebrews 9:11–14; Mark 10:32–45. (Our Holy Mother Mary of Egypt: Galatians 3:23–29; Luke 7:36–50).

The Saturday before Palm Sunday: Hebrews 12:28–13:8; John 11:1–45 (The Saturday of Lazarus).

Palm Sunday: Philippians 4:4–9; John 12:1–18.

Having examined the structure of Lent in the Orthodox Church, we should now consider its content. The discipline of fasting, prayer and alms-giving is integral to this season. All the Lenten observances are intended to bring our bodies and souls, our hearts and wills into a loving and co-operative obedience to the will of God. External discipline and interior purification go hand in hand, and are set within the strong theological framework of the liturgical season that has its climax in the Paschal celebration. This whole season has been described as 'the journey to Pascha'[2]; it is a journey in which the Church re-lives the story of Adam's fall and expulsion from Paradise, the story of the Passover and the Exodus, the witness of the prophets, and the redeeming work of Christ in his Passion and Resurrection. The Church re-lives this story both as a commemoration of past history and as a present reality, focusing on our own fall and loss of grace, our repentance and return to God, and our own experience of salvation through the Cross of Christ. The frequent use of Psalm 137 [136] expresses this mood of exile and penitence: 'By the waters of Babylon, there we sat down and wept'. The commemoration of saints during Lent provides inspiration through the examples of those who have been victorious in the spiritual conflict.

The whole Psalter is recited twice each week, as the Church immerses itself in the prayers and other Scriptures that did so much to shape our Lord's own understanding and life of prayer. The book of Genesis not only introduces the theme of Paradise which figures so prominently in the Lenten season, it also includes the story of Joseph whose innocent sufferings are seen as foreshadowing the suffering of Christ. In the book of Exodus Moses and the deliverance wrought through him foreshadow the new redemption and passover achieved through Christ's death and Resurrection. The themes of repentance and glory are developed in Isaiah and Ezekiel. Ethical amendment of life and conduct is the Lenten message received from the book of Proverbs, while Job's patience in suffering again points forward to the redemptive suffering voluntarily accepted by Christ.

≪ **II** ≫

The period before the great fast begins is a preparation for Lent. The tone of expectation and a desire to see Christ is set on the Sunday of Zacchaeus (Luke 19: 1–10) which is the last of the Sundays before the specifically pre-Lenten period. Clarity of vision, a sense of purpose, and a determination to enter more fully into a life of repentance and obedience are the qualities set before us in the Zacchaeus story, qualities which are demanded of everyone who embarks on the Lenten journey.

The Sunday of the Publican and Pharisee (Luke 18:10–14) develops the theme of repentance in the light of Christ's parable. True repentance involves a change of heart and mind, an inner transformation of motives that will lead to greater love for God and humanity. The publican's penitence contrasts sharply with the vainglory of the Pharisee, and the Church's prayer is for that quality of repentance which gives access to the abundant grace of God, as can be seen in the following extracts from the liturgical texts.

Open to me, O Giver of Life, the gates of repentance.[3]

A Pharisee, overcome with vainglory, and a Publican, bowed down in repentance, came to Thee the only Master. The one boasted and was deprived of blessings, while the other kept silent and was counted worthy of gifts. Confirm me, O Christ our God, in these his cries of sorrow, for Thou lovest mankind.[4]

The Publican used humility as a ladder and was raised to the heights of heaven; but the wretched Pharisee was lifted up on the rotten emptiness of pride and fell into the snare of hell . . .[5]

In our prayer let us fall down before God, with tears and fervent cries of sorrow, emulating the Publican in the humility which lifted him on high . . .[6]

The theme of repentance is developed again on the Sunday of the Prodigal Son (Luke 15:11–32). The departure of the Prodigal from the father's home into the depths of sin and exile is in many ways a parallel in the Lord's teaching to the loss of Paradise by Adam and Eve, and the Israelites' experience of exile in Babylon. The Prodigal's repentance and return is an inspiration for the Christian people's determination of will to repent and return to God in the Lenten observance.

> As the Prodigal Son I come to Thee, merciful Lord. I have wasted my whole life in a foreign land; I have scattered the wealth which thou gavest me, O Father. Receive me in repentance, O God, and have mercy upon me.[7]

> Utterly beside myself, I have clung in madness to the sins suggested to me by the passions. But accept me, O Christ, as the Prodigal . . .
> Open thine arms, O Christ, and in thy loving-kindness receive me as I return from a far country of sin and passions.[8]

> I was enslaved to strangers, an exile in the land of corruption, and I was filled with shame. But now I return, merciful Lord, and cry to Thee: I have sinned.[9]

This week ends with the Saturday of the Dead, on the eve of the Sunday of the Last Judgement. The prayer for mercy for the dead is permeated with a spirit of hope because of the Resurrection:

> Give rest to Thy servants, O Lord, in the land of the living from which pain, sorrow and sighing have fled away. In Thy love for mankind be merciful to the sins that they committed in this life: for Thou alone art sinless and merciful, O Master of the dead and the living.[10]

> Christ is risen, releasing from bondage Adam the first-formed man and destroying the power of hell. Be of good courage, all ye dead, for death is slain and hell despoiled; the crucified and risen Christ is King. He has given incorruption to our flesh; He counts worthy of His joy and glory all who, with a faith that wavers not, have trusted fervently in Him.[11]

Next in the pre-Lenten sequence comes the Sunday of the Last Judgement (Matthew 25:31–46), and here again we find interwoven with the theme of the Last Judgement the theme of repentance and an anticipation of the Paschal Mystery.

> Knowing the commandments of the Lord, let this be our way of life: let us feed the hungry, let us give the thirsty drink, let us clothe the naked, let us welcome strangers, let us visit those in prison and the sick. Then the Judge of all the earth will say even to us: 'Come, ye blessed of my Father, inherit the Kingdom prepared for you'.[12]

Through greed we underwent the first stripping, overcome by the bitter tasting of the fruit, and we became exiles from God. But let us turn back to repentance and, fasting from the food that gives us pleasure, let us cleanse our senses on which the enemy makes war. Let us strengthen our hearts with the hope of grace, and not with foods which brought no benefit to those who trusted in them. Our food shall be the Lamb of God, on the holy and radiant night of His Awakening: The Victim offered for us, given in communion to the disciples on the evening of the Mystery, who disperses the darkness of ignorance by the Light of his Resurrection.[13]

The last Sunday before Lent is the Sunday of Forgiveness, when the Church commemorates the casting out of Adam from Paradise. Here Adam's expulsion from Paradise is closely linked to our own fall from grace; the liturgical texts put words into the mouth of Adam, not only as his prayer for forgiveness and restoration, but as the prayer on the lips of the whole of fallen humanity as we cry out for the opportunity to enter once more into full communion with God. A reiterated plea echoes through the liturgical texts for this Sunday like the repeated tolling of a bell:

But, Master, in compassion call me back again.
But, Lord, who in the last times wast made flesh of a Virgin,
call me back again, and bring me into Paradise.[14]

Despise me not, O God my Saviour, but call me back.
Despise me not, O God of Love, but call me back.
In thy loving compassion despise me not, O God my Saviour, but call me back.
Despise me not, O good Virgin, but call me back.[15]

This plea becomes transformed and, as it were, put into a different key to become a cry of welcome on Palm Sunday:

Blessed art thou that comest to call back Adam.[16]

In this commemoration of the casting out of Adam from Paradise the liturgical texts have a remarkable tenacity as they draw together so many of the themes of the Lenten season which is about to begin – themes which are kept firmly in the light of the life-giving death and Resurrection of Christ. The prominence of Adam in these texts should be remembered when we come to the Easter icon, for there we see Christ releasing Adam from Hades and raising him up, grasping him firmly with his right hand (see **Plate 18**).

O precious Paradise, unsurpassed in beauty, tabernacle built by God, unending gladness and delight, glory of the righteous, joy of the prophets, and dwelling of the saints, with the sound of thy leaves pray to the Maker of all: may He open unto me the gates which I closed by my transgression, and may He count me worthy to partake of the Tree of Life and of the joy which was mine when I dwelt in thee before.

Adam was banished from Paradise through disobedience and cast out from delight, beguiled by the words of a woman. Naked he sat outside the garden, lamenting 'Woe is me!' Therefore let us all make haste to accept the season of the Fast and hearken to the teaching of the Gospel, that we may gain Christ's mercy and receive once more a dwelling-place in Paradise.[17]

Through Thy Blood Thou hast sanctified the nature of mortal man, O loving Lord, and hast opened unto those that worship Thee the gates of Paradise that of old were closed to Adam.[18]

Let us set out with joy upon the season of the Fast, and prepare ourselves for spiritual combat. Let us purify our soul and cleanse our flesh; and as we fast from food, let us abstain also from every passion. Rejoicing in the virtues of the Spirit may we persevere with love, and so be counted worthy to see the solemn Passion of Christ our God, and with great spiritual gladness to behold His holy Passover.[19]

⊰ III ⊱

The liturgical texts for the services throughout Lent manifest the same urgency of repentance that we have seen in the pre-Lenten services, and there are additional observances that greatly increase the sense of joy and triumph that permeates the whole Lenten fast. The following extracts convey something of the sense of penitential urgency and devotion that is at the heart of the Orthodox observance of Lent, and show how biblical texts, imagery and allusions permeate the prayer of the Church in this season.

The First Week of Lent

Behold, the appointed time; behold, the day of salvation, the entrance to the Fast. O my Soul, be watchful, close all the doors through which the passions enter, and look up towards the Lord.[20]

The Fast shines upon all of us more brightly than the sun, bringing us the light of grace and proclaiming the good news of the Cross, of the precious Passion and the saving day of Resurrection.[21]

Great is the power of Thy Cross! It has made the flower of abstinence to grow within the Church; it has stripped bare and uprooted the sinful greed that Adam showed in Eden. Adam's greed brought death to men, but the Cross brings immortality and incorruption to the world. As though from some new river of Paradise, there flows from it the quickening stream of Thy Blood mingled with water, restoring all to life. Through this Thy Cross make sweet the Fast for us, O God of Israel, great in mercy.[22]

The Saturday in the first week of Lent is dedicated to the commemoration of St Theodore the Recruit, a soldier who was martyred early in the fourth century, and whose posthumous intervention through a dream helped Archbishop Eudoxios to uphold the observance of Lent in Constantinople against the attempts of Julian the Apostate (Emperor 361–363) to defile the food in the markets with blood from pagan sacrifices. The commemoration of this great martyr and of other saints throughout Lent acts as an encouragement in the unseen spiritual warfare that is being undertaken by the faithful through prayer, fasting and almsgiving.

I shall sing the praises of Theodore, great among martyrs, the spiritual athlete, illustrious and renowned, famed for his miracles from one end of earth to the other. A day of gladness has dawned in this season of mourning, and with its light it has dispersed the gloom. Through the grace of the holy martyr, it heralds from afar the coming feast of the Resurrection.

    The Lord, who was Himself offered in sacrifice, has accepted the sacrifice of the martyr who suffered for the glory of God; and with the blood of this holy victim He purifies the Church.[23]

Thou hast carried as a shield the faith of Christ within thy heart, and trampled underfoot the power of the enemy, O greatly-suffering martyr; thou hast received a heavenly and eternal crown, for thou wast undefeated in battle. (Kontakion) [24]

Rightly art thou named 'Gift of God', for to all who ask thou dost grant divine gifts and the grace of healing. O victorious martyr Theodore, intercede with Christ our God. that we who celebrate thy holy memory with love may receive remission of our sins.[25]

The first Sunday in Lent is a celebration of the Triumph of Orthodoxy in 843 at the end of the iconoclast period. The Triumph of Orthodoxy affirmed that Christ could be depicted in icons, and that icons had a place in the Church's worship. This affirmation was seen as an integral part of the Orthodox faith. Those who had suffered exile, torture or death in defending the use of the holy icons were seen as defenders of Orthodoxy, and consequently many who died for this aspect of the faith were honoured as martyrs. Here again we find a spiritual link between the honouring of those who suffered for Orthodoxy during the iconoclast conflict and the invisible martyrdom involved in the keeping of Lent: both involve a witness to the truth as it has been revealed in Orthodoxy. The Kontakion for this Sunday is addressed to the Mother of God and affirms the reality of the Incarnation, the truth of the restoration of the image of God in man, and the depiction of this salvation in icons:

> The uncircumscribed Word of the Father became circumscribed, taking flesh from thee, O Theotokos, and He has restored the sullied image to its ancient glory, filling it with the divine beauty. This our salvation we confess in deed and word, and we depict it in the holy ikons.[26]

The quotations that follow express different aspects of this celebration – with considerable theological precision:

> Thou who art uncircumscribed, O Master, in Thy divine nature, wast pleased in the last times to take flesh and be circumscribed; and in assuming flesh, Thou hast also taken on Thyself all its distinctive properties. Therefore we depict the likeness of Thine outward form, venerating it with an honour that is relative. So we are exalted to the love of Thee, and following the holy traditions handed down by the apostles, from Thine icon we receive the grace of healing.
>
> As a precious adornment the Church of Christ has received the venerable and holy ikons of the Saviour Christ, of God's Mother and of all the saints. Celebrating now their triumphant restoration, she is made bright with grace and splendour, and drives away all heretics. With great rejoicing she gives glory unto God who loves mankind, and who for her sake has endured His voluntary Passion.[27]

> The grace of truth has shone forth upon us; the mysteries darkly prefigured in the times of old have now been openly fulfilled. For behold, the Church is clothed in a beauty that surpasses all things earthly, through the ikon of the incarnate Christ that was foreshadowed by the ark of testimony. This is the safeguard of the Orthodox faith; for if we hold fast to the ikon of the Saviour whom we worship, we shall not go astray. Let all who do not share this faith be covered with shame; but we shall glory in the ikon of the Word made flesh, which we venerate but

do not worship as an idol. So let us kiss it, and with all the faithful cry aloud: O God, save Thy people and bless Thine inheritance.[28]

The heavenly Zion, our mother, is made beautiful with the holy ikons of the prophets, the apostles and the martyrs, and of all the saints: and she is brightly adorned with the glory of the spiritual Bridegroom and the Bride.[29]

In **Plate 12** we have an icon for the Sunday of Orthodoxy; this panel, now in the British Museum, was probably painted in Constantinople about 1400.[30] The upper section is dominated by the representation of another icon: the celebrated miracle-working Hodegitria★ icon is shown in the centre on a stand covered with decorated red material, and with red curtains drawn back to reveal the painting; two winged figures guard the icon and use their hands to draw our attention to the central image. On the left in the upper section we see the young Emperor Michael III accompanied by his mother, the regent Empress Theodora, whose influence helped to bring the iconoclast controversy to an end in 843; on the right stands the Patriarch Methodios, appointed after the deposition of the iconoclast Patriarch John VII Grammatikos; behind Methodios and in the lower half of the icon are other heroes of the struggle to defend and restore the use of icons. At the bottom left St Theodosia holds a panel icon of Christ; in the centre St Theophanes the Confessor and St Theodore of Studium hold another image of the Saviour.

The three images within this icon of the Triumph of Orthodoxy are of great significance for the overall message conveyed by the scene. The original Hodegitria icon was believed to have been painted by St Luke, and was said to have been kept at Constantinople from ancient times; the image was well known before the iconoclast period. The belief that St Luke had painted an icon of the Mother of God, and that this had been blessed by the Virgin herself, was a powerful weapon for the defenders of the icons: this Evangelist had transmitted the Gospel not only by the written word but also through the painted image. It was seen as a natural development that the work of artists should be used by the Church to convey the Orthodox faith, and after the resolution of the iconoclast controversy the ultimate control of images lay, at least in theory, with the bishops. The original Hodegitria icon that was kept in Constantinople was a major focus for devotion; it was carried in procession through the city in times of emergency or triumph; in the late Byzantine period it was taken from the Hodegon Monastery in procession through the streets on Tuesdays and was greeted by large crowds. Stephen, a Russian pilgrim to Constantinople in 1348 or 1349, describes the welcome given to the icon:

Since it was Tuesday we went . . . to the procession of the icon of the Holy Mother of God. Luke the Evangelist painted this icon while looking at Our Lady the Virgin Mother of God herself while she was still alive. They bring this icon out every

Tuesday. It is quite wonderful to see. All the people from the city congregate. The icon is very large and highly ornamented, and they sing a very beautiful chant in front of it, while all the people cry out in tears, 'Kyrie eleison'.[31]

The icon was widely copied and became familiar throughout the Orthodox world; the original is said to have been cut up into four pieces when Constantinople fell to the Turks in 1453. The representation of the Hodegitria icon within a late fourteenth-century painting of the Triumph of Orthodoxy shows the close links between the traditions associated with the Hodegitria, the theological defence of icons articulated during the eighth and ninth centuries, and the continuing celebration of the Triumph of Orthodoxy.

The icon of Christ held by St Theodosia is intended to be seen as the image that had been on the Chalke Gate of the Imperial Palace, and had been destroyed by the iconoclasts at the outbreak of the conflict in 730; according to the iconodules St Theodosia had died with other martyrs while trying to save the image. The image of Christ in the centre of the group in the lower half of the icon is similar to the circular images of Christ that were commonly used in the marginal illustrations in Psalters produced during the ninth century; these manuscripts contain many illustrations as powerful anti-iconoclast propaganda.

This icon of the Triumph of Orthodoxy appears to be the earliest surviving example of this subject. In it we see the faith articulated at the Seventh Ecumenical Council in 787 in defence of the holy icons, and expressed in the liturgical texts already quoted. This same theology underlies the whole Orthodox practice of the painting and veneration of icons. It is worth looking at the icon in conjunction with the Kontakion for this Sunday, quoted above (page 80).

The second Sunday in Lent is a commemoration of St Gregory Palamas (1296–1359) – the Archbishop of Thessalonica who in his day defended Orthodoxy, especially in matters connected with hesychast theology. On this Sunday the theme of repentance is enriched by the use of the parable of the Prodigal Son in the hymns for the day.

With reference to St Gregory Palamas

What hymns of praise shall we sing in honour of the holy bishop? He is a trumpet of theology, the herald of the fire of grace, the honoured vessel of the Spirit, the unshaken pillar of the Church, the great joy of the inhabited earth, the river of wisdom, the candlestick of the light, the shining star that makes glorious the whole creation.

What words of song shall we weave as a garland, to crown the holy bishop? He is the champion of true devotion and the adversary of ungodliness, the fervent protector of the Faith, the great guide and teacher, the well-tuned harp of the Spirit, the golden tongue, the fountain that flows with waters of healing for the faithful, Gregory the great and marvellous.[32]

With reference to the Parable of the Prodigal Son

I kneel before Thee, as the Prodigal Son of old, O Lord and Master: run out to meet me and receive me, and taking me in Thine embrace grant me the tokens of Thy salvation. Instead of a hired servant make me once again Thy son, O Saviour who lovest mankind.[33]

When I was an exile far from Thee, Thou hast taken on Thyself my poverty. Thou hast assumed all my human nature in Thyself, and for my sake Thou offerest Thy divine body in sacrifice out of love for man, making it, O Word of God, my restoration and my joy.[34]

The third Sunday of Lent is known as the Sunday of the Cross, because of the veneration of the Cross that occurs at the end of Mattins. In this celebration the light of Christ's Cross and Resurrection illuminates the Lenten observances, beckoning the faithful to share in the Paschal Feast.

This is a day of festival: at the Awakening of Christ, death has fled away and the light of life has dawned; Adam has arisen and dances for joy. Therefore let us cry aloud and sing a song of victory. This is the day of the veneration of the Precious Cross. Now it is placed before us and shines with the brightness of Christ's Resurrection. Let us all draw near and kiss it with great rejoicing in our souls.[35]

The fiery sword no longer guards the gate of Eden, for in a strange and glorious way the wood of the Cross has quenched its flames. The sting of death and the victory of hell are now destroyed, for Thou art come, my Saviour, crying unto those in hell: 'Return again to Paradise'.[36]

Thy tomb, O Christ, has brought me life: for Thou, the Lord of life, hast come and cried to those who were dwelling in the grave: 'O all who are in bonds, be loosed: for I am come, The Ransom of the world.'[37]

The fourth Sunday of Lent sees the commemoration of St John Climacus, the sixth-century Abbot of St Katherine's Monastery on Sinai who wrote *The Ladder of Divine Ascent*.[38] He is seen as the great exemplar of the ascetic life, and in manuscripts and icons the ladder of ascent has often been illustrated. A famous late twelfth-century icon at the Monastery of St Katherine shows the ladder stretching up from earth to heaven; monks make the ascent assisted by the prayers of the community and the saints, but some are being attacked and dragged off the ladder by a variety of demons; St John Climacus leads the ascent and is being welcomed into heaven by Christ; the ladder has 30 rungs in keeping with the 30 stages of the monastic ascent and the 30 chapters of St John's book.[39] The liturgical texts for this Sunday use the parable of the Good Samaritan with much eloquence and urgency.

With reference to St John Climacus

> With the fiery coal of thine ascetic warfare, O saint, thou hast burnt up the thorns of the passions, giving warmth through thy fervour to all who follow the monastic life. Through thine ascetic labours, O saint, thou hast become myrrh of sanctification, offered up as sweet-smelling fragrance to God.
>
> Attentive to the laws of asceticism, with the waters of thy tears thou hast drowned the passions, as the soldiers of Pharaoh once were drowned in the Red Sea.[40]

> For all who follow the ascetic and monastic way, thou art in truth a lawgiver like Moses, a meek and gentle ruler like David; and we bless thee, Father.
> Planted beside the waters of abstinence, O blessed father, thou art become a fruitful vine, bearing the grapes of true sanctity.[41]

With reference to the Parable of the Good Samaritan

> Journeying on the path of life, O Christ, I have been sorely wounded by thieves because of my passions: I pray Thee, raise me up.
>
> Thieves have robbed my mind and left me half dead, wounded by my sins: but heal me, O Lord.
>
> My passions have stripped me bare of Thy commandments, O Saviour Christ, and I have been scourged by sensual pleasures. But pour oil upon my wounds.[42]

> Adam fell among thieving thoughts: his mind was robbed, his soul wounded, and he lay naked with none to help. The priest that was before the Law did not attend to him; the Levite that came after the Law did not look upon him. Thou alone hast helped him, O God who camest not from Samaria but from the Theotokos: glory be to Thee.[43]

> Departing from Thy divine commandments as from Jerusalem, and going down to the passions of Jericho, I was led astray by the false glory of the cares of this life. I fell among the thieves of my own thoughts; they stripped me of the robe of sonship that was mine by grace, and now I lie wounded, as though without the breath of life. The priest drew near and saw my body, but he took no heed; the Levite

looked at it with loathing and passed by on the other side. But Thou, O Lord who ineffably hast taken flesh from the Virgin, Thou hast of Thine own will poured out blood and water from Thy side for my salvation, and as with oil Thou hast anointed me. O Christ my God, bind up my wounds with linen, and in Thy compassion bring me to Thy heavenly Kingdom.[44]

From the Great Canon of St Andrew of Crete (used in its entirety on the Thursday of the Fifth Week)

The end draws near, my soul, the end draws near; yet thou dost not care or make ready. The time grows short, rise up: the Judge is at the door. The days of our life pass swiftly, as a dream, as a flower. Why do we trouble ourselves in vain.[45]

O Creator, Thou hast worked salvation in the midst of the earth, that we might be saved. Thou wast crucified of Thine own will upon the Tree; and Eden, closed till then, was opened. Things above and things below, the creation and all peoples have been saved and worship Thee.[46]

Two major liturgical texts have a conspicuous place in the Lenten services, and have two special days dedicated to them. The Great Canon of St Andrew of Crete is a long penitential prayer with immensely rich imagery drawn from many parts of the Bible. The Great Canon is used in its entirety at Mattins on Thursday of the fifth week of Lent; it is incorporated into Great Compline from Monday to Thursday during the first week of Lent. Similarly, in the Greek usage sections of the Akathistos Hymn to the Mother of God are used at Small Compline on the first four Fridays of Lent, but the whole hymn is sung on the Saturday of the fifth week. The Feast of the Annunciation (25th March) nearly always falls in Lent; this is not only an additional opportunity for devotion to the Mother of God but is a major celebration of the Incarnation in the midst of the season that comes to its climax in the celebration of the Lord's saving Passion and Resurrection.

The Fifth Sunday in Lent includes the commemoration of St Mary of Egypt (possibly fifth century) who is celebrated as a major example of repentance and asceticism. She is often depicted in paintings as an aged, emaciated and naked figure living in the desert, and about to receive Communion from Bishop Zosimas shortly before her death. Appropriately, the parable of the Rich Man and Lazarus (Luke 16:19–31) forms the basis for much reflection on the true riches that are gained through repentance, and the dangers of a misdirected pursuit of worldly wealth.

With reference to St Mary of Egypt

Through thy sinful actions thou hast drawn near to the gates of destruction; but He who of old broke in pieces the gates of hell by the power of His Godhead, opened to thee the gates of repentance, O all-honoured Saint; for He is Himself the Gate of life.[47]

With the baited hook of the flesh and through the lust of the eyes she took many men prisoner, and by means of short-lived sensual pleasure she made them food for the devil; but now she has herself been taken prisoner, in all truth, by the divine grace of the Holy Cross, and she has been brought as a sweet spiritual offering to Christ.[48]

With reference to the parable of the Rich Man and Lazarus

O Christ, as Thou hast saved Lazarus from the flame, deliver me, Thine unworthy servant, from the fire of Gehenna.
O Lord, in passions and lusts I am as wealthy as the rich man, yet in my lack of virtues I am as poor as Lazarus. But do Thou save me.[49]

I am rich in the deceptive joys of this life, like the rich man who spent all his days in pleasure; but, I pray Thee, loving Lord, in Thy compassion deliver me from the fire as Thou hast saved Lazarus.[50]

A final quotation from the Lenten liturgical texts reminds us that we are approaching Palm Sunday, and that Christ comes to Jerusalem 'that he may slay death':

As we begin with eagerness, O ye faithful, the sixth week of the holy Fast, let us sing a hymn in preparation for the Feast of Palms, to the Lord who comes with glory to Jerusalem in the power of the Godhead, that He may slay death. So with reverence let us prepare the branches of the virtues, as emblems of victory; and let us cry Hosanna! to the Creator of all.[51]

The Raising of Lazarus forms a prelude to the drama of Holy Week, as the belly of Hades is broken open to release the dead brother of Mary and Martha. As we shall see in some of the texts quoted in connection with Good Friday, emphasis is laid on the initiative of Christ in coming to the Cross in order to find Adam and accomplish the work of redemption.

≪ 9 ≫

Thou Hast Broken the Belly of Hell

THE RAISING OF LAZARUS

Wishing in Thy love to reveal the meaning of Thy Passion and Thy Cross, Thou hast broken open the belly of hell that never can be satisfied, and as God Thou hast raised up a man four days dead.[1]

Christ, the joy of all, the truth, the light, the resurrection of the world, in His love appeared to those on earth; and He became the pattern of our resurrection, granting divine forgiveness to all. (Kontakion)[2]

≪ I ≫

The Raising of Lazarus as recounted in St John's Gospel (11:1–44) is the last of the miracles worked by Jesus, the culmination of a series of signs selected by St John as manifestations of the glory and divinity of Jesus. After this great event, there is only the greatest sign of all to be recounted: the Resurrection of Jesus himself. These events precipitate controversy, a fact which is most conspicuous in chapters 6, 9, and 11 of this Gospel. The actions which manifest the glory of Christ meet with resistance from those who will not believe, and in the case of the Raising of Lazarus the resistance is more determined than ever (11:45–57). While the Jews are planning to control or remove Jesus, Caiaphas the High Priest says to the Council, 'You do not understand that it is expedient for you that one man should die for the people, and that the whole nation should not perish' (John 11:50). St John interprets this as a High Priestly prophecy 'that Jesus should die for the nation, and not for the nation only, but to gather into one the children of God who are scattered abroad', and adds that 'from that day on they took counsel how to put him to death' (John 11:51–53). Christ must die because Lazarus lives. The Raising of Lazarus takes us straight into the arena of Holy Week, where the final conflict takes place, and the Life Giver who raised Lazarus from the dead brings new life and salvation to the world through his own entry into death and the tomb.

In the Gospel, the raising of Lazarus is shown as a public act, a clear manifestation of the power of Christ the Life-Giver. But as with the other signs, so here the eyes of faith are invited to look beyond the external event. So the feeding of the multitude had become the occasion when the true identity of Jesus as the bread of life was revealed, the true bread that the Father gives to the world (John 6); the healing of the blind man had become an occasion for seeing of a different kind – the recognition that Jesus is the Son of Man, whose coming brings judgement to this world, enlightening those who cannot see and revealing the blindness of those who claim to be able to discern the mind of God (John 9:35–41). Now the restoration of Lazarus to life confirms the faith of Martha that Jesus is the Christ, the Son of God, and leads many others to believe in him; but it is also the final act of life-giving power that leads those who will not believe in him to take counsel about how to put him to death.

⊰ II ⊱

The Saturday of Holy and Righteous Lazarus is the first day after the end of Lent, and together with Palm Sunday marks the transition from Lent into Holy Week. The liturgical texts for Lazarus Saturday develop many themes from the Gospel account of the raising of Lazarus, and its implications for Christian theology, spirituality and liturgy. At Vespers on Friday evening there is a keen sense of anticipation of the events to be celebrated on the Saturday and the Sunday, and the transition from Lent into Holy Week:

> Having completed the forty days that bring profit to our soul, let us cry: Rejoice, city of Bethany, home of Lazarus. Rejoice, Martha and Mary, his sisters. Tomorrow Christ will come, by His word to bring your dead brother to life. Hearing his voice, bitter hell that is never satisfied will tremble and groan aloud, and it will release Lazarus bound in his grave-clothes. Amazed by this miracle, a multitude of Jews will come to meet Him with palms and branches; though their fathers look on Him with malicious envy, yet shall the children praise Him, saying: Blessed is He that comes in the Name of the Lord, the King of Israel.[3]

The Raising of Lazarus has universal implications.

> Before Thine own death, O Christ, Thou hast raised from hell Lazarus that was four days dead, and hast shaken the dominion of death. Through this one man whom Thou hast loved, Thou hast foretold the deliverance of all men from corruption. We therefore worship Thine almighty power and cry: Blessed art Thou, O Saviour, have mercy upon us.[4]

Christ's victory over the power of death and hell is plainly stated, even before his own resurrection, but we need to be aware of some of the terminology that is employed to express this truth. The English word 'hell' refers largely to a place of punishment. The Greek term *hades*, which is generally used in these texts, refers rather to the place and dominion of death to which all men were doomed before the coming of Christ.

> Hell, that had received so many, was unable to resist Thy sovereign command, O Jesus, but trembling it surrendered Lazarus, four days dead yet brought to life by Thy voice.[5]

> Thou hast broken open the all-devouring belly of hell and snatched me out, O Saviour, by Thy power; and Thou hast raised me from the dead by Thy command.[6]

Teaching about the divine and human natures of Christ is also conveyed:

> O Lord, Thou hast shed tears for Lazarus, showing that Thou art man; and Thou hast raised him from the dead, O Master, showing to the peoples that Thou art the Son of God.[7]

> O Christ, who art the Resurrection and the Life of man, standing by the tomb of Lazarus Thou hast confirmed our faith in Thy two natures, O forbearing Lord, proving that Thou wast born from the pure Virgin as both God and man. For as man Thou hast asked, 'Where is he buried?' and as God by Thy life-giving command Thou hast raised him from the dead on the fourth day.[8]

The deliverance of Lazarus from the grave is the basis for our pleas for deliverance from the passions and from sin:

> O Lord, Thou hast said to Martha, 'I am the Resurrection'; and Thou hast confirmed Thy words by actions, calling Lazarus from hell. Through my passions I am dead: raise me also, I beseech Thee, in Thy tender love for mankind.[9]

> O Master, Thou hast raised a dead man bound in grave clothes . . . I am held fast in the bonds of sin, raise me up and I shall sing: O God of our fathers, blessed art Thou.[10]

The tears of Jesus and the healing power of his Passion are linked:

> Shedding tears over Thy friend, O merciful Lord, Thou hast made the tears of Martha cease, and by Thy voluntary Passion Thou hast wiped away all tears from the face of Thy people. O God of our fathers, blessed art Thou.[11]

The imagery used in the Creation story (Genesis 2:7) and Ezekiel's vision of the Valley of Dry Bones (Ezekiel 37:5–6) is also developed:

> Joining dust to spirit, O Word, by Thy word in the beginning Thou hast breathed into the clay a living soul. And now by Thy word Thou has raised up Thy friend from corruption and from the depths of the earth. [12]

> Thou hast breathed life into my flesh, O Saviour, when there was no breath within it: Thou hast bound it fast with bones and sinews, and Thou hast raised me from the dead by Thy command.[13]

⋘ III ⋙

Some of the earliest examples of Christian illustrative art consist of 'image signs' found in the catacombs in Rome. These are images 'which imply more than they actually show'[14] – they allude to events in which God's power to save has been demonstrated, and they act as an incentive to faith in the face of death or some other crisis situation. Daniel among the lions, Jonah escaping from the whale, and the three children surviving in the fiery furnace are the examples most frequently taken from the Old Testament. From the New Testament, the Adoration of the Magi (an acknowledgement by the Gentiles of the presence of the Incarnate God), the healing of the paralytic and the Raising of Lazarus are the commonest salvation signs. In all cases the past event is evidence of the saving power of God – and it is not surprising that allusions to these events have been made in Christian rites for the dying and the dead from the earliest days of the Church. The transition from the early image signs of the Raising of Lazarus in the second century to the later icons is a long historical development from simple figures of only Christ and Lazarus, to images where much of the detail of the story is portrayed. Not only is the representational content of the icons much fuller, but also the icons seem to be greatly enriched by the fruit of theological reflection on the significance of the Lazarus story. The emphasis is on the public event of the miracle of the Raising of Lazarus, but theological implications can be discerned in the way the event is depicted.

Plate 13 shows a late fifteenth-century icon from the Novgorod area. This is a composition with a great sense of balance and harmony. Between the peaks of two sections of rocky landscape we can see the wall of Jerusalem, to which Jesus would soon be going for the Feast of Passover. The three groups of people in the icon are carefully arranged. On the left is the group of disciples led by Jesus. On the right, the group includes Lazarus bound in his grave-clothes and the man preparing to loose the burial garments, and also the Jews who have gathered at the grave. Lower on the right are the two sisters bowing down at the feet of Jesus, and a man struggling to remove the stone from the tomb of Lazarus. We shall look at each of these groups in turn.

At the lowest level of the icon we have the sisters on the right prostrated before Christ. Their words in St John's Gospel seem to be embodied in their posture: 'Lord, if you have been here, my brother would not have died. And even now I know that whatever you ask from God, God will give you' (John 11:21–22, 32). There is a sense of profound grief, loss and trust in the way Martha and Mary are bowed down before Christ. Above them a man is bent double, struggling to remove the stone from the top of the tomb of Lazarus in obedience to the Lord's command, 'Take away the stone' (John 11:39). The struggle to remove the stone seems almost incidental compared with the key elements of the story portrayed in the icon.

At the extreme right of the composition is the figure of Lazarus, bound in his white burial cloths; to his left stands a man ready to pull the cloths from the body, but with his right hand raised to his face in a gesture of horror at the stench of death. Behind this man stands a group of eight or nine other people who have gathered at the tomb. In this icon the whole group – Lazarus and the crowd – are placed against the mouth of the dark cave. In other icons the crowd stands some distance from the entrance to the cave, and the white figure of Lazarus alone stands out against the darkness of the cave. In all icons of this subject we need to bear in mind the symbolic significance of the cave (as in the Nativity icons): a place which evokes a sense of the darkness of evil and ignorance, as well as of death and corruption. The earliest developed images of the Raising of Lazarus show Lazarus alone against the mouth of the cave, and this representation continues to be used (see **Plate 8b** and comments towards the end of this chapter); but the assimilation of the crowd and the figure of Lazarus together against the background of the cave in the Novgorod icon may imply that the crowd who have witnessed the miracle are tainted with ignorance, evil and death, and that while some there may believe in Jesus because of this miracle, others will be party to the plans to eliminate Jesus and bring about his death. The white figure of Lazarus stands out not only against the darkness of the cave, but also against the crowd which is close to him: his Resurrection shows up the fickleness, darkness and malice of some of those who have been witnesses to the event.

On the left of the icon stands a group of disciples behind the tall, elegant figure of Christ; in his left hand he holds a scroll, which can symbolize his wisdom, his authority to teach and give the Law; his right hand is raised in a gesture of speech towards Lazarus, implying the great command, 'Lazarus, come forth!' (11:43 AV). The dominant posture and gaze of Christ are balanced by the white standing figure of Lazarus, still bound, his head inclined towards Christ in a gesture of obedience. The faces of the disciples are turned towards Lazarus, while those in the crowd look towards Jesus or Lazarus; all have expressions of great amazement, which reinforce the central relationship between the resurrected Lazarus and the Life-Giver whose voluntary death will in fact be precipitated by this miraculous gift of new life to his friend.

While many commentators stress the fact that this icon portrays a public event, and claim that it is not concerned with making known hidden truths by symbolic methods, I believe this icon does present us with theological truths that go beyond the specific details of the incident portrayed. This is partly because of the place this event has acquired in the Church's festival cycle. The liturgical texts for Lazarus Saturday look beyond the events at Bethany to the final accomplishment of the Saviour's work of redemption through his voluntary death on Good Friday and his Resurrection; and St John's Gospel itself is such a complex and integrated theological work that it is impossible to look at chapter 11 in isolation from the rest of the Gospel and the theological themes that permeate the whole work. If the Gospel was written 'that you may believe that Jesus is the Christ the Son of God, and that believing you may have life in his name' (20:31), then we can assume that the details of the story point to the nature of the life that we are called to share. In his High Priestly prayer, Jesus says, 'And this is eternal life, that they know thee the only God, and Jesus Christ whom thou hast sent' (17:3). The life we are called to share is one that is formed through our relationship with Christ; it is a life which begins through Baptism and faith, and is nourished by the Scriptures, the Tradition, and the Sacraments of the Church; it is a life which is 'in communion' with Christ and his people. Frequently in St John's Gospel the interaction between Christ and a particular person becomes a pattern for the Christian community, so when we come to the raising of Lazarus we shall naturally move on to explore the implications of what is set before us.

In the icon a central relationship is established between the Saviour and Lazarus – a relationship of grace and redeeming love; the Saviour comes to summon Lazarus from death into life, to bring him back to a relationship with Christ himself. Christ is shown not alone, but with his disciples, the nucleus of the Christian Church; there is also the crowd that has gathered at the tomb, which includes those who will welcome him as well as those who will reject him. One man prepares to loose the grave clothes of Lazarus, another removes the stone, and the sisters pour out their hearts to the Lord in grief and faith, and intercede for their dead brother. (These figures in their very human attitudes and actions are reminiscent of the figures in the lower level of the Nativity icon; see **Plate 6**.) All these reflect the Christian's situation. Through Baptism we die to sin and rise to a new life in Christ, a life in communion with his Church, where we are supported by the prayers of others and share with them the privileges and burdens of the Christian life in the world. As with Lazarus and his sisters, in all the complexities of life the essential relationship is that established with us by Christ himself who is the Life-Giver, and calls out of darkness into the light of his presence.

For many years I have associated with this icon various parts of the letter to the Colossians, particularly the following verses:

May you be strengthened with all power, according to his glorious might, for all endurance and patience with joy, giving thanks to the Father, who has qualified us to share in the inheritance of the saints in light. He has delivered us from the dominion of darkness and transferred us to the kingdom of his beloved Son, in whom we have redemption, the forgiveness of sins. (1:11–14)

These words about the baptismal relationship are an apt comment on the relationships implied within the icon of the raising of Lazarus.

Plate 8b shows a fresco painted in 1105–6 in the Church of the Panagia Phorbiotissa at Asinou in Cyprus. Compared with the panel icon, the fresco presents a less compact design and the figures are less tall and commanding, but the essential relationships are still placed before us with clarity. Christ has a determined look as he comes to the tomb with his right hand raised and with the scroll in his left hand; the disciples follow closely behind him. The other group of people are compressed into a narrow space behind the handsome entrance to the tomb, within which Lazarus stands, being released from the grave-clothes by one man, after the other has removed the stone from the tomb. One sister kneels at the feet of Jesus while the other sits up looking with amazement at the miracle that is taking place. The presentation of the scene in this fresco may not have the sophistication and elegance of the Novgorod icon, but it celebrates the event and its significance with considerable drama and a good range of colour.

★　　　★　　　★

Biblical readings for Lazarus Saturday:

At Vespers: Genesis 49:33–50:26; Proverbs 31: 8–31.
At the Divine Liturgy: Hebrews 12:28–13:8; John 11:1–45.

✦ 10 ✦

Thy King Comes Unto Thee

PALM SUNDAY

> Let us also come today, all the new Israel, the Church of the Gentiles, and let us
> cry with the Prophet Zechariah: Rejoice greatly, O daughter of Zion; shout
> aloud, O daughter of Jerusalem; for behold, thy King comes unto thee: he is meek
> and brings salvation, and He rides upon the colt of an ass, the foal of a beast of
> burden. Keep the feast with the children, and holding branches in your hands
> sing His praises: Hosanna to the highest; blessed is He that comes, the King of
> Israel.[1]

The Palm Sunday Gospel (John 12:1–18) makes clear the causal links between the
raising of Lazarus and the triumphal entry of Jesus into Jerusalem. It also makes clear
the intimate connections linking the whole series of events that take place between
the raising of Lazarus and the death and Resurrection of Jesus himself; the plans to
kill Jesus are undertaken with great seriousness after the raising of Lazarus. After a
brief time of withdrawal to the edge of the wilderness, Jesus returns to Bethany, and
there at dinner Mary anoints his feet and wipes them with her hair – an action which
Jesus interprets as a preparation for his burial. A crowd gathers in order to see Jesus
and Lazarus, and a great crowd welcomes Jesus when he arrives in Jerusalem the following day, because they have heard of the raising of Lazarus from the dead. Christ's
action in riding on the foal is seen as a fulfilment of Zechariah 9:9, and the entry into
the city becomes a messianic triumphal procession. The tension between the Lord
and his enemies is increased, and leads to his arrest and crucifixion; but Christ's death
occurs only after he has prepared the context for his death by his prophetic actions
at the Last Supper with his disciples. The sequence of events that begins with Christ's
visit to the tomb of the dead Lazarus comes to a climax with the Lord's own death,
entombment and Resurrection.

By the late fourth century the liturgical celebrations in Jerusalem, as recorded
by the pilgrim Egeria, made explicit links between the events at Bethany and those

in Jerusalem. After the commemoration of the raising of Lazarus in Bethany on the Saturday, John 12:1ff was read on Saturday afternoon, and on Sunday a procession made its way from the Mount of Olives to the Church of the Resurrection with people carrying palms and singing,'Blessed is he who comes'. Away from Jerusalem the causal links between the events of Lazarus Saturday and Palm Sunday were less dramatically represented, but each day came to have great significance for the Church. The carrying of palms on Palm Sunday became a widely used liturgical practice to commemorate the Lord's triumphal entry into the Holy City. By the ninth century Baptisms had become common on Lazarus Saturday, and this is seen in the chant, 'As many of you as were baptized into Christ, have put on Christ, Alleluia'.[2] The 'surety of the general resurrection' implied in the raising of Lazarus meant that the events of this weekend looked forward to the Resurrection as their culmination.

The Old Testament readings used at Great Vespers provide the background of Messianic expectations which find their fulfilment with Christ's triumphal entry into Jerusalem. The Gospel readings at Mattins and at the Divine Liturgy deal with the events of Palm Sunday and the children in the Temple welcoming Jesus as the Messianic Son of David. Psalm 8:1–2 is used at Great Vespers and Mattins, and is echoed in the hymnody of the Feast. The Epistle at the Divine Liturgy places the Church's celebration of Palm Sunday in the context of the expectation of the second coming of Christ (see details at the end of the chapter). The hymnody for the Feast builds on this and much other biblical material, reiterating the historicity of the events and their theological significance in the economy of salvation.

The following extracts from the liturgical texts for Palm Sunday show how the events celebrated and their theological significance are closely interwoven.

1. The Church's celebration of the events of Palm Sunday can be looked at from three perspectives:

(a) The Church in her worship unites herself with the events which are being celebrated, and with those who welcomed Christ at his triumphal entry into Jerusalem:

> Rejoice and be glad, O city of Zion; exult and be exceeding joyful, O Church of God. For behold, thy King has come in righteousness, seated on a foal, and the children sing His praises: Hosanna in the highest! Blessed art Thou who showest great compassion: have mercy upon us.[3]

> With our souls cleansed and in spirit carrying branches, with faith let us sing Christ's praises like the children, crying with a loud voice to the Master, 'Blessed art Thou, O Saviour, who hast come into the world to save Adam . . .'[4]

(b) The link between the Raising of Lazarus and the events of Palm Sunday is made clear, and we find references to Baptism that probably derive from the time when Baptisms took place on Lazarus Saturday:

> Giving us before Thy Passion an assurance of the general resurrection, Thou hast raised Lazarus from the dead, O Christ our God. Therefore, like the children, we also carry tokens of victory, and cry to Thee, the Conqueror of death: Hosanna in the highest; blessed is He that comes in the Name of the Lord.[5]

> Buried with Thee through Baptism, O Christ our God, we have been granted immortal life by Thy Resurrection, and we sing Thy praises, saying: Hosanna in the highest! Blessed is He that comes in the Name of the Lord.[6]

(c) The link between the events that begin and those that end Holy Week is kept in sight:

> Passing from one divine Feast to another, from palms and branches let us now make haste, ye faithful, to the solemn and saving celebration of Christ's Passion. Let us behold Him undergo voluntary suffering for our sake, and let us sing to Him with thankfulness a fitting hymn: Fountain of tender mercy and haven of salvation, O Lord, glory to Thee.[7]

2. The hymn-writers emphasize that the events of Palm Sunday represent the fulfilment of prophecy.

> With Thy disciples Thou hast entered the Holy City, seated upon the foal of an ass as though upon the cherubim, and so Thou hast fulfilled the preaching of the prophets.[8]

3. The One who fulfils prophecy is 'He who comes', God Incarnate, the One who brings victory and salvation to his people, the One who comes 'to call back Adam':

> First they sang in praise of Christ our God with branches, but then the ungrateful Jews seized Him and crucified Him on the Cross. But with faith unchanging let us ever honour Him as Benefactor, crying always to Him: Blessed art Thou that comest to call back Adam.[9]

> Greatly rejoice, O Zion, for Christ thy God shall reign for ever. As it is written, He is meek and brings salvation. Our righteous Deliverer has come riding on a foal, that He may destroy the proud arrogance of His enemies who will not cry: O all ye works of the Lord, praise ye the Lord.[10]

4. The humility and the glory of Christ are seen in the fact that he whose throne is in heaven lowers himself to be seated on a dumb foal, and to be welcomed by children:

> He who sits upon the throne of the cherubim, for our sake sits upon a foal; and coming to His voluntary Passion, today He hears the children cry 'Hosanna!'[11]

> Seated in heaven upon Thy throne and on earth upon a foal, O Christ our God, Thou hast accepted the praise of the angels and the songs of the children who cried out to Thee: Blessed art Thou that comest to call back Adam.[12]

5. The different responses to Christ's triumphant entry into Jerusalem included welcome and hostility, yet in spite of this paradoxical response to his coming Christ 'weds the New Zion', bringing into existence the Church that celebrates his triumph:

> Come forth, ye nations, and come forth, ye peoples: look today upon the King of heaven, who enters Jerusalem seated upon a humble colt as though upon a lofty throne. O unbelieving and adulterous generation of Jews, draw near and look on Him whom once Isaiah saw: he is come for our sakes in the flesh. See how he weds the New Zion, for she is chaste, and rejects the synagogue that is condemned. As at a marriage pure and undefiled, the pure and innocent children gather and sing praises. Let us also sing with them the hymn of the angels: Hosanna in the highest to Him that has great mercy.[13]

6. This last quotation points us on to the theme of the revelation to the Gentiles, for it is out of the Gentile nations and peoples that the New Zion is created. The inclusion of the Gentiles is implied in the reading from Genesis 49: 'To him shall be the obedience of the peoples' (v. 10); the Gospel reading, John 12:1–18 stops short of the passage where the Pharisees say, 'The world has gone after him' (v. 19) and some of the Greeks at the festival 'wish to see Jesus' (v. 21), but the implications of this chapter for the universal mission of the Church seem to permeate much of the hymnody of this Feast. The single detail of the Palm Sunday events that is most frequently used to express the revelation to the Gentiles is quite simply the fact of Christ riding on the untamed foal. The implication is that the untamed foal represents the nations that are as yet 'untamed and uninstructed' through the Law and the Prophets. In the following quotations we can see how varied imagery from the Scriptures is used to express the faith that the Messiah who comes to his people Israel also comes to gather the nations into the same peace and salvation.

> Thy riding on a foal prefigured how the Gentiles, as yet untamed and uninstructed, were to pass from unbelief to faith. Glory be to Thee, O Christ, who alone art merciful and lovest mankind.[14]

The daughter of Zion is glad, and the nations of the earth rejoice exceedingly. The children hold branches and the disciples spread their garments in the way; and all the inhabited earth is taught to cry aloud to Thee: Blessed art Thou, O Saviour; have mercy upon us.[15]

In **Plate 14** we have an early sixteenth-century Russian icon of the entry into Jerusalem. Christ is seated on the donkey, side-saddle, with his legs over on the left side of the beast; he holds a scroll in his left hand, and his body is turned so that he faces straight out from the icon, although his posture at first sight seems to suggest that he is looking back at the group of disciples behind him. This group, led by St Peter, is tightly compressed into the left side of the icon, and is balanced by another group of people on the right coming out from Jerusalem to greet the Lord; at the front of this group two men greet the Lord with palm branches, while at their feet children cast clothes to the ground before the Lord. The presence of the children is significant, and is emphasized in the hymns; both the hymns and the icons use the presence of the children crying out in the Temple, 'Hosanna to the Son of David', and Christ's words, 'Have you never read, "Out of the mouths of babes and suck-lings thou hast brought perfect praise"', quoting Psalm 8:2 (Matthew 21:15–16). These details from the incident within the Temple seem to have been transferred in the icons to the approach to the Holy City. In the upper section of the icon on the left we see the Mount of Olives – a background that sweeps down into the centre of the icon; next there is a tall tree with two children among its branches; and then, on the right, there is Jerusalem, depicted as a compact city, with towers and walls that enclose many buildings; the crowd emerges from a large gateway in the city walls. In the centre of the whole composition the donkey seems to float, upholding the Lord between the disciples and the crowd:

> Seated in heaven upon Thy throne and on earth upon a foal, O Christ our God, Thou hast accepted the praise of the angels and the songs of the children who cried out to Thee: Blessed art Thou that comest to call back Adam. (The Kon-takion for the Feast)[16]

The background features of the mountain, the tree and the city are directly related to the events commemorated on Palm Sunday, but it is interesting to note that they may bear a reference to the mountain, tree and building that appear in some icons of the Holy Trinity. The symbolism embedded in the Christian tradition has its roots in the landscape, geography and history of the people of the Holy Land; dif-ferent events involve similar environmental details which create cross-references within this tradition of symbolism. Thus the Mount of Olives evokes the memory of other 'mountain top' experiences of divine revelation at Sinai, Horeb or Tabor; the tree with the children gathering palm branches evokes the memory of the oak of Mamre and the Tree of Life; the stylized city is reminiscent of the house of Abraham, each in their own way different forms of human dwelling places, and each capable of becoming a symbol for the Father who is the source and origin of all life and community.

In the context of the Palm Sunday entrance into Jerusalem the image of the Holy City in the icon calls to mind both the historical city of Jerusalem that was destroyed within 40 years of the Lord's crucifixion, and the New Jerusalem of the book of Revelation (Revelation 21:2), the great symbol of the perfect communion of God and his human creation. Thus, while commemorating the particular events of Palm Sunday, the icon has an eschatological dimension that looks beyond the specific historical event to its fulfilment in 'the holy city Jerusalem coming down out of heaven from God, its radiance like a most rare jewel' (Revelation 21:11).

In the central portion of the icon there is little strong colouring; darker and brighter tones are present in the two groups at the outer edges of the icon. There is a sense of tranquillity and luminosity in the icon, which is perhaps surprising in view of the energetic and emotional nature of the events of Palm Sunday. The icon is not intended to arouse emotions; rather to allow the mystery of Christ's entry into Jerusalem to be set before us, so that he may be able to enter our hearts and bring to us the joy and peace of his Kingdom.

We end this chapter with an extract from one of the addresses of St Andrew of Crete (c. 660–740), one of the great Byzantine hymn-writers. This emphasizes the Christian's participation in the events depicted in the icon.

> Come then, let us run with him as he presses on to his passion. Let us imitate those who have gone out to meet him, not scattering olive branches or palms in his path, but spreading ourselves before him as best we can, with humility of soul and upright purpose. So may we welcome the Word as he comes, so may God who cannot be contained within any bounds, be contained within us. . .
>
> Today let us too give voice with the children to that sacred chant, as we wave the spiritual branches of our soul: 'Blessed is he who comes in the name of the Lord, the King of Israel'.[17]

★   ★   ★

The main biblical readings for Palm Sunday are:

At Great Vespers: Genesis 49:1–2, 8–12; Zephaniah 3:14–19; Zechariah 9:9–15.
At Mattins: Matthew 21:1–11, 15–17.
At the Divine Liturgy: Philippians 4:4–9; John 12:1–18.

✦ 11 ✦

His Voluntary Passion and Life-giving Cross

HOLY AND GREAT FRIDAY, AND THE UNIVERSAL EXALTATION OF
THE PRECIOUS AND LIFE-GIVING CROSS (14TH SEPTEMBER)

In haste to suffer for the world, Jesus goes up of His own will with His disciples to the city of Jerusalem, where he will undergo His voluntary Passion . . . He who suffers for us heals our passions by His Passion; for willingly He undergoes in our human nature His life-giving sufferings, that we may be saved.[1]

Hail! guide of the blind, physician of the sick and resurrection of all the dead. O precious Cross, thou hast lifted us up when we were fallen into mortality.[2]

✦ I ✦

The events of Good Friday have left their mark on the Christian faith as no other day has. Without Christ's death by crucifixion the Cross would never have become *the* Christian symbol; without the link between the Last Supper and the death of Christ we would not have the Divine Liturgy; and without the theological framework that interprets Christ's death as sacrificial and of benefit to humanity the Christian faith and religion would be devoid of its power to redeem and transform human life. And of course, without the Resurrection the victory won on Good Friday would have remained hidden; there would have been no Gospel rooted in what God has done through the death and Resurrection of his Son. So intimately linked are the events in the final days of the ministry of Jesus that it is hard to attribute greater or lesser significance to individual events or days. It is therefore not surprising that the Church has found a variety of ways to refer to the whole sequence: Holy Week and Easter; the Paschal celebration; the Easter Triduum.

The over-arching significance of Christ's Passion, death and Resurrection for the New Testament writers can be seen in the way that this narrative forms a major part of all the Gospels, and is prefaced by the journey up to Jerusalem and the tri-

umphal entry into the holy city. In terms of the length of the life of Jesus a dispro-
portionate amount of attention is devoted to the last few days of his life – for the
simple reason that in those last few days the Church has seen the 'full extent of his
love' (John 13:1 NEB), and recognized that the drama of redemption was accomplished on the Cross.

The death and Resurrection of Jesus were key elements in the earliest Christian preaching (Acts 2:22–24, 3:14–15, 4:1–2. 1 Corinthians 15:3–4). It was almost
inevitable that interest in the details of those last days in the Lord's life should grow,
and that sayings of Christ predicting his Passion should become a part of the Gospel
narrative as converts took up the Cross and followed Christ (cf Mark 8:31–34, 9:31,
10:33–34). The individual writers of the New Testament have their own distinctive
appreciation of the significance of the Cross. For St John, the Cross is the place above
all others where we can see the glory of Christ (cf 13:30–32): where the light shines
triumphant in the darkness, and where Christ's work is accomplished (cf John 19:30
'It is finished', or 'It is achieved' – Knox[3]). For St Mark, Jesus is the Messiah who
accepts the vocation of the suffering Servant of God, who takes up his cross and asks
his disciples to do the same; only through the Cross can the Master and the disciple
come to the joy of Resurrection. For St Paul, most of the key theological themes of
the Israelite faith had to be reinterpreted in the light of the Cross of Christ. So it is in
Christ crucified that we see the wisdom and power of God (1 Corinthians 1:18,
22–25), and that we find the righteousness of God demonstrated to humanity
(Romans 3:21–25). It is in the Cross of Christ that we see the love and forgiveness
of God made manifest (Romans 5:6–8). And such is the significance of the events of
Christ's death and Resurrection at the time of Passover in Jerusalem that Paul can say
that 'Christ our Passover has been sacrificed for us' (1 Corinthians 5:7 AV) – Christ
himself is the very pass-over from death into life for those who believe and are baptized. The One who is the new Passover has brought into existence a New Covenant,
and given his followers the sacred rite whereby they can be united in his sacrifice
through the gift of his Body and Blood.

There is little reliable information about the nature of the celebration of the
Christian Passover until the second century; then it becomes reasonably clear that the
Christian Passover generally took place on the Sunday after the Jewish Passover, thus
honouring the day of the Resurrection; this celebration was preceded by two days of
fasting. In some places, however, the celebration occurred on the same date as the
Jewish Passover, the fourteenth day of the month Nisan, whatever the day of the
week. In the year 325 the Council of Nicaea decided on Sunday as the day for celebrating the Christian Passover; in practice this meant a fast on the Friday, and the
Easter liturgy beginning with a Paschal Vigil on the Saturday night, going through
until Sunday morning.

Throughout the third and fourth centuries there was an increasing interest
in the history of the events that marked the beginnings of Christianity, and their

liturgical commemoration in some sort of historical order develops during this period. This time saw the expansion of the pre-Easter fast days and ceremonies; a fast of six days before Easter was common by the mid-third century, and towards the end of the fourth century Great Week or Holy Week was beginning to be established in Jerusalem under the influence of its bishop, St Cyril (Bishop of Jerusalem c. 348/50–386/7). By this time Jerusalem had gained a prominence in the Christian world which it had not really enjoyed before. After the conversion of the Emperor Constantine and the official recognition of Christianity as the major religion of the Roman Empire, the places in Palestine associated with Jesus Christ became important sites and pilgrimage centres. Jerusalem gained in status at the expense of Caesarea (the Roman city on the Mediterranean coast of Palestine, and the episcopal see made famous by its bishop Eusebius [c. 260–340], who was known as the 'Father of Church History' because of his *Ecclesiastical History*).

Imperial interest in the holy places and investment in church building on these sites created a situation in which the dramatic celebration of the events of the Lord's life could be promoted. In Jerusalem the main sites associated with the last days of Christ on earth were endowed with churches and facilities for coping with large numbers of pilgrims, and among these pride of place fell to the site of Christ's crucifixion and burial. Under the inspiration of the Emperor Constantine and his mother St Helen the area known as Golgotha or Calvary was greatly modified to allow the sites of the crucifixion and the burial to be integrated into one complex of buildings capable of accommodating large numbers of pilgrims. Here by the late fourth century the Good Friday liturgy included lengthy readings from the Gospel accounts of Christ's Passion and death, and the veneration of the Cross of Christ, which had been discovered by St Helen; the burial of Christ was then commemorated in the church of the Anastasis (Resurrection).

The pattern of Holy Week ceremonies that developed in Jerusalem gradually influenced observances elsewhere in the Byzantine Empire, and by the ninth century the more dramatic Jerusalem ceremonies replaced other rites in Constantinople. Also in the capital there was a great devotion to the Sacred Lance which had pierced the side of Christ; huge crowds were attracted to Hagia Sophia to venerate the lance and other relics of the Passion, but by 1200 this popular devotion had declined, and no longer took place in Hagia Sophia.

Another significant development in Constantinople was the growth of intense devotion to the Passion of Christ in some of the smaller monasteries during the twelfth century. At this time there was an increasing interest in human psychology and emotion, and this led to reflection on the relationship between the Theotokos and Christ during the last stages of his earthly life. Much poetry was written on this subject, and some has found a place in the liturgical texts for Good Friday and Holy Saturday. This in turn had its influence on icon painting. Many icons and frescoes of this period (from a wide geographical area, including Russia, the Balkans, Cyprus, and Anatolia) show great pathos in the depiction of the Entombment of Christ, the image of Christ as the Man of Sorrows, the Dormition of the Mother of God, and in the developing 'eleousa' image of the Mother of God with the young Christ enfolded in her arms. The most famous example of this influence is the icon which has come to be known as the Vladimir Mother of God; it was painted in Constantinople about 1130, commissioned by Prince Izyaslav of Kiev for the church in his capital city. This remarkable icon became, and has remained, the most important visible focus for the prayer and faith of the Russian peoples through over eight centuries of turbulent history; in this century it has attracted the devotion of millions of Christians beyond the confines of Russia.

In contemporary Orthodox observance, the first Good Friday services take place on the Thursday evening; twelve Gospel readings take the worshippers from Christ's final discourse at the Last Supper, through the whole story of the Passion to the account of Christ's burial. In Greek practice, just before the sixth reading a large cross is brought from the sanctuary by the priest, and set up in the centre of the church; this practice was adopted from Antioch by the Church in Constantinople in 1824. In the Russian Church a large crucifix is placed in the centre of the church before the service begins; the clergy assemble here for most of the service during which the twelve readings from the Gospels are interspersed with meditative hymns and readings on the subject of Christ's Passion. On Good Friday morning the solemn celebration of the Hours takes place, with Old Testament reading, Epistle and Gospel at each Hour. Vespers concludes with a dramatic veneration of the dead Christ. An embroidered icon known as the 'Epitaphion' (depicting the dead Christ with his Mother and St John bent over him and angels hovering above) is brought in procession from the sanctuary for veneration by the faithful in the centre of the church, where it remains until just before Easter Mattins. A similar procession with the Epitaphion concludes Mattins on Holy Saturday. These processions appear to date from the fifteenth or sixteenth centuries. In current practice on Good Friday there is no celebration of the Divine Liturgy or of the Liturgy of the Presanctified.

II

The following quotations from the liturgical texts express the depth of understanding that is present in the Orthodox celebration of Christ's suffering and death.

1. The Crucifixion is celebrated in the light of the Resurrection; we are not allowed to lose sight of these two sides of the story. We are reminded also that this redemptive event has cosmic consequences.

When Thou wast crucified, O Christ, all the creation saw and trembled. The foundations of the earth quaked in fear of Thy power. The lights of heaven hid themselves and the veil of the temple was rent in twain, the mountains trembled and the rocks were split.[4]

O Lord, upon the Cross Thou hast torn up the record of our sins; numbered among the departed, Thou hast bound fast the ruler of hell, delivering all men from the chains of death by Thy Resurrection. Through this Thy Resurrection, O Lord, who lovest mankind, we have been granted light, and cry to Thee: Remember us also, Saviour in Thy Kingdom.[5]

2. Christ's willing acceptance of crucifixion and death is stressed, as is the central paradox that it is 'the Master of Creation', 'the Creator of all', who is mocked and judged by those he has created.

Today the Master of Creation stands before Pilate; today the Maker of all things is given up to the Cross, and of His own will He is led as a lamb to the slaughter.[6]

Today He who hung the earth upon the waters is hung upon the Cross
He who is King of the angels is arrayed in a crown of thorns.
He who wraps the heaven in clouds is wrapped in the purple of mockery.
He who in Jordan set Adam free receives blows upon His face.
The Bridegroom of the Church is transfixed with nails.
The Son of the Virgin is pierced with a spear.
We venerate Thy Passion, O Christ.
Show us also Thy glorious Resurrection.[7]

3. The penitent thief and his entry into Paradise are significant elements in the Passion story; he is depicted in a number of complex late Russian icons, sometimes leading others into Paradise, and sometimes welcoming them there. In the Kariye Djami in Istanbul the penitent thief is depicted close to the Anastasis fresco. He is a sign of hope, for Christ's compassion enable the pardoned thief to open the gate of Paradise.

O Lord thou hast taken as Thy companion the thief who had soiled his hands with blood: in Thy goodness and love for mankind, number us also with him. Few were the words that the thief uttered upon the Cross, yet great was the faith that he showed. In one moment he was saved: he opened the gate of Paradise and was the first to enter in. O Lord who hast accepted his repentance, glory to Thee.[8]

4. The Crucifixion bears fruit in the new life of the Church, and the renewal of the world through the Gospel.

> Thy life-giving side, O Christ, flowing as a river from Eden, waters Thy Church as a living Paradise. Then, dividing into the four branches of the Gospels, with its streams it refreshes the world, making glad the creation and teaching the nations to venerate Thy Kingdom with faith.[9]

5. The removal of Christ's body from the Cross, and the burial in the new tomb are events which create a sense of wonder and awe.

> Down from the Tree Joseph of Arimathea took Thee dead, who art the Life of all, and he wrapped Thee, O Christ, in a linen cloth with spices. Moved in his heart by love, he kissed Thy most pure body with his lips; yet, drawing back in fear, he cried to Thee rejoicing: 'Glory to Thy self-abasement, O Thou who lovest mankind.'[10]

> When Thou, the Redeemer of all, wast laid for the sake of all in a new tomb, hell was brought to scorn and, seeing Thee, drew back in fear. The bars were opened and the dead arose. Then Adam in thanksgiving and rejoicing cried to Thee: 'Glory to Thy self-abasement, O Thou who lovest mankind.'[11]

6. The place of the Mother of God in the events of Good Friday is the subject of reflection and imaginative contemplation (see **Plate 17**). Her presence with Christ at his death and burial gave rise to some of the most profound poetry in the Byzantine liturgical tradition. There was an increased appreciation of the dynamics of human emotion during the twelfth century in Byzantium, which found expression in liturgical poetry and iconography. These quotations from the Lament of the Virgin show some of the insights that come from this creative period in Byzantine Church history.

> 'By Thy strange and fearful birth, my Son, I have been magnified above all mothers; but woe is me! Inwardly I burn as I see thee now upon the Cross.'[12]

> Broken and distraught by grief, Joseph and Nicodemus took down the all-pure temple of the Master, His body, from the Cross; and they made lamentation and sang His praises as their Lord.
> The pure Virgin Mother wept as she took Him on her knees; her tears flowed down upon Him, and with bitter cries of grief she kissed Him.
> 'My Son, my Lord and God, Thou wast the only hope of Thine handmaiden, my life and the light of mine eyes; and now, alas, I have lost Thee, my sweet and most beloved Child.'

'Woe is me! Anguish and affliction and sighing have taken hold of me,' cried the pure Virgin, bitterly lamenting, 'for I see Thee, my beloved Child, stripped, broken, anointed for burial, a corpse.'

'In my arms I hold Thee a corpse, O loving Lord, who hast brought the dead to life; grievously is my heart wounded and I long to die with Thee', said the All-Pure, 'for I cannot bear to look upon Thee lifeless and without breath.'

'Where, O my Son and God, are the good tidings of the Annunciation that Gabriel brought to me? He called Thee King and God and Son of the Most High; and now, O my sweet Light, I behold Thee naked, wounded, lifeless.'

'Release me from my agony and take me with Thee, O my Son and God. Let me descend also with Thee, O Master, into hell. Leave me not to live alone, for I cannot bear to look upon Thee, my sweet Light.'[13]

⋞ III ⋟

Representations of the Cross and the Crucifixion of Christ are extremely rare before the fourth and even the fifth centuries. At first the stress was on the glory of Christ and the universal salvation achieved through the Cross.[14] Only later was there a greater artistic interest in the death of Jesus and a more realistic representation of Christ crucified. Interest in the significance of the Cross is heightened as theologians see it in relation to various Old Testament *types* or prefigurations of the Cross, such as the wood cast into the bitter waters of Marah to make them sweet (Exodus 15:22–25), the bronze serpent that was raised up by Moses in the wilderness to bring healing to those bitten by serpents (Numbers 21:4–9; John 3:13–15), the Tree of Life (Genesis 2:9; Revelation 22:1–2), and the wood for the burnt offering carried by Isaac as Abraham goes to offer him in sacrifice (Genesis 22:6).

St John Chrysostom developed a theology of the Cross that helped to increase its popularity in Christian art. For this great theologian the Cross was central to God's loving kindness towards humanity; it was a symbol of his providential care for his creation; and the salvation of the world was rooted in the Cross of Christ. Baptism and the Cross free us from bondage to the Law of the old covenant; the erection of the Cross purified the air of demons and destroyed the power of the devil; the Cross thus becomes a monument to the banishment of the enemy. As the devil conquered Adam by tempting him with the fruit of the tree of the knowledge of good and evil, so Christ conquered the devil by the wood of the Cross.

Other factors also helped promote devotion to the Cross: Constantine's vision of the Cross in the sky came just before his victory over his enemies in 312; the basilica in honour of the Resurrection was dedicated in Jerusalem in 335; according to tradition St Helen, the mother of Constantine, discovered the True Cross in Jerusalem in the course of her investigation of the sites associated with Jesus. In 614 the True Cross was taken from Jerusalem by the conquering Persians, and restored to the holy city in 631; this loss and recovery of the Cross, and the spread of relics of the Cross throughout the Christian world, led to increased devotion to the Cross, and its use as an image on reliquaries.

One of the most important early images of the Crucifixion is found in the Syrian Rabula Gospels (586). Christ is shown on a central cross between the two crucified thieves; the thieves are shown wearing loincloths, but Christ is clothed in a *colobion* or tunic; he is alive, upright, with his eyes wide open; one soldier holds a sponge up to Christ, and another pierces his side; the Mother of God and St John are placed on the left of the scene, the other women on the right, and three soldiers beneath the feet of Christ. Beneath this scene of the Passion is the Easter scene: the tomb and sleeping soldiers are central; on the left an angel addresses the women coming to the tomb; and on the right two women kneel before Christ in the garden. The whole composition of this illustration in the Rabula Gospels testifies to a theology of the victory of the Cross – Christ ascends the Cross in order to accomplish his work of redemption. By the eleventh century Byzantine artists had developed a different representation of the crucifixion: Christ is shown dead, with his eyes closed, head bent, and his body naked except for a loincloth. Attention was being drawn to the suffering of Christ in a new way, and a realism is expressed in powerful images of the dead Christ. Prominent among these images is the Man of Sorrows, where the dead Christ's head and naked torso are shown upright in a sarcophagus, with the Cross in the background; in Greek the image is known as *The Akra Tapeinosis*, 'the peak of humiliation', alluding to the Septuagint version of Isaiah 53:8. Nevertheless, the Orthodox Church never expresses the extreme torments of the dying Christ that have become a common feature of Western Church art. During the eleventh century relations between Rome and the Byzantine Church became strained over a variety of issues, one of which was the new representation of Christ dead on the Cross. At this time in the West, loyalty to the Christus Victor image was strong, and the new developments in Byzantium were viewed with considerable suspicion, as the Papal legates made clear in 1054. However, by the end of the thirteenth century the Man of Sorrows image was making a big impression in Western circles as icons looted from Constantinople during the fourth Crusade were brought back to Italy.[15]

⪻ **IV** ⪼

Plate 15 shows an eighteenth-century icon of the Crucifixion from northern Greece. The figure of Christ crucified stands out against a gold ochre upper background, raised above a lower background of warm grey and red walls. The crucifixion is shown as taking place outside the city walls, on the hill of Calvary or Golgotha. In many icons a cave is shown beneath the cross in which lies the skull of Adam. This traditional detail (which is not included in this icon) showing the blood of Christ falling into the grave of Adam, expresses visually the truth that Christ's death is redemptive for the whole of humanity, and that he has by his death on the Cross truly gone 'in search of Adam'.

On the left stands the Mother of God; her undergarment is dark blue, with highlights and gold cuffs, and the outer garment is vermilion with black shading and gold fringes. On the right stands St John with a bright vermilion mantle and a tunic similar in colour to that of the Mother of God. The bold colours and simplicity of design help to give this icon considerable spiritual impact. The Mother of God stands in a dignified posture, her right hand raised and pointing to her Son; her left hand is raised to her face in a gesture that is associated with the expression of grief in the tradition of Byzantine rhetoric and painting; the restraint with which the Mother of God is depicted helps to convey the elements of both grief and confidence – grief at the suffering and death of her Son, and confidence that this death is the Sacrifice which takes away the sins of the world and opens the way to new life. St John similarly stands in a contemplative posture which expresses the same sense of wonder at the mystery of Christ's voluntary suffering and death. Christ is shown with his eyes closed in death, yet his posture is that of willing acceptance: he has mounted the Cross to fulfil his work, and his hands are stretched out in a gesture of prayer and self-oblation.

The icon encourages us to reflect on this climax to our Lord's earthly life; his work has been accomplished, and he commends himself to the Father. The following verses come to mind: 'I glorified thee on earth, having accomplished the work that thou gavest me to do' (John 17:4); 'It is finished' (John 19:30); 'Father, into thy hands, I commit my spirit' (Luke 23:46). And these verses from the letter to the Hebrews seem equally appropriate: 'Let us run with perseverance the race that is set before us, looking to Jesus the pioneer and perfecter of our faith' (Hebrews 12:1–2); 'So Jesus also suffered outside the gate in order to sanctify the people through his own blood. Therefore let us go forth to him outside the camp, bearing abuse for him. For here we have no abiding city, but we seek the city which is to come' (Hebrews 13:12–14).

The following extract from St Theodore the Studite's *On the Adoration of the Cross* shows how the victorious nature of Christ's death on the Cross was interpreted by a great teacher of Orthodox theology (759–826):

> How precious is the gift of the cross! See, how beautiful it is to behold! . . . It is
> a tree which brings forth life, not death. It is the source of light, not darkness. It
> offers you a home in Eden. It does not cast you out. It is the tree which Christ
> mounted as a king his chariot, and so destroyed the devil, the lord of death, and

rescued the human race from slavery to the tyrant. It is the tree on which the Lord, like a great warrior with his hands and feet and his divine side pierced in battle, healed the wounds of our sins, healed our nature that had been wounded by the evil serpent. Of old we were poisoned by a tree; now we have found immortality through a tree . . .

. . . By the cross death was killed and Adam restored to life. In the cross every apostle has gloried; by it every martyr has been crowned and every saint made holy. We have put on the cross of Christ, and laid aside the old man. Through the cross we have joined Christ's flock, and are granted a place in the sheepfold of heaven.[16]

Plate 16 shows a Russian icon of the Novgorod School, c. 1500, depicting the theme of the Descent from the Cross, also known as the Deposition. This had become a popular subject in Orthodox Church art by the fourteenth century, and formed part of a Passion cycle which was sometimes incorporated into the iconostasis as it became more developed in Russia during subsequent centuries. The details of this icon are in keeping with other icons and manuscript illustrations of this period from the Novgorod area, with bright colours and strength of form in the depiction of human figures. The inspiration of this Novgorod style of icon painting came in part from the Byzantine classical revivals in the thirteenth and fourteenth centuries, with the sculptured appearance of the figures and three-dimensional depiction of robes in the Hellenistic tradition; it also derived from a local tradition of bright colours and simplicity of form – contrasts of light and dark colours combined with a popular style to convey religious intensity.

At first sight this icon seems to present a very busy scene. However, the more one contemplates this icon the more one is impressed by the harmony and tranquillity that it conveys. The scene clearly takes place on the hill of Calvary; despite the damage to the lower part of the icon one can still see the dark cave and part of the skull of Adam. The cross is raised outside and above the city wall, and Joseph of Arimathea is engaged with others in the task of taking down the body of Christ. Two unusual details help to emphasize the role of the people involved: the ladder and the tool used for the removal of the nails are simply shown by line drawings; to have given them more substantial representation would have distracted attention from the essential task and the people fulfilling it. The seven people gathered around the cross and the dead body of Christ form a harmonious group. The outer two women (Mary Magdalene on the left) are standing almost upright; the Mother of God and the woman on the right of the cross bend slightly inwards towards the body of Christ. The curve of Christ's body is echoed in the bending figure of Joseph of Arimathea, while St John and Nicodemus, engaged in freeing Christ's feet from the nails, face each other in a way that balances the lower part of the composition.

The painter of this icon has used many shades of the main colours to create subtle tones; their distribution over the panel helps to create a sense of harmony and unity. A wide range of reds is used: subdued vermilion in the outer garment of Mary Magdalene, on the feet of Christ, in the undergarments of Nicodemus and the woman on the extreme right; crimson-brown on the outer garment of the Mother of God; and light red with varied tonalities in the outer garment of St John; light red, in a wide variety of tones is used in the walls behind the people around the cross. Varied shades of yellow are used in the icon, including burnt sienna and raw sienna in the upper background and in the outer garment of the woman holding the body of Christ. A pewter colour is used for the undergarments of the Mother of God, St John, and the woman assisting with the removal of Christ's body, and for the outer garments of Joseph of Arimathea and the woman on the extreme right. Brown is used for the outer garment of Nicodemus, and a warm grey with raw sienna is used for the mountain.

The two women at the outer edges of the group seem to float in the air, rather than being firmly placed on the ground like the two men in the centre; and the elevated status and significance of the Mother of God seem to be emphasized by the two-stepped pedestal on which she stands. The attention of St John and Nicodemus is directed to the task in hand – the removal of the nails which have held Christ to the cross; in contrast with them the attention of the rest of the group is on Christ, with their eyes lovingly turned towards him. Joseph's face is thoughtful and compassionate, while the face of the Mother of God expresses a tranquil confidence in the salvation which is being accomplished by her Son, even as she is tenderly engaged in the removal of his body from the cross in preparation for burial.

In **Plate 17** we have a small detail from a twelfth-century fresco in the Cathedral of the Transfiguration of Our Saviour at the Mirozhsky Monastery in Pskov, Russia. The fresco of the Lamentation over the dead Christ is an outstanding example of the way in which the twelfth-century Orthodox artists were able to express pathos and depth of human emotion. (Another famous example of this theme is found at the Church of St Panteleimon at Nerezi near Skopje in the Former Yugoslav Republic of Macedonia.) The head of the Mother of God is placed against the head of the dead Christ; this seems to express in a visual form the sentiments that were expressed in the extracts from the Lament of the Virgin quoted earlier in this chapter. The Mother of God is inseparable from her Son; together they share in the pain and suffering that has to be endured by redemptive love; the intensity of the gaze of the Mother of God expresses both the questioning that is there in the Lament, and at the same time a courage and trust that sustains her in her grief. Looking at this scene, one feels caught up in an endless moment of intense love and pain. It is not difficult to imagine the impact of such painting on the people who would contemplate these scenes during their time in church: God incarnate is present with us in our most vulnerable moments of life, gathering up the pain and suffering of the world into his work of redemption.

V

The Feast of the Universal Exaltation of the Precious and Life-Giving Cross has its origins in the dedication of the Church of the Resurrection (The Anastasis) in Jerusalem and in the discovery of the True Cross at Golgotha. The significance of this Feast on 14th September was reinforced by the recovery of the True Cross from the Persians in 631 after it had been taken by them at their conquest of Jerusalem in 614; it was transferred to Constantinople in 633 and the Feast there was celebrated with great solemnity. From the capital city this feast spread throughout the Christian Commonwealth, and was celebrated in Rome by Pope Sergius before the end of the seventh century.

The Feast is an opportunity outside the observances of Holy Week to celebrate the full significance of the victory of the Cross over the powers of the world, and the triumph of the wisdom of God through the Cross over the wisdom of this world. Away from the intensity of the Holy Week observances, this Feast gives the Church an opportunity to relish the full glory of the Cross as a source of light, hope and victory for Christ's people. It is also a time to celebrate the universality of the work of redemption accomplished through the Cross: the entire universe is seen through the light of the Cross, the new Tree of Life which provides nourishment for those who have been redeemed in Christ. At Mattins during the Great Doxology the Precious Cross is placed on the Holy Table on a tray with branches of basil or flowers; it is censed from four sides, and then taken in solemn procession to the centre of the church; in the Greek use the priest turns to face the four points of the compass and with the cross makes the sign of the Cross over the people in each of the four directions. After this the cross is venerated by all the clergy and people present. During this ceremony the Troparion* and Kontakion of the Feast are sung several times; these texts reflect the shared concerns of Church and State in the Byzantine Commonwealth:

> O Lord, save Thy people and bless Thine inheritance, granting Orthodox Christians victory over their enemies, and guarding Thy commonwealth by Thy Cross. [17]

> Lifted up of Thine own will upon the Cross, do Thou bestow Thy mercy upon the new commonwealth that bears Thy Name. Make the Orthodox people glad in Thy strength, giving them victory over their enemies: may Thy Cross assist them in battle, weapon of peace and unconquerable ensign of victory. [18]

In the following quotations we see how the liturgical texts for this Feast evoke a sense of wonder at what has been accomplished through the Cross:

Hail! guide of the blind, physician of the sick and resurrection of the dead. O precious Cross, thou hast lifted us up when we were fallen into mortality. Through Thee corruption has been destroyed, and incorruption has flowered forth; we mortal men are made divine and the devil is utterly cast down.[19]

The Cross is the guardian of the whole earth; the Cross is the beauty of the Church. The Cross is the strength of kings; the Cross is the support of the faithful. The Cross is the glory of angels and the wounder of demons.[20]

In this liturgy as elsewhere we find the person of Adam often mentioned as representing the whole human race that has been raised up with Christ. So wonderful is the Cross that it moves the 'whole assembly of those born on earth' and all creation to sing the praises of the Lord's passion; true human beauty has been restored and we are counted worthy to be citizens of heaven:

Lifted high upon the Cross, O Master, with Thyself Thou didst raise up Adam and the whole of fallen nature.[21]

As an unconquerable token of victory, an invincible shield and a divine sceptre, we worship Thy most Holy Cross, O Christ, whereby the world has been saved and Adam filled with joy. With the whole assembly of those born on earth we honour it, singing its praises, and as we celebrate its divine Exaltation, we entreat Thee for forgiveness.[22]

The use of imagery and types drawn from the Old Testament is extensive. Here we draw attention to four examples of this typology:

1. The wood of the True Cross is the focal point of devotion, but devotion to the Cross does not depend on the relic being present; within the complex tapestry of biblical and later Christian literature certain events and images resonate with others in our consciousness; hence the use of the wood images and allusions in the following texts is able to convey a profound awareness of the work of redemption that has been accomplished through the Cross of Christ; this becomes the Tree of Life through which we gain the fruits of Christ's sacrificial love. In reflecting on these texts it is worth bearing in mind the importance of the discovery of the True Cross in Jerusalem, the building of the church known as Martyrium over the site of Golgotha, the building of the Church of the Resurrection over the tomb of Christ, and the veneration of the True Cross in Hagia Sophia in Constantinople after its recovery from the Persians.

The Tree of true life was planted in the place of the skull, and upon it hast Thou, the eternal King, worked salvation in the midst of the earth. Exalted today, it sanctifies the ends of the world, and the Church of the Resurrection celebrates its dedication.[23]

Today is lifted up from the hidden places of the earth the Tree of life on which Christ was nailed, confirming our faith in the Resurrection. And exalted on high by priestly hands, it proclaims His Ascension into heaven, whereby our nature, lifted from its fallen state on earth, is made a citizen of heaven.[24]

2. We can see how use is made of the incident in Exodus 17:8–13 where Moses holds out his hands to support and bless the children of Israel as they fight against Amalek. Moses with his outstretched arms becomes a type of the Cross itself. Because of Christ's incarnation and redemption we can say 'now is the fulfilment of these images'.

Moses prefigured the power of the precious Cross, O Christ, when he put to flight Amalek, his adversary, in the wilderness of Sinai: for when he stretched out his arms in the form of a cross, the people became strong again. And now the fulfilment of these images has come to pass for us. Today is the Cross exalted and devils are put to flight; today the whole creation is set free from corruption: for through the Cross every gift of grace has shone upon us.[25]

3. In a similar way the wood cast into the waters of Marah to take away their bitterness becomes a type of the transforming power of the Cross to transform human life, and bring Gentiles to the true faith (cf Exodus 15:22–25):

Not suffering the deadly bitterness of the tree still to remain, Thou hast utterly destroyed it through the Cross. In like manner of old did wood once destroy the bitterness of the waters of Marah, prefiguring the strength of the Cross that all the powers of heaven magnify.[26]

In days of old Moses transformed with wood the bitter wells in the wilderness, prefiguring the bringing of the Gentiles to the true faith through the Cross.[27]

4. In the New Testament St John makes use of the story of Moses and the serpents, using the raising up of the bronze serpent to make the point that Christ raised up on the Cross takes away the sting of death and gives hope of new life (cf Numbers 21:4–9 and John 3:13–15). This same typology appears in the hymns for this Feast.

Moses set upon a pole a cure against the deadly and poisonous bite of the serpents: for crosswise upon the wood – as a symbol of the Cross – he placed a serpent
that creeps about the earth, and thereby he triumphed over calamity. Therefore
let us sing to Christ our God, for he has been glorified.[28]

So great was the influence of the Emperor Constantine on the development of
the Church's presence within the Byzantine state, and his mother St Helen's influence on the development of pilgrimage sites and relics associated with the origins of
Christianity, that these two key figures from the beginnings of the Byzantine theoc-
racy are honoured as saints in the Orthodox tradition. St Helen and St Constantine
are often represented together in icons and frescoes on either side of the True Cross;
they appear in icons of the Elevation of the Cross; and it is no surprise that they find
a significant place in the hymns for this Feast. St Constantine's vision of the Cross in
the heavens and St Helen's recovery of the True Cross from the site of Golgotha have
left a permanent impression on the Orthodox tradition.

Divine treasure hidden in the earth, the Cross of the Giver of Life appeared in
the heavens to the godly King, and its inscription spiritually signified his victory
over the enemy. Rejoicing with faith and love, inspired by God he made haste
to raise on high the Cross which he had seen in his vision; and with great zeal he
brought it forth from the bosom of the earth, for the deliverance of the world
and the salvation of souls.[29]

O Cross, sign radiant with light among the stars, thou hast in prophecy revealed
a trophy of victory to the godly King; and when his mother Helen found thee,
she displayed thee in the sight of the world.[30]

Finally, we draw attention to the sense of joy and hope that is conveyed through
this celebration of the significance of the Cross of Christ for the life and society of
the Christian world.

Shining with pure rays, the holy Cross sheds its divine light upon the peoples
darkened by the beguilement of error, and it reconciles them to Christ who was
crucified upon it, granting peace unto our souls.[31]

Lifted up of Thine own will upon the Cross, do Thou bestow Thy mercy upon
the new commonwealth that bears Thy Name. Make the Orthodox peoples glad
in Thy strength, giving them victory over their enemies: may Thy Cross assist
them in battle, weapon of peace and unconquerable ensign of victory.[32]

The icons associated with this Feast usually show Bishop Macarius of Jerusalem with deacons at his side as he raises the True Cross; in the background is the Church of the Resurrection; St Constantine and St Helen form part of the usual scene. St Helen discovering the three crosses on Golgotha, and a healing miracle associated with the True Cross, may also be shown.

★   ★   ★

The main biblical readings on Good Friday are:

At Mattins: The Office of the Holy and Redeeming Passion of our Lord Jesus Christ, otherwise known as The Service of the Twelve Gospels: (8 p.m. on Holy Thursday evening): John 13:31–18:1, 18:1–28; Matthew 26:57–75; John 18:28–19:16; Matthew 27:3–32; Mark 15:16–32; Matthew 27:33–54; Luke 23:32–49; John 19:25–37; Mark 15:43–47; John 19:38–42; Matthew 27:62–66.

At the Royal Hours, beginning at 8 a.m. on Good Friday morning.
At the First Hour: Psalms 5, 2, 22 [21]; Zechariah 11:10–13; Galatians 6:14–18; Matthew 27:1–56.
At the Third Hour: Psalms 35 [34], 109 [108], 51 [50]; Isaiah 50:4–11; Romans 5:6–10; Mark 15:16–41.
At the Sixth Hour: Psalms 54 [53], 140 [139], 91 [90]; Isaiah 52:13–54:1; Hebrews 2:11–18; Luke 23:32–49.
At the Ninth Hour: Psalms 69 [68], 70 [69], 86 [85]; Jeremiah 11:18–23; 12:1–5, 9–11,14–15. Hebrews 10:19–31; John 18:28–19:37.

At Vespers, beginning at 4 p.m.
Psalm 104 [103], Exodus 33:11–23; Job 42:12–17; Isaiah 52:13–54:1; 1 Corinthians 1:18–2:2; Matthew 27:1–38; Luke 23:39–43; Matthew 27:39–54; John 19:31–37; Matthew 27:55–61.

For the Exaltation of the Cross the main biblical readings are:
At Great Vespers: Exodus 15:22–16:1; Proverbs 3:11–18; Isaiah 60:11–16.
At Mattins: Psalm 51 [50]; John 12:28–36.
At the Divine Liturgy: 1 Corinthians 1:18–24; John 19:6–11, 13–20, 25–28, 30–35.

⫸ 12 ⫷

Now Are All Things Filled with Light

THE HOLY AND GREAT SUNDAY OF PASCHA
(EASTER SUNDAY)

Now are all things filled with light; heaven, and earth, and the places under the earth. All Creation doth celebrate the Resurrection of Christ.[1]

⫸ I ⫷

'This is to us a Feast of feasts and a Solemnity of solemnities as far exalted above all others as the Sun is above the stars . . . Today we are celebrating the Resurrection itself, no longer as an object of expectation, but as having already come to pass, and gathering the whole world unto itself.'[2] Thus St Gregory Nazianzen (c. 329–390) states the great dignity of Easter. Similar sentiments are expressed in the hymns for Easter: 'This chosen and holy day is the first of the sabbaths, the queen and lady, the feast of feasts, and the festival of festivals, wherein we bless Christ unto the ages'.[3] By the time of St Gregory the liturgical observance of the Christian Passover had been expanded to include the separate celebration of the Lord's Passion on Good Friday, and the Baptism of Catechumens at the Easter Vigil. Easter as a separate liturgical day could thus become the climax of a series of celebrations during which it had been 'an object of expectation'.

The present Orthodox celebration of Easter begins at midnight, but follows on from the services of Holy Saturday. Mattins of Holy Saturday is usually celebrated on Good Friday evening, and concludes with a procession of the Epitaphion round the outside of the church, a reminder of Christ's descent to the darkness of hades. On Saturday morning and afternoon Vespers and the Divine Liturgy of St Basil are celebrated – now brought forward from their previous later time; the fifteen Old Testament readings at Vespers are related to the themes of Passover, Resurrection and Baptism. At about 11.30 p.m. the Midnight Office begins in total darkness, except for a single lamp in the sanctuary; the senior priest reads the Canon of Holy Saturday in the body of the church before the Epitaphion. After this the Epitaphion is removed from its stand and taken in procession through the Royal Doors into the sanctuary and placed on the Holy Table (where it remains until the Ascension). At midnight the priest leads a procession with the book of the Gospels, the icon of the Resurrection and candles to the narthex (a reminder of the women going to the tomb on Easter morning); the Resurrection is proclaimed outside the main door of the church, and then the joyful procession enters the church which is now filled with light. Mattins for Easter Day now begins, and consists mainly of texts composed in the eighth century by St John of Damascus. The heart of the Easter message is expressed in the Paschal Troparion: 'Christ is risen from the dead, trampling down Death by death, and upon those in the tomb bestowing life,'[4] and the Troparion 'Now are all things filled with light . . .'

After the fast of Great Lent and the intensity of Holy Week, the celebration that crowns the Paschal Mystery is an outpouring of light and joy. Like a ray of light dispersed into its component colours when it is passes through a prism, the following extracts from the liturgical texts show the different elements in the composition of the Church's Easter celebration and the wide-ranging implications of Christ's triumph over sin and death.

1. The events of Easter morning as narrated in the Gospels are referred to within the overall context of the Church's celebration of the work of redemption.

> Though Thou didst descend into the grave, O Immortal One, yet didst Thou destroy the power of Hades, and didst arise as victor, O Christ God, calling to the myrrh-bearing women, Rejoice, and giving peace unto Thine Apostles, O Thou who dost grant resurrection to the fallen. (Kontakion for Easter)[5]

> When they who were with Mary came, anticipating the dawn, and found the stone rolled away from the sepulchre, they heard from the Angel: Why seek ye among the dead, as though He were mortal man, Him who abideth in everlasting light? Behold the grave-clothes. Go quickly and proclaim to the world that the Lord is risen, and hath put death to death. For He is the Son of God, Who saveth the race of man.[6]

2. Christ's suffering and death have been accepted *voluntarily* in order to bring about the redemption of Adam.

> O my Saviour, the life-giving and unslain Sacrifice, when, as God, Thou of Thine own will, hadst offered up Thyself unto the Father, Thou didst raise up with Thyself the whole race of Adam when Thou didst rise from the grave.[7]

3. The dramatic nature of Christ's descent into the underworld is plainly stated, but the hymns do not dwell on this excessively. It is as if Hades was broken open *en passant* in the process of rescuing Adam, who represents us. *We* are included among the redeemed: 'Thou didst shatter the bars that held fast those that were fettered'; 'Thou didst lead *us* out of darkness and the shadow of death'. Psalm 107:16 [106] and Isaiah 45:2–3 proved powerful imagery for hymn-writers and icon painters alike.

> Thou didst descend into the deepest parts of the earth, and didst shatter the bars that held fast those that were fettered, O Christ. And on the third day, like Jonas from the sea monster, Thou didst arise from the grave.[8]

> Out of fear, the gates of death opened unto Thee, O Lord; and on beholding Thee, the gate-keepers of Hades trembled; for Thou didst crush the brazen gates, and didst break the iron bars. And Thou didst lead us out of darkness and the shadow of death, and didst break our bonds asunder.[9]

4. The Resurrection brings light and joy to the whole creation:

> Today the whole creation is glad and doth rejoice, for Christ is risen, and Hades hath been despoiled.[10]

5. Light and joy permeate the Church's worship, and bear fruit in reconciliation and forgiveness:

> Bearing lights, let us go forth to meet Christ, Who cometh forth from the grave like a bridegroom. And with the ranks of them that love and keep this festival, let us celebrate the saving Pascha of God.[11]

> It is the day of Resurrection: let us be radiant for the festival, and let us embrace one another. Let us say, O brethren, even to those that hate us: Let us forgive all things on the Resurrection; and thus let us cry: Christ is risen from the dead, by death hath He trampled down death, and on those in the graves hath He bestowed life.[12]

6. The celebration of Pascha looks forward to the fullness of God's Kingdom:

> O Great and most sacred Pascha, Christ; O Wisdom and Word and Power of God! Grant that we partake of Thee fully in the unwaning day of Thy Kingdom.[13]

7. The Gospel reading at the Divine Liturgy (John 1:1–17) stresses the divinity of the Incarnate Logos. The hymns stress that the two natures of Christ, God and man, remain united even in death and hades:

In the grave bodily; in Hades with Thy soul, though Thou wast God; in Paradise
with the thief; and on the Throne with the Father and the Spirit wast Thou Who
fillest all things, O Christ the Uncircumscribable.[14]

8. Finally we have an extract from a Resurrection homily traditionally attributed to
St John Chrysostom, which forms an integral part of the liturgical texts for the celebration of Easter. It summarizes not only themes that have already been quoted, but
also the imagery and message of the Anastasis icon:

> Let no one fear death, for the death of our Saviour has set us free: He has destroyed
> it by enduring it, He has despoiled Hades by going down into its kingdom, He
> has angered it by allowing it to taste of his flesh. When Isaias foresaw all this, he
> cried out: 'O Hades, you have been angered by encountering Him in the nether
> world.' Hades . . . is angered because it has been reduced to naught, it is angered
> because it is now captive. It seized a body, and, lo! it discovered God; it seized
> earth, and, behold! it encountered heaven; it seized the visible, and was over-
> come by the invisible. O death, where is your sting? O Hades, where is your
> victory? Christ is risen and you are abolished, Christ is risen and the demons are
> cast down, Christ is risen and the angels rejoice, Christ is risen and life is freed,
> Christ is risen and the tomb is emptied of the dead.[15]

⋘ **II** ⋙

We now turn to the development of the iconography associated with the Resurrection of Christ. André Grabar described the earliest images of the Resurrection as
'juridical and evangelical':[16] they functioned as evidence for the Resurrection, and
were drawn from the Gospel narratives. We are told that the Myrrophores (the spice-
bearing women) came to the tomb, found it empty, and were told of the Resurrection
by an angel (Matthew 28:1ff; Mark 16:1ff; Luke 24:1ff); the number of the women
mentioned in the Gospels is either two or three, an appropriate number of witnesses
in matters of Jewish Law. From the fourth Gospel we have the account of Christ's
appearance to Thomas (John 20:24–29); his experience of seeing and touching the
risen Lord's wounded hands and side becomes a powerful witness to the reality of
the Resurrection. Images representing the women at the tomb were extant from at
least the fourth century, and from the sixth to seventh centuries were commonly used
together with images of Christ and St Thomas, on the pilgrimage ampullae (small
vessels of metal or clay used by pilgrims to carry oil, water or earth etc. from the holy
places). On Roman sarcophagi of the fourth century the Cross with a triumphal
wreath and the *Chi-Ro* monogram are used to symbolize the Resurrection, sometimes flanked by sleeping soldiers. As pilgrimage to the holy places became more

common, a representation of the Church of the Resurrection in Jerusalem, some-times with sleeping soldiers, was used to signify the Resurrection. From this early range of Resurrection images, those of the women at the tomb and Christ with St Thomas have remained a constant feature in the art of the Orthodox Church to this day. However, the main icon for Easter is quite different.

The common Easter icon is referred to simply as the Anastasis[17] (Resurrection), and the scene depicts Christ triumphant over hades and raising Adam with himself. It has long been assumed that the imagery for this icon is largely derived from the apocryphal *Gospel of Nicodemus*,[18] and this is still asserted. However, it seems rather to be the case that the relevant section of the so called *Gospel of Nicodemus* is a later addition, and that the major sources for the Anastasis image are to be found in the homilies and liturgical texts that were in use from the fourth and fifth centuries onwards. St John of Damascus, in his major work the *Exposition of the Orthodox Faith*, devotes a section to this theme which was clearly well established by the eighth cen-tury, and provides the imagery pictorialized in the icon. While Christ's body remains in the tomb, his soul descends to hades:

> The soul when it was deified descended into Hades, in order that, just as the Sun of Righteousness rose for those upon the earth, so likewise He might bring light to those who sit under the earth in darkness and shadow of death: in order that just as He brought the message of peace to those upon the earth, and of release to the prisoners, and of sight to the blind, and became to those who believed the Author of everlasting salvation and to those who did not believe a reproach of their unbelief, so He might become the same to those in Hades: 'that every knee should bow to Him, of things in heaven, and things in earth and things under the earth' (Philippians 2:10). And thus after He had freed those who had been bound for ages, straightway He rose again from the dead, showing us the way of resur-rection.[19]

We can see how the teaching of this great theologian is in keeping with the teach-ing of St Peter in Acts 2 and in 1 Peter 3:18–19. Christ's descent is a mission to the dead, and the Resurrection begins from hades: 'Christ is risen from the dead, tram-pling down Death by death, and upon those in the tomb bestowing life.'

The earliest type of Anastasis image is exemplified by the now much decayed fresco at the Palatine ramp in the Church of Sta. Maria Antiqua in Rome c. 705–707. Christ makes a dramatic entry into the underworld of death; with his right hand he takes hold of Adam's left hand, and with his right foot tramples on the personified Hades. Eve stands alongside Adam, with her left hand raised up towards Christ; beneath Adam is an open tomb, and the hand of Hades is stretched out to hold back Adam. Christ holds a scroll in his left hand, his large halo is marked with the Cross, and there remain traces of an oval mandorla around him. Scholars regard this fresco as evidence of a well-developed iconographic theme, and one which survived throughout the Byzantine period. The emphasis in this type is on Christ's dynamic passage through death to rescue Adam. A second type of this image is described as the victory type, where the triumphant Christ pulls Adam out of hades and holds the Cross as a trophy. A good example of this is the mosaic at Hosios Loukas, c. 1030. Much less common is a type in which Christ shows his wounded hands to Adam and Eve, emphasizing the means whereby salvation has been achieved. Further variants on the theme include Christ shown bending deeply to raise up Adam, and an even-handed type where Christ stands in the centre and raises Adam and Eve who are on his right and left.

The Anastasis image developed at a time when there was increased interest in the possibilities of depicting Christ at the key moments of his work of redemption: his death and Resurrection. Changes took place in the way Christ crucified is depicted, and the Anastasis image depicted Christ accomplishing the release of Adam – a major conceptual advance from the images of the angel appearing to the Myrrophores and Christ appearing to Thomas. Some formal elements in the development of the image have been traced to imperial images of triumph and also to themes from classical mythology such as Hercules pulling Cerebus out of hades. External elements of form and style were at hand to enable the theology to be expressed in an image. Jill Storer comments: 'The Anastasis has the character of an image devised deliberately to express a complex of ideas and combining a number of formulae.'[20]

In the ninth and tenth centuries after the end of the iconoclast controversy, evidence for this image becomes much more plentiful; in Psalters and other manuscripts, on reliquaries, and in church wall paintings in Cappadocia the image becomes familiar. From the tenth century St John the Forerunner, King David and King Solomon begin to appear as part of the image, and over the ensuing centuries the cast of attendant figures is increased to include such characters as Abel and Samuel (even, mysteriously, Cain in some provincial areas). Variations in the representation of the underworld are also noticeable, with more or less prominence being given to Hades, the broken gates, bolts, bars, locks and keys, and angels who bind Satan or Hades. On the whole, reticence about giving prominence to images of evil means that the underworld and its contents do not intrude too much into the main scene, but occasionally it seems that fascination with the details of the underworld overcame a sense of reticence. The early fourteenth century in Byzantium was a period of great intellectual ferment and artistic experiment; to this period belong some monumental paintings of the Anastasis including that in the Kariye Djami in Istanbul (c 1315–21). Here the central figure of Christ stands dramatically over hades, vigorously rescuing Adam and Eve who seem to float out of their tombs while a large number of the righteous dead stand on either side. The central figure of Christ from this fresco is illustrated on the front cover of this book.

In **Plate 18** we have a fifteenth-century Russian icon of the Anastasis. There is no doubt about the central relationship in this icon: Christ has descended even to the underworld to bring back Adam to himself. Christ is depicted not as the victim of mortality and evil, but as the victorious Son of God, clothed in glory, who by death has conquered death, and has released those who have been held captive in hades. It is as if Christ has come at speed to rescue Adam: the Saviour's gold-flecked yellow ochre robes billow out behind him as he bends towards Adam; he grasps the left wrist of Adam whose arms are stretched out to welcome the Redeemer. Behind the figure of Christ is a circular mandorla – the symbol of the divine presence; the outer circle is in blue, the next circle towards the centre is in various shades of blue-green; across the darker central section lines of gold radiating from the bottom left suggest the dawn of the Resurrection, and it is into this central section of the mandorla that the figure of Adam is drawn by Christ. The darkness of hades has been filled with light, and Adam's yellow ochre clothing represents the garment of glory, indicating the new life into which he has been raised; in the same way the white robes of the newly baptized symbolize their new life in Christ.

Behind Adam stand King David and King Solomon, ancestors and prophets of the Saviour. Behind Solomon we see John the Baptist. He is the Forerunner who prepared the way of the Lord, preceded him in a martyr's death, and preceded his entry to hades; similarly John's baptism preceded and prepared for the Church's sacrament of Christian Baptism. On the right Eve kneels with her hands raised in prayer and looks attentively towards Christ; she is clothed in a rich vermilion garment and shares with Adam in the freedom which Christ has brought to the underworld. The figure of Eve, in posture and clothing, is reminiscent of the Mother of God; it is appropriate that the 'mother of all living' should evoke the figure of her who is Mother of the Incarnate God, and Mother of the new humanity which comes to life in Christ. This link between Eve and Mary is stated by St Ephraim the Syrian: 'He entered Sheol and plundered its storehouses and emptied its treasures. He came then to Eve the Mother of all living . . . [who] became the well-spring of death to all living. But Mary budded forth, a new shoot from Eve the ancient vine.'[21] Behind Eve in the icon we see Moses, with the tablets of the Law; the exodus and covenant associated with Moses have found fulfilment in this new exodus from hades and death, and in the New Covenant inaugurated by Christ. Behind Moses are other righteous dead who await liberation from hades. Beneath the figure of Christ the gates of hades have been broken down, and the personification of Hades is seen in the darkness of the underworld, having lost those who had been in subjection to him and the power of death. The darkness of hades is reminiscent of the cave in the icons of the Nativity, the Raising of Lazarus and the Crucifixion.

In the upper section of the icon the two peaks of rock remind us that 'the earth shook and the rocks were split' (Matthew 27:51) in the earth-shattering aftermath of the death of Christ. The dividing of the rocks in the Anastasis icon seems to recall the division involved in the earlier Passover mystery – the dividing of the waters of the

Red Sea as the people of Israel move from slavery in Egypt towards the freedom of the Promised Land. In each instance God makes a way for his people to pass from bondage to freedom: the ending of servitude in Egypt prefigures the ending of the tyranny of sin and death accomplished in the Christ's Paschal Mystery.

In **Plate 19** we have a modern version of the Anastasis from the wall paintings of Fr Gregory Kroug in the Skete of the Holy Spirit at Mesnil-St-Denis near Paris.[22] It is interesting to note what is *not* represented in this icon: the dark depths of hades are not seen, and there is no personified figure of Hades either; the rocky landscape familiar in many icons is absent, and the dividing of the rocks can be seen at the lower outer edges only; and none of the extra cast of attendant figures which had been assimilated into the Anastasis scene are present. Christ is represented with Adam and Eve – the New Man emerging from hades, and raising up with him the old human-ity. Fr Gregory seems to have returned to the origins of the image, and with great simplicity has created an icon which conveys a powerful sense of Christ's compas-sion: the Saviour who came to earth for our redemption has descended to the underworld in search of Adam; Christ's whole posture and expression radiate love and compassion. The expression on the face of Adam is one of loving adoration. The words from Psalm 34:5 [34] seem appropriate: 'Look to him, and be radiant.' It is as if the imagery in the parable of the Prodigal Son has been transformed: the old man Adam, the father of our race, welcomes the Son of Man who comes as his redeemer, and he is clothed by the Son with the garments of glory. God the Son embodies and reveals the Father's redeeming love to the father of our race, and that love is recip-rocated by the adoration of Adam as his hand is taken by the Son. One sentence from the hymnody of the Feast sums up the relationship: 'Adam, who fell and has now been raised up, was terrified when God walked in Paradise, but rejoices when He descends into Hades.'[23] In this icon Adam sees the face of God and is glad. The hand of Christ reaches down to raise up Adam; compared with many icons where Christ grasps the wrist of Adam and wrenches him out of hades, in this icon Fr Gregory shows Christ lifting up Adam as if he were a child needing help after a fall. The hand and posture of Adam express gladness and willingness to be lifted from where he has fallen. The figure of Eve is closely associated with Adam; she is at his side, 'bone of my bones and flesh of my flesh' (Genesis 2:23), and although it is the hand of Adam that Christ takes, Eve is an integral part of the redeemed humanity that is raised up. God has come to restore his image, and Adam and Eve are raised together, for 'in the image of God he created him; male and female he created them' (Genesis 1:27).

The whole scene is set within an arch in the wall; the mandorla with its three distinct areas forms the background; rays of light pass across the blue background from the figure of Christ. The subtle colours used to depict the three figures are all enhanced by highlights which make the whole icon radiant in a manner similar to the work of Andrei Rublev. The letters IC XC towards the top of the icon, as always indicate the person of Christ; his halo is marked with a Cross and bears the Greek inscription *Ho On* ('The One Who Is') to indicate his divinity, for he is the One who makes all things new (cf Revelation 21:5). In Christ's left hand is the scroll, the symbol of the teacher and his wisdom, and, unusually, Adam too is shown with a scroll in his left hand – perhaps indicating that he has grown in wisdom and understanding, and is able to bring wisdom to others. This icon is truly remarkable, and one which merits much contemplative attention.

The descent of Christ into the underworld to release Adam and Eve from their bondage to death is sometimes used as a type through which to understand the work of Christ in the individual soul. Just as Christ descends to the realm of the dead to save sinners and bring light and life to the dead, so he enters into the depths of the human heart in order to free our capacity to respond to the love of God. The following quotation develops this idea:

> When you hear that Christ descended into hell in order to deliver the souls dwelling there, do not think that what happens now is very different. The heart is a tomb and there our thoughts and our intellect are buried, imprisoned in heavy darkness. And so Christ comes to the souls in hell that call upon Him, descending, that is to say, into the depths of the heart; and there He commands death to release the imprisoned souls that call upon Him, for He has power to deliver us. Then, lifting up the heavy stone that oppresses the soul, and opening the tomb, He resurrects us – for we were truly dead – and releases our imprisoned soul from its lightless prison . . .
>
> . . . What was the purpose of His descent to earth except to save sinners, to bring light to those in darkness and life to the dead?'[24]

In many icons of the Anastasis the representation of the depths of the underworld being opened up by Christ is shown in a very dramatic way, and sometimes this seems to mirror a spiritual experience of the opening up of one's own interior world; the depths and powers of one's heart and soul are laid open to the light of Christ, to his healing love and forgiveness, and are transformed by Christ. Just as in the icons Adam and Eve are attracted to Christ and raised up by him, so the human heart is released to respond in love and adoration to the Saviour who takes us by the hand and leads us into the light and peace of his Kingdom; the broken and disparate elements of our humanity are integrated and restored to a new wholeness as we are raised to life in Christ. Through some icons this influence can be very powerfully felt.

★　　　★　　　★

The main biblical readings on Holy Saturday are

At Vespers, the readings connected with the themes of Passover, Resurrection and Baptismal initiation: Genesis 1:1–13; Isaiah 60:1–16; Exodus 12:1–11; Jonah 1:1–4, 11; Joshua 5:10–15; Exodus 13:20–15:19; Zephaniah 3: 8–15; 1 Kings 17:8–24; Isaiah 61:10 – 62:5; Genesis 22:1–18; Isaiah 61:1–9; 2 Kings 4:8–37; Isaiah 63:11–64:5; Jeremiah 31:31–34; Daniel 3:1–23; The Song of the Three Children, vv 1–66.
At the Divine Liturgy of St Basil: Romans 6:3–11; Matthew 28:1–18.

The main biblical readings for the Easter services are:

At Mattins: Mark 16:1–8.
At the Divine Liturgy: Acts 1:1–8; John 1:1–17.

❧ 13 ❧

Living Waters of Wisdom and Endless Life

Thou, O Saviour, dost pour out for all the world living waters of wisdom and endless life, inviting all to partake and to drink of these saving streams.[1]

❧ I ❧

This Feast of the Church has been described as a 'festival of an idea'[2] – in the sense that it is a complex one which draws together images and texts expressing a theological insight, rather than a Feast that commemorates a specific event. The fact that this Feast is not part of the Western Christian tradition means that it is not immediately obvious to non-Orthodox Christians what it really concerns.

Within the whole Christian Church there is an awareness that two of the major Jewish festivals have been transformed into Christian feasts. The Jewish Feast of Passover provides a basis for the Christian celebration of the death and Resurrection of Christ, and the Jewish Feast of Pentecost provides a basis for the Christian celebration of the outpouring of the Holy Spirit. In these cases the events of the death and Resurrection of Christ and the gift of the Holy Spirit were from the beginning associated with the Feasts of Passover and Pentecost because the events actually took place at the time of those Feasts in Jerusalem. The third great Jewish festival, the Feast of Tabernacles, was not historically the occasion of an event which has passed into universal Christian liturgical observance. However, the Feast of Tabernacles is the time when the events spoken of in chapters 7 and 8 of St John's Gospel took place (the controversy with the Jews that arises over the growing number of believers in Jesus, the possibility that he might be the Christ, his promise of the Spirit, and his claim to be the light of the world). In a way, the Orthodox Mid-Pentecost Feast could well be regarded as a Christianization of the Feast of Tabernacles, in that this Orthodox Feast is centred on the events and teaching contained in John 7, but placed in a liturgical context which is at the mid-point between Easter and Pentecost where the scripture is actually part of the continuous course of reading. The Gospel reading for Mid-Pentecost is from John 7, as is that for Pentecost itself; these Gospel readings are concerned with the identity of Christ and his promise of the Spirit; the symbolism of water is conspicuous, and recurs throughout the liturgical texts for the Feast of Mid-Pentecost.

It should be pointed out at this stage that there is a great contrast between the richness of imagery and themes in the liturgical texts for Mid-Pentecost and the economy and simplicity of the icon for this Feast, where we simply see the youthful Christ seated in the Temple with the teachers. In comparison with the developed imagery of the texts, the icon is remarkably restrained. At first sight it may not be clear how the verbal and visual imagery associated with this Feast do in fact fit together, so it will be necessary to look in detail at the biblical background material that is incorporated into the texts and their imagery, and that which is incorporated into the icon of this Feast.

≼ II ≽

The Feast of Tabernacles was one of the very popular Jewish festivals, and during its long history it had come to be associated with many aspects of Jewish faith and experience. As a harvest festival it involved thanksgiving for crops including grain and fruit, but especially for wheat and grapes. As a New Year festival it looked forward to the gift of rain and the need for water to sustain both crops and community in another year. Remembering the experience of the Exodus wanderings in the wilderness, giving thanks for the gift of the promised land, celebrating the Davidic dynasty and the existence of the Temple in Jerusalem – all these elements added to the richness of what was celebrated in this festival; there was also an apocalyptic aspect which looked forward to the coming of the Messiah and his Kingdom. Zechariah 9–14 was associated with the Feast of Tabernacles, as it expressed the triumph of God and the coming of the Messianic king (9:9); Zechariah speaks of God pouring out a spirit of compassion and supplication on Jerusalem (12:10), opening up a fountain that will cleanse Jerusalem (13:1), and providing living waters that flow from Jerusalem to the Mediterranean and the Dead Sea (14:8). This part of Zechariah is believed to be relevant background not only for John 7:38 but also for Revelation 22. Rituals that took place during the seven or eight days of the Feast involved light and water. The Temple area was illuminated with lamps and torches; bunches of myrtle and willow together with lemons or other citrons were carried in the daily processions around the altar; water was carried from the spring that supplied the Pool of Siloam and poured out before the altar of offering. Psalm 118 [117] was sung in procession, and Isaiah 12:3 was sung as the priests offered water at the altar: 'With joy you will draw water from the wells of salvation.'

One would have to be very ignorant of the Bible to be unaware of the way water is mentioned in it with great frequency. In the Middle East it is obvious that where there is water there is life, and the reverse is true: where there is no water there is no life. This awareness permeates the Holy Scriptures and enables water to become a symbol of many aspects of life. A few examples will help to make this point. Genesis 2:10–14 speaks of the four rivers flowing out of Eden to water the whole earth; Genesis 6-8 is the account of the flood; in Exodus 17:2–7 and Numbers 20 Moses brings forth water from the rock in the wilderness; in Isaiah water and the imagery of water refer to renewal, salvation, and the outpouring of the Spirit (12:3–4; 35:6–7; 44:3–4; 55:1); water comes from the side of the Temple in Ezekiel 47, and is a frequent image in the Psalms (e.g. Psalm 63:1[62]). In the New Testament water is of particular significance in the Johannine writings (cf John 4:5–42 [the Gospel for the Sunday of the Samaritan Woman, which comes after Mid-Pentecost]; 5:2–9; 7:37–39; 19:34; 1 John 5:8; Revelation 21:6, 22:1–2, 17). The imagery of water, life and Spirit continues to play a significant part in the whole Christian tradition of theology and spirituality, especially in those parts of the Church where imagery and symbolism have been a key part of the language of theology and spirituality.

The key text in John 7 which needs to be examined is verses 37–39, part of the Gospel for Mid-Pentecost:

> On the last day of the feast, the great day, Jesus stood up and proclaimed, 'If any one thirst, let him come to me and drink. He who believes in me, as the scripture has said, "Out of his heart shall flow rivers of living water."' Now this he said about the Spirit, which those who believed in him were to receive; for as yet the Spirit had not been given, because Jesus was not yet glorified.

In his commentary on St John's Gospel, Raymond Brown[3] looks at the range of possible Old Testament background texts to which this passage in the Gospel might refer. Interesting possibilities from the Wisdom tradition are suggested: Proverbs 18:4 'The words of a man's mouth are deep waters; the fountain of wisdom is a gushing stream'; Sirach 24:30–33 'I [Wisdom] went forth like a canal from a river and like a water channel into a garden . . . I will again make instruction shine forth like the dawn, and I will make it shine afar; I will again pour out teaching like prophecy'; and one of the Qumran hymns is quoted: 'You, O my God, have put into my mouth, as it were, rain for all [who thirst], and a fount of living waters which shall not fail.' Interesting though these texts may be, Brown moves on to another group of texts which have greater consonance with the whole mystery of salvation and redemption. The account of Moses bringing water from the rock in the Exodus story (Exodus 17:1–7 and Numbers 20:2–13) is closely linked with other elements in the Exodus story which are alluded to in the fourth Gospel (the paschal lamb, the brazen serpent, and the gift of manna), and this rock is seen in the early Church as a type of Christ (cf 1 Corinthians 10:4). In the Psalms there is a linking of the gifts of manna and water from the rock: 'They asked, and he brought quails, and gave them bread from heaven in abundance. He opened the rock, and water gushed forth; it flowed through the desert like a river' (Psalm 105:40–41 [104]). 'Tremble, O earth, at the presence of the Lord, . . . who turns the rock into a pool of water, the flint into a spring of water' (Psalm 114:7–8 [113]). Elsewhere the same imagery occurs: 'The wild beasts will honour me, the jackals and the ostriches; for I give water in the wilderness, rivers in the desert, to give drink to my chosen people' (Isaiah 43:20). 'For I will pour water on the thirsty land, and streams on the dry ground; I will pour my Spirit upon your descendants, and my blessing on your offspring' (Isaiah 44:3). 'They thirsted not when he led them through the deserts; he made water flow for them from the rock; he cleft the rock and the water gushed out' (Isaiah 48:21). 'He cleft rocks in the wilderness, and gave them drink abundantly as from the deep. He made streams come out of the rock, and caused waters to flow down like rivers' (Psalm 78:15–16 [77]). Many of these texts actually formed part of the synagogue readings when the Feast of Tabernacles was celebrated.

The importance of Zechariah 14 has already been mentioned, but alongside this we need to place Ezekiel 47, the vision of water flowing from the side of the Temple. Both passages seem to influence Revelation 22, and it is argued that their influence should also be recognized in John 7:37–38. Brown quotes Daniélou's thesis that John is highly dependent on Ezekiel 47:1–11, and that Jesus is the Temple rock from which, in Ezekiel's imagery, flows the river which is the source of life. In the fourth Gospel, Jesus is identified as the Temple (John 2:19–22), and in the patristic period Jesus is often identified with the Temple rock.

Both the imagery of the Exodus tradition and of the apocalyptic tradition contribute to the way in which Jesus is presented in St John's Gospel as the source of the waters of life. While the Wisdom tradition may not be directly involved, it is nevertheless part of the living background within which the imagery of water, food and wine, wisdom and teaching is used to convey the reality of God's presence and revelation. 'If the water is a symbol of the revelation that Jesus gives to those who believe in him, it is also the symbol of the Spirit that the resurrected Jesus will give, as v. 39 specifies.'[4] The Johannine connection between Spirit, water and blood (cf 1 John 5; John 19:34) leads us to recognize the Church's sacramental life as part of the context in which all this teaching is given, received and lived.

≼ **III** ≽

From this examination of the biblical background in the Feast of Tabernacles and parts of John 7 we now move on to look at some of the varied themes that are present in the liturgical celebration of the Orthodox feast of Mid-Pentecost. Texts have been selected according to various themes, but it should be emphasized that within *The Pentecostarion* the texts are not presented thematically; there they form a rich tapestry where ideas, themes and images are interwoven in ways that allow the heart, mind and soul to be continuously touched and shaped by the liturgical hymns and chants.

1. The links between the Paschal Mystery, the Ascension and Pentecost are reiterated in the texts, as is the presence of Jesus in the Temple at the mid-point of the Feast of Tabernacles.

> The mid-point of Pentecost is come this day. By the former feast it is illumined with the most divine radiance of the divine Pascha, and by the latter feast it is made to shine with the grace of the Comforter.[5]

> Today the mid-point of two hallowed days hath illumined us with an effulgent light, O Thou Life-giver, Jesus, gracious Benefactor of our souls.[6]

> Thou, at Mid-feast, didst stand in the Temple's court in a manner befitting God and didst cry: Let him who doth suffer thirst now draw nigh unto Me and drink.[7]

2. The imagery of water and the Spirit permeates this Feast and forms an integral part of the language of prayer.

> Thou who art rest for all didst grow weary in the flesh; Thou Who art the Wellspring of miracles didst willingly thirst. Thou didst seek after water, O Jesus, promising living water.[8]

> O Sovereign Master and Creator of all things, O Christ our God, Thou didst cry unto those present at the Judaic Mid-feast and address them thus: Come hither and draw ye forth immortality's water. Wherefore, we fall down before Thee and faithfully cry out: Grant Thy compassion unto us, O Lord, for Thou art truly the Well-spring of life for all. (Kontakion)[9]

3. Wisdom, teaching and truth were concepts linked with water and the Spirit in the Wisdom tradition, as we have seen. Naturally they are conspicuous in the texts for this Feast.

> He that drinketh of this divine water that I shall give, from within him the springs of My teachings shall issue forth. Whoso doth believe that the Divine Father sent Me, and that I came forth from Him, he with Me shall be glorified. Therefore do we cry unto Thee: Glory to Thee, O Christ God, Who dost cause the streams of Thy great love for man to well forth in all abundance to us . . .[10]

> Thou, O Saviour, dost pour out for all the world living waters of wisdom and
> endless life, inviting all to partake of these saving streams; for the man who
> receiveth and keepeth Thy holy law thereby quencheth the coals of dark error
> and fallacy.[11]

4. Conflict with the Jews and questions about the identity of Jesus as Messiah abound
in St John's Gospel, and are certainly brought into focus in chapter 7. This also is
reflected in the liturgical texts.

> The Messiah and Lord of all put to silence the lawless scribes and rebuked the Jews
> as He cried out unto them: Judge not according to mere appearances, O ye
> unrighteous ones.[12]

5. The Church receives the gift of living waters.

> Thou didst open unto the Church the springs of life-creating waters, O Good
> One, and didst cry: If any zealous man thirst, let him go and drink.
> > Thou saidest plainly that Thou wouldst be lifted up from earth unto Heaven,
> and Thou didst promise to send the Holy Spirit from thence.[13]

6. Healings by Christ on the Sabbath precipitated much of the conflict that surrounded
his ministry, and led to some of the attempts to arrest Jesus. The theme of healing
is prominent in the texts for this Feast, partly because the Sunday before Mid-
Pentecost is the Sunday of the Paralytic when the Gospel is John 5:1–15; here again
water is involved, as the healing takes place at the Pool of Bethesda. Some of the texts
for Mid-Pentecost include petitions for various kinds of healing.

> O Word, Who didst heal the withered hand by a word, do Thou heal the earth
> of my heart, which hath long ago become parched, and show me forth as one
> fruitful, that I also might bring forth fruit in fervent repentance, O Saviour.[14]

> I lie . . . in the pain of my offences, weakened in the members of my body and
> my soul. But, O most merciful Christ, my God, who didst become man by Thine
> own will in Thy boundless love for man, do Thou now invisibly raise me up,
> make me whole, as Thou didst him who was paralysed.[15]

7. Human thirst for the Spirit is poignantly expressed in many parts of the Bible.
Because of Christ's words in the Temple at the Feast of Tabernacles, and because the
Feast of Mid-Pentecost looks forward to Pentecost itself, this longing and thirst for
the living waters of the Spirit finds expression in the texts of this Feast. We should
remember that the Gospel readings for the Divine Liturgy at Mid-Pentecost and at

Pentecost are both from John 7: verses 14–36 at Mid-Pentecost and verses 37–52 and 8:12 at Pentecost.

> With the streams of Thy Blood do Thou water my soul, which is grown dry and barren because of mine iniquities and offences, and show it to be fruitful in virtues. For Thou didst tell all to draw nigh Thee, O all-holy Word of God, and to draw forth the water of incorruption, which is living and washeth away the sins of them that praise Thy glorious and divine arising. Unto them that know Thee as God, O Good One, grant from on high the strength of the Spirit, which verily was borne by Thy disciples, for Thou art truly the Well-spring of life for all.[16]

> Almighty Saviour . . . Thou didst cry unto all: Should some one be pained by thirst, let him resort to Me . . . For I grant streams of wisdom, strength and life unto all that draw nigh unto Me in faith, since I took on man's likeness of Mine own will, as the Friend of man.[17]

❧ IV ❧

After looking at many of the spiritual and theological themes that are presented to us within the celebration of the Feast of Mid-Pentecost, what do we see when we look at the icon associated with the Feast, and how do we respond to the icon?

The illustration in **Plate 20** is of a fifteenth-century Russian icon of the Novgorod School. The background is a stylized representation of the Temple buildings, in front of which the young Christ is seated in the centre, with a group of three teachers on either side. After all that has been said thus far about the Feast of Tabernacles and its significance for the Feast of Mid-Pentecost, the icon represents a completely different event: the event narrated in St Luke's Gospel (2:41–51), where Christ as an adolescent boy is found in the Temple, 'sitting among the teachers, listening to them and asking them questions; and all who heard him were amazed at his understanding and his answers' (vv. 46–47). In the icon Christ is shown as a beardless youth, as the 'Christ-Emmanuel' who manifests his wisdom by teaching in the Temple; the right hand of Christ, raised in an explanatory gesture, and the scroll in his left hand suggest that he embodies and imparts the Word and Wisdom of God. The fact that he is seated, and in a higher position reinforces his role as teacher, since this was a conventional way of presenting the philosopher and teacher. The teachers by their posture and gestures express amazement 'at his understanding and his answers', a response echoed later in the Mid-Pentecost Gospel when the Jews at the Feast of Tabernacles marvel saying, 'How is it that this man has learning, when he has never studied?' (John 7:15).

The key to this icon is the portrayal of Christ-Emmanuel, the embodiment of the Word and expositor of divine Wisdom. He is in his 'Father's house' at the age of twelve. Later he is again in the Temple at the Feast of Tabernacles as the adult teacher of divine Wisdom who explicitly speaks about God's authority for his teaching and action (John 7:16–18); he speaks of his return to the Father (John 7:34), claims to be the One to whom the thirsty should come for refreshment and to experience the living waters of the Spirit (John 7:37–38); as the Light of the World he promises that all who follow him 'will not walk in darkness, but will have the light of life' (John 8:12). The figure of the Christ-Emmanuel as teacher brings together all the 'water imagery' of Mid-Pentecost concerned with a thirst for wisdom, and the teaching, revelation, and the gift of the Spirit which are given in response. In a simple and concentrated way the icon expresses all that has been said above – or to put it conversely: all that has been said above unfolds what is presented with great economy in the icon.

It is well worth examining this icon in conjunction with the icon of the gift of the Spirit at Pentecost (see **Plate 23**). In the Mid-Pentecost icon the semi-circular bench has Christ-Emmanuel seated in the centre with the Jewish teachers on either side. In the Pentecost icon of the descent of the Spirit a similar semi-circular form has been extended into an elongated horseshoe shape, and the bench is occupied by the assembled apostles. From Christ-Emmanuel teaching in the Temple we move to the apostles of Christ receiving the gift of the Spirit in tongues of fire to enable them to become the teachers of the nations.

★   ★   ★

The Scripture readings for the main services at the Feast of Mid-Pentecost are:

At Vespers: Micah 4:2–3, 5, 6:2–5, 5:4; Isaiah 55:1–2, 12:3–4, 55:2–3, 6–13 and Proverbs 9:1–11.
At the Divine Liturgy: Acts 14:6–18; 17:14–36.

❧ 14 ❧

The Cloud Took Thee Up and Heaven Received Thee

THE ASCENSION OF OUR LORD AND GOD
AND SAVIOUR JESUS CHRIST

When Thou, O Christ, didst come unto the Mount of Olives to accomplish the good will of the Father, the heavenly Angels were amazed and the nethermost regions shuddered with fear. The disciples stood by with joy and trembling as Thou spakest unto them, and a cloud prepared as a throne awaited opposite them; and Heaven, throwing open the gates, shone with comeliness; . . . the cloud took Thee up and Heaven received Thee within itself. Thou hast wrought this great and strange deed, O Lord, for the salvation of our souls.[1]

❧ I ❧

Until the late fourth century the ascent of Christ into heaven and the descent of the Holy Spirit were celebrated together at the end of the great 50-day period of Pentecost; the term 'Pentecost' in those early centuries applied definitely to the whole 50-day period of rejoicing at the Resurrection, rather than signifying the fortieth day after the Resurrection, as happens in current Western liturgical usage. The development of a separate celebration of Christ's Ascension on the fortieth day after Easter began in Syria and Asia Minor during the latter part of the fourth century, and seems to have become almost universal practice by the seventh or eighth centuries. The Feast rounds off the celebration of the Lord's earthly life and ministry, and in many ways has a lot in common with the Feast of Christ's Nativity. Whereas Christmas celebrates the beginning of the economy of salvation with the human birth of the Incarnate Son of God, and explores the paradoxes and theological implications that are involved, the Ascension celebrates the accomplishment of salvation through Christ, and the taking of our humanity up to the throne of God. Man is seated at the right hand of the Father in the Person of the Incarnate Son, our great High Priest, whose ministry as Mediator between God and humanity provides access into the divine life.

The liturgical texts rejoice at the consummation of the work of salvation with Christ's Ascension:

> Marvellous is Thy birth, marvellous Thy resurrection, marvellous and amazing Thy divine ascension, O Life-giver.[2]

> Having appeared in the likeness of the flesh, Thou didst gather together into one the things that were formerly separated, O Friend of man. And while the disciples were watching, O Compassionate One, Thou wast taken up into the Heavens.[3]

God's search for Adam led to the Incarnation, Christ's humiliation on the Cross and his descent to the depths of Hades; it involved Christ's triumphant resurrection from the dead, his liberation of Adam from the bondage of sin and death, and his raising of Adam up to heaven:

> Having come down from Heaven unto the things of earth, O Christ, as God, with Thyself, Thou didst resurrect Adam's form, which lay prostrate in the nether holds of Hades' vault; in Thine Ascension to the heights Thou didst lead it up unto the Heavens and Thou didst seat it upon the throne of Thy Father, since Thou, the Friend of man, art merciful.[4]

> O Christ, having taken upon Thy shoulders our nature, which had gone astray, Thou didst ascend and bring it unto God the Father.[5]

Other texts develop the implications of the Ascension for the disciples of the Lord. Three key consequences stand out:

1. Christ's Ascension will lead to the Father's gift of the Holy Spirit, the Comforter:

> Thou hast ascended in glory, O Christ our God, and gladdened Thy disciples with the promise of the Holy Spirit; and they were assured by the blessing that Thou art the Son of God and Redeemer of the world.[6]

2. The Ascension will lead to other gifts that will enable the Church's ministry to develop (cf Ephesians 4:8–16), and there is also the assurance that 'I am not separated from you'. ' I am with you, and none shall prevail against you':

> When Thou hadst fulfilled Thy dispensation for our sakes, uniting things on earth with things in the Heavens, Thou didst ascend in glory, O Christ our God, departing not hence, but remaining inseparable from us and crying unto them that love Thee: I am with you, and no one can be against you. (Kontakion)[7]

3. As a consequence of the Ascension the Church lives in expectation of the Second Coming of Christ in judgement. Although judgement is not mentioned by the angels in Acts 1:11, it is implied in their reference to the Second Coming, and is given prominence in the hymnody of the Feast:

> Having mounted upon heaven's clouds, O Christ, Thou didst leave peace unto those upon the earth; and Thou didst ascend and sit at the Father's right hand on high . . . Wherefore Thou now waitest till the last consummation, when Thou shalt return to judge all mankind upon the earth. O Thou most righteous Judge and Lord, since Thou art a most merciful God, do Thou spare our souls and do Thou grant to us, Thy lowly servants, the pardon of our failings and our sins.[8]

The events that mark the end of the Lord's earthly life and ministry are seen in the light of Old Testament passages that celebrate the sovereignty of God. One particular text which is not read, but had a great influence on the imagery associated with the Ascension in early homilies and in icons, is Psalm 24:7–10 [23]:

> Lift up your heads, O gates! and be lifted up, O ancient doors! that the King of glory may come in.
>> Who is the King of glory? The Lord, strong and mighty, the Lord, mighty in battle!
>> Lift up your heads, O gates! and be lifted up, O ancient doors! that the King of glory may come in.
>> Who is this King of glory? The Lord of hosts, he is the King of glory!

The imagery of gates and doors and processions in this Psalm is related in Christian tradition first to Christ's ascent into heaven, and then also to his descent into Hades, and forms part of the way in which the Church celebrates Christ's accomplishment of salvation for the human race. This same imagery is an active ingredient in Orthodox liturgical celebrations: the doors in the iconostasis facilitate movement between the nave and the sanctuary and also symbolize the interaction between heaven and earth. The movement through the doors at various points in the liturgy, while a functional necessity, also increases awareness of the spiritual thresholds that have to be crossed in the course of our worship; the Divine Liturgy takes us across a threshold into the life of the Kingdom and the Communion of Saints, and also requires that barriers within our hearts and souls be removed to prepare for the entry of the Heavenly King, the Life-Giver and Lover of mankind who seeks to dwell with his people.

II

The iconography of the Ascension as we know it was established in the sixth century, and by the ninth century the Ascension was depicted in the domes of churches. The seventeenth-century Russian icon in **Plate 21** is a typical panel icon of the Ascension. In the upper section of the icon Christ is enthroned against the background of an oval mandorla which is supported by two angels; shafts of white light radiate across the grey-blue outer section of the mandorla; the halo is inscribed with the Cross and the words *Ho On* ('The One Who Is'). Christ's right hand is raised in blessing (in accordance with Luke 24:50, 'and lifting up his hands he blessed them'), and in his left hand is the scroll, the symbol of the wisdom and teaching that Christ brings. This depiction of Christ sets before us not only the event of Christ's Ascension as it is given to us in the Scriptures, but also the continuing reality of Christ's relationship with the Church: he continues to be the source of its teaching and message; he continues to bless and guide those to whom he has entrusted his work. Beneath Christ and the escorting angels is the larger section of the icon which presents three groups of figures set against the background of the Mount of Olives.

The Mother of God is very much at the centre. The icon, like many of the liturgical texts, expresses the Orthodox belief that the Mother of God was present with the apostles not only in the upper room after the Ascension, but also at the Ascension itself:

> O Lord, having fulfilled the mystery that was hidden from before the ages and from all generations, as Thou art good, Thou didst come with Thy disciples to the Mount of Olives, having together with Thyself her that gave birth to Thee, the Creator and Fashioner of all things; for it was meet that she who, as Thy Mother, suffered at Thy Passion more than all, should also enjoy the surpassing joy of the glorification of Thy flesh, O Master . . .[9]

Just as the upper section of the icon sets forth continuing truths about Christ and the Church, so does the lower section. The group of twelve apostles includes St Paul, who was certainly not present at the time of the Ascension; his inclusion here makes it clear that in the icon the apostolic group represents the Church rather than the particular individuals who, historically speaking, were present on the Mount of Olives at the time of the Ascension. Peter and Paul are placed on either side of the Mother of God, and the apostolic group in this icon are shown all with heads and eyes raised towards Christ in glory; he is the focal point of their attention. In some icons we see varied focal points, with some apostles looking towards Christ and others looking towards the Mother of God or the two angels; similarly there may be animated expressions of amazement, with a variety of gestures and postures. In this icon only Peter and Paul raise their hands towards Christ, but in other icons the hands of many apostles may be raised. The 'two men . . . in white robes' (Acts 1:11) are represented as angels, and their raised hands point to Christ as they give their message to the apostles: 'Men of Galilee, why do you stand looking into heaven? This Jesus, who was taken up from you into heaven, will come in the same way as you saw him go into heaven.' The iconographic presentation of Christ in glory with angels originated as a reference to his Second Coming in glory with the angels, and was subsequently used in connection with the Ascension. The apostles have been given their final commission by Christ (Acts 1:7–8): they are to receive the gift of the Spirit, and to become Christ's witnesses to the ends of the earth; their ministry is to be fulfilled in dependence on the Lord's promises, and in expectation of his return. The icon, like the Feast itself and the liturgical texts, marks the completion of the Lord's earthly ministry and the inauguration of the ministry of the Church.

The understanding of the Church set forth in the Ascension icon is succinctly expressed by Paul Evdokimov: 'Christ is the head of the Church, the Mother of God is its image, and the apostles are its foundation'.[10] The icon expresses the sovereignty of Christ over his Church; he is its Head, its guide, its source of inspiration and teaching; it receives its commission and ministry from him, and fulfils it in the power of the Holy Spirit. The Mother of God, as the image of the Church, stands under Christ. She from whom the Incarnate Son took his humanity stands rooted on the earth in the midst of the apostles, with her hands raised in the gesture of the orant, signifying prayer and intercession; Mary intercedes for humanity, and in this she embodies an important aspect of the Church's vocation – to intercede, to be the mediating channel of divine grace and love in a fallen world. Mary represents the holiness of the Church, which already shares the divine life and knows the reality of Christ's triumph over sin and death. Sometimes the hands of the Mother of God are shown with palms facing forward, as if defending the faith against deception and error. In many icons of the Ascension the figure of the Mother of God is striking in its elongation, suggesting the way in which she forms a link between earth and heaven, both in her own person and as an image of the Church. In this respect one is reminded of the image of the Mother of God in apses of churches where the tall static figure with upraised hands suggests the role of Ladder or Bridge linking the earthly and heavenly worshipping communities. In the Akathistos Hymn, as in many other texts, three particularly relevant images applied to the Mother of God are worth quoting here: 'Hail, heavenly ladder by which God came down. Hail, bridge leading men from earth to heaven.' 'Hail, pillar of fire, guiding those in darkness'.[11]

This icon of the Ascension is permeated by a great sense of harmony; others may depict more movement and animation; but the icons and the hymns convey a sense of joy at the Lord's promise and triumph: 'I am not separated from you; I am with you';[12] 'Thou, O Lover of men, hast joined into one what was formerly separated';[13] 'The earth doth celebrate and dance for joy, and Heaven doth rejoice today on the Ascension of the Maker of creation, Who by His volition clearly united that which was separated'.[14] The harmony of colours and the balance of forms and gestures in the icon create a works of great beauty which expresses the theological truth that he who became Incarnate is now ascended into the glory of heaven, and that the Church is to experience the peace and unity of the Kingdom.

★   ★   ★

The main biblical readings for the Ascension are:

> *At Vespers:* Isaiah 2:2–3, 62:10–63:9; Zechariah 14:1, 4, 8–11.
> *At Mattins:* Mark 16:9–20.
> *At the Divine Liturgy:* Acts 1:1–12; Luke 24:36–53.

≼ 15 ≽

We Have Seen the True Light

We have seen the true Light; we have received the Heavenly Spirit; we have found the true Faith, in worshipping the indivisible Trinity; for He hath saved us.[1]

≼ I ≽

THE FEAST

The Feast of Pentecost marks the end of the Paschal season, and looks forward to the Feast of All Saints on the following Sunday. Pentecost is the 'post-festal and last feast', the feast that crowns and completes the Paschal celebrations, and therefore it is rightly celebrated 'most radiantly'[2] as the Church continues to rejoice at the great things that have been accomplished through the death and Resurrection of the Son of God. The texts for the celebration of Pentecost are filled with a sense of joyful wonder, a sense of awe that moves us to praise and adoration.

The origins of this Feast derive from the Jewish Feast of Weeks, which is otherwise known as the Feast of Pentecost; it was the time when the first-fruits of the corn harvest were presented to the Lord (Deuteronomy 16:9), and later became the commemoration of the giving of the Law by Moses, 50 days after the Passover celebrations. The Jewish Feast stressed the Sinai covenant and Law, and the identity of the chosen people in their relationship with God. The fact that the gift of the Holy Spirit to Christ's apostles took place at Pentecost enabled this Jewish Feast to take on great significance for Christians: it became the occasion to celebrate the role of the Holy Spirit in the creation of the new chosen people and the new law that was to become operative within the life of the Church. 'Pentecost' referred originally to the 50-day period after the Resurrection, which was seen as a 50-day-long Sunday; this was a time of extended rejoicing in which fasting was out of place, and where the practice of kneeling was forbidden as out of keeping with the fact that Christians were already raised up to new life in Christ. Christ had been raised and glorified, and the Spirit had been poured out on the Church, and the number symbolism of seven times seven, plus one, to make the 50 days of Pentecost expressed a fullness and perfection that were appropriate for the extended celebration of Christ's triumph over sin and death. To this day, the name of the service book for this period is *The Pentecostarion*. The earliest accounts of this Christian liturgical period come from the mid-second century. By the fourth century the Ascension had become a separate commemoration at the fortieth day after Easter, and by the fifth century Pentecost Sunday had begun to become more associated with the events spoken of in chapter 2 of the Acts of the Apostles.

One aspect of the Orthodox celebration of Pentecost which is markedly different from the Western observances is the way in which this Feast is seen as the culmination of the revelation of the Holy Trinity. Through the gift of the Spirit at Pentecost, the revelation of the Holy Trinity is brought to fulfilment. Hence, 'the mighty works of God' which are heard of by the assembled multi-national crowd in Jerusalem on the Day of Pentecost (cf Acts 2:11) are interpreted as the making known of the Holy Trinity, the unfolding of the Triune nature of God, together with the implication that this divine unfolding is a process that enfolds humanity within the divine life. Deification or theosis, the raising up of human life into the life of the Godhead, becomes possible because of the Incarnation and the manifestation of the Trinity. The celebration of this Feast is, like the others, not only about past events, but about the present reality that has been brought about through God's self-revelation and work of redemption. We take part in the liturgy as beneficiaries who 'are made luminous and radiant as lightning, and are transformed with an extraordinary transformation of exceeding beauty'[3] as we take part in the worship and adoration of the Holy Trinity.

The Trinity icon is in fact the primary Pentecost icon. The icon of the Descent of the Holy Spirit, which most non-Orthodox Christians might well assume is the key to the celebration of Pentecost, is associated with the Monday, not the Sunday, of Pentecost. In the Orthodox world there is no 'Trinity Sunday' separate from Pentecost; Pentecost Sunday is often called 'Trinity Day', and the Monday of Pentecost may be called 'Spirit Day'. This does not mean that these two aspects of Pentecost are celebrated exclusively on these separate days. On each day the liturgical texts reflect a wide range of themes. However, the icons used on the two days do differ. The Trinity icon is venerated on the Sunday, and the icon of the Descent of the Spirit upon the Apostles is given prominence on the Monday. This gives a sense of priority to the revelation of the Holy Trinity, without neglecting the outpouring of the Spirit on the Church.

One of the prayers associated with Pentecost has become part of the daily prayer of Orthodox Christians, and of many other Christians as well. It is concise and eloquent, recognizing the bounty of the Holy Spirit, and seeks to allow our lives to be transformed by his indwelling:

> Heavenly King, O Comforter, the Spirit of truth, who art everywhere present and fillest all things, O Treasury of every good and Bestower of life: come and dwell in us, and cleanse us from every stain, and save our souls, O Good One.[4]

The following selection from the liturgical texts for Pentecost has been arranged to illustrate the wide variety of themes in these hymns. Such an arrangement is in some ways artificial, but it does present the broad spectrum of what is being celebrated.

✦ **II** ✦

EXTRACTS FROM THE LITURGICAL TEXTS

1. This first quotation shows the range of themes present in this Feast:

> The Holy Spirit provides every gift: He inspires prophecy, perfects the priesthood, grants wisdom to the illiterate, makes simple fishermen to become wise theologians, and establishes perfect order in the organization of the Church. Wherefore, O Comforter, equal in nature and majesty with the Father and the Son, glory to You![5]

2. The fulfilment of prophecy and of the hope generated in the Old Testament period are a prominent part of the understanding of this Feast:

> That which was proclaimed in the Prophets and in the Law of old hath been fulfilled; for on this day the grace of the Divine Spirit is poured on all the faithful.[6]

3. Similarly, the gift of the Holy Spirit is described as a fulfilment of Christ's personal promise:

> Thou didst say unto Thy disciples, O Christ: Tarry ye in Jerusalem till ye be clothed with power from on high, and I will send you another Comforter like unto Me, Who is My Spirit and the Spirit of the Father, in Whom ye shall be established.[7]

4. The events that occurred in Jerusalem on the day of Pentecost, are celebrated with reference to the revelation of the Holy Trinity:

Today all the nations beheld strange things in the city of David, when the Holy Spirit descended in fiery tongues, as Luke, the herald of things divine, declared; for he said: As the disciples of Christ were gathered together, there came a sound as of a mighty wind, and it filled the house where they were sitting; and all began to articulate strange and foreign words, doctrines strange and new, strange and new teachings of the Holy Trinity.[8]

5. The gift of tongues, of wisdom and of teaching, are often mentioned – along with the accusations that the strange behaviour of the apostles was due to drunkenness:

O Lord, when You sent down your Spirit upon the assembled apostles, the Hebrews were struck with awe as they heard them speak in many tongues, as the Spirit inspired them. They knew them to be illiterate and now saw them wise, speaking divine truths and bringing Gentiles to believe. Wherefore we also cry out to You: 'O Lord who have appeared on earth and saved us from error, glory to You!'[9]

When the Apostles spake eloquently concerning the divine and mighty deeds, the Spirit's power, whereby the Trinity is known as the one God of our Fathers, was thought to be drunkenness by them that believed not.[10]

6. Worship of the Holy Trinity becomes possible as a result of the divine revelation at Pentecost. The hymn-writers relish the wonder of this revelation:

> All things bow their knee before the Comforter,
> And the Offspring of the Father, and the Consubstantial Father;
> For they acknowledge in Three Persons,
> The One, Infallible, Unapproachable and Timeless Essence;
> For the grace of the Spirit hath shined forth illumination.[11]

7. The story of the Tower of Babel forms a point of comparison for the Pentecost events: one brought division and confusion, the other brings reconciliation and harmony:

In days of old, pride brought confusion of tongues to the builders of the tower of Babel, but now the diversity of tongues enlightened the minds and gave knowledge for the glory of God. There, God punished infidels for their sin, while here Christ enlightened fishermen through his Spirit; there, the confusion of tongues was for the sake of vengeance, while here there was variety so that voices could be joined in unison for the salvation of our souls.[12]

8. The outpouring of the Holy Spirit leads to life in the Church through Baptism, and there are many texts which link these aspects of the Feast. Baptism is rarely mentioned directly, but the references to water, fire and Spirit leave no doubt as to their sacramental reference:

> Coming down to those on earth, the Holy Spirit's spring was seen in the form of fiery streams apportioned spiritually to all, as it bedewed and enlightened the Lord's Apostles. And thus, the fire became a cloud bedewing them, filling them with light, and raining flames on them. And through them, grace hath been vouchsafed to us by fire and water in very truth. Behold, the Comforter's light is come and hath illumined the whole world.[13]

9. Illumination and sanctification are continuing aspects of the work of the Spirit in the Church, bringing successive generations into the fullness of the Trinitarian life.

> The Father is Light; the Word is Light; and the Holy Spirit is Light, Who was sent to the Apostles in the form of fiery tongues; and thus through Him all creation is illuminated and guided to worship the Holy Trinity.[14]

⫷ III ⫸

THE HOLY TRINITY ICON – THE HOSPITALITY OF ABRAHAM
THEOLOGICAL BACKGROUND

Most Western Christians are familiar with images and symbols of the Holy Trinity, in the form of a triangle, a clover leaf, or a group consisting of an old man, a crucified Christ and a dove. These are part of the visual repertoire of Western Christianity. In the East, things are different. The primary image used in connection with the Holy Trinity is derived from the account in Genesis 18 of Abraham's hospitality to the three mysterious visitors; the presence of these visitors is seen as a theophany, a manifestation of God the Holy Trinity to Abraham. Leonid Ouspensky explains the Orthodox tradition:

> Only at the blessing of the Old Testament icon is the following sticheron chanted: 'Come, O peoples, let us worship God in three Persons.' At the blessing of other Trinitarian icons [e.g. the Theophany and the Transfiguration] the troparion and kontakion of the corresponding feasts are sung.

Apart from these icons,

the ritual of blessing knows of no others. Is not this because in the New Testament it is not possible to have an image of God 'glorified in the Holy Trinity, the One no mind can reach and no word can express, the One never seen by men anywhere' (the rite of blessing for Trinitarian icons)? A visible image of the divine Trinity, in whatever iconographic variant, according to whatever abstract concept, is impossible. Of the three Persons of the Divinity, only the second hypostasis can be represented in human form in the Son of God who became the Son of Man. The world only knows God in the Son through the Holy Spirit. In the New Testament, Pentecost is the apex of the revelation of the Trinity – a revelation not in an image but within man himself, by his deification. Divinization, then, is 'the action of the Spirit . . . through Whom the Trinity is known' (Ode 7 of the first canon of Pentecost). In other words, the dogma of the Trinity is not an abstract doctrine . . . Knowledge of the Trinity is not gained by external teaching but by an inward, living experience of the Christian life . . . It is not by chance that it is precisely in the wake of St Sergius of Radonezh, himself a 'dwelling place of the Trinity' (troparion of the saint), that this image of the Old Testament Trinity is shown with a new fullness, a new vision and a new theological content in the icon of St Andrei Rublev. The icon of the Old Testament Trinity links the beginning of the Church in the Old Testament, the promise made to Abraham, to the moment at which the New Testament Church was founded. The beginning of divine revelation is joined to its consummation on the day of Pentecost, to the supreme revelation of the tri-hypostatic Divinity. It is precisely in this image that the 'action of the Spirit' unfolded to Andrei the monk the meaning of the Old Testament revelation, a new vision of Trinitarian life.[15]

The underlying theological principle behind this use of an Old Testament event to express the significance of later revelation is often designated as 'typology': a particular event is seen as a type, a pattern or example that foreshadows something that will be fully revealed at another stage. Thus, ideas of redemption and salvation have their roots in the Old Testament experience of the Hebrew people, but take on a richer significance in the New Testament where they are linked to Christ's life, death and Resurrection as saving acts of God which have universal significance. Particular events, such as the crossing of the Red Sea, the gift of manna in the wilderness and water from the rock become types through which the significance of Christ's work of redemption and nourishment are understood and expressed. So, early in the Church's reflection, the manifestation of God to Abraham in Genesis 18 is seen as a foreshadowing of the revelation that will be completed at Pentecost. Genesis 18 begins by stating that 'the Lord' appeared to Abraham at the oaks of Mamre, and then goes on to speak of three men standing in front of him; Abraham bows down before the three men and addresses them as 'My Lord'. Two main types of interpretation are linked to this passage: one stressing Abraham's hospitality, the other stressing the manifestation of God to Abraham; some writers use both types of interpretation. If we look at some of the texts in which theologians have reflected on this passage we shall appreciate how wide a range of understanding has been crystallized in the icons showing the Hospitality of Abraham. To recognize this long tradition of interpretation, and the way it creates links with other dimensions of theology, will enrich our appreciation of these icons.

Origen (c.185–c.254) was one of the early theologians whose use of the Old and New Testaments was greatly shaped by what has come to be known as *allegorical* or *mystical* interpretation of Scripture: the realization that various levels of meaning are to be sought and can be found in individual stories and details, and their relationship to other parts of Scripture examined. This approach to Scripture is uncommon in the Western Churches today, but for much of the Church's history it was a normal way of approaching Holy Scripture as the vehicle of Divine Revelation.

Origen's interpretation of Genesis 18 in his *Fourth Homily on Genesis*[16] is thoroughly allegorical; few details in the story escape interpretation. He links what to us appear like insignificant details to the revelation that has been completed in Christ: Abraham

> serves, therefore, bread mixed 'with three measures of fine wheat flour'. He received three men, he mixed the bread 'with three measures of fine wheat flour.' Everything he does is mystical, everything is filled with mystery. A calf is served; behold, another mystery. The calf itself is not tough, but 'good and tender.' And what is so tender, what so good as that one who 'humbled himself' for us 'to death' and 'laid down his life' 'for his friends'? He is the 'fatted calf' which the father slaughtered to receive his repentant son. 'For he so loved this world, as to give his only son' for the life of this world.

Abraham, the wise man, 'is not ignorant of whom he has received. He runs to three men and adores one.' And to this recognition of the divine nature of his guests is added a further understanding of the significance of the feet-washing: 'Abraham, the father and teacher of nations, is, indeed teaching you by these things how you ought to receive guests and that you should wash the feet of guests. Nevertheless he said this mysteriously. For he knew that the mysteries of the Lord were not to be completed except in the washing of feet.' The homily ends with a call to the living of a life worthy of the mystery of what has been revealed and entrusted to us:

> Let us give our attention to make our acts such, our manner of life such, that we may be held worthy of knowledge of God, that he may see fit to know us, that we may be held worthy of knowledge of his Son Jesus Christ and knowledge of the Holy Spirit, that we, known by the Trinity, might also deserve to know the mystery of the Trinity fully, completely and perfectly, the Lord Jesus revealing it to us. 'His is the glory and sovereignty forever and ever, Amen'.[17]

However unfamiliar this type of biblical interpretation may seem to us, it is worth noting the way that Revelation, Incarnation and Theosis are present in this homily. The particular theophany under consideration becomes the basis for a Christian interpretation that closely links the Old Testament event to the teaching and revelation of the New Testament; virtues involved in Christian living are considered along with spiritual conflict; and the culmination of the homily looks to the fulfilment of the process of being known by God, knowing 'the mystery of the Trinity fully, completely and perfectly'. In this homily we can see a spiritual and theological structure that is at the very heart of Orthodoxy, even though some of Origen's teaching was later condemned as unorthodox.

St John Chrysostom (c.347–407) took a much less allegorical approach to the Hospitality of Abraham, stressing the virtue of hospitality extended towards strangers, and linking the example of Abraham to the teaching given by Christ in his parable of the Last Judgement (Matthew 25:31–46). In the same period, St Ambrose (c. 339–397), Archbishop of Milan, offers a Trinitarian interpretation of the story:

> Abraham, ready to receive strangers, faithful towards God, devoted in ministering, quick in his service, saw the Trinity in a type; he added religious duty to hospitality, when beholding Three he worshipped One, and preserving the distinction of the Persons, yet addressed one Lord, he offered to Three the honour of his gift, while acknowledging one Power. It was not learning but grace which spoke in him, and he believed better what he had not learnt than we who have learnt. No one had falsified the representation of the truth, and so he sees Three, but worships the Unity.[18]

Evidence of another allegorical interpretation can be found in the writings of St John of Damascus (c. 675–c. 749); at the end of his treatises *On the Divine Images* he quotes Eusebius of Caesarea (c. 260–c. 339):

> Even now the inhabitants of those regions near where Abraham worshipped those who appeared to him honour it as a holy place. Indeed, the oak tree is still to be seen there, and there is a picture of those whom Abraham entertained reclining at table, one shown on each side and the most august and honourable guest in the middle. Through him is signified to us our Lord and Saviour, whom simple men honour and whose divine words they believe. Hidden in human appearance and form, he showed himself to Abraham the Godloving forefather, and gave him knowledge of the Father. Thus through Abraham He planted the seed of righteousness in men.[19]

This less Trinitarian interpretation is sometimes found in icons and frescoes where Christ is the central figure and is accompanied by angels on either side.

THE HOLY TRINITY ICON – THE HOSPITALITY OF ABRAHAM
ICONOGRAPHIC DEVELOPMENT

Having looked at some of the theological developments associated with the Hospitality of Abraham, it is now time to turn to the iconography that is derived from this theological tradition.

Our earliest evidence comes from the catacombs of the Via Latina in Rome, a painted scene showing Abraham greeting three identical men, without haloes; the paintings in these catacombs are dated to about 320–350. Then there is a mosaic panel in Sta. Maria Maggiore in Rome as part of an Old Testament cycle placed there during the pontificate of Sixtus III (432–440). In the upper level of the panel Abraham welcomes the approaching visitors; each has a halo, but the central figure is shown as more important, and is surrounded by an oval aureole. In the lower level of the panel on the left, Abraham turns and points to Sarah who is preparing the three loaves outside the door of the house/tent, while on the right the three haloed figures, now represented as identical, are seated at the table, being served by Abraham; behind the figure of Abraham is the tree adjacent to the house/tent.

The outstanding example of this theme to survive from early times is included in the mosaics of the choir of San Vitale in Ravenna (sixth century). Here on the south wall are depicted the sacrifices of Abel and Melchizedek, and on the north wall is a mosaic composition of considerable theological subtlety which brings together the hospitality of Abraham in Genesis 18 and his sacrifice of Isaac in Genesis 22. At the extreme left of the scene stands the figure of Sarah, not actively involved in the meal-serving, but musing on the promise of a son, whose birth has been announced to her. At the extreme right Isaac is placed on an altar ready to be sacrificed by Abraham; a ram stands just in front of Abraham, whose face and right arm are raised toward the hand of God which appears through the clouds. Thus the scenes at the left and right present an Old Testament annunciation and sacrifice, which foreshadow the New Testament Annunciation and Sacrifice of the Son of God. In the centre of the panel the three visitors are depicted in identical form, all with haloes, seated in a row behind the table on which are placed three loaves of bread; to the left, Abraham stands presenting the calf which has been prepared. The house/tent of Abraham and Sarah, the oak of Mamre, and the mountain (Mount Moriah) are conspicuous in this panel, and are details which recur throughout the centuries in this composition. The panel is placed in the choir of the church near other representations of sacrifice and food, and suggests references to the Eucharist.

These three early examples of the iconography of the Hospitality of Abraham are all in Italy, in the western part of the Byzantine-Roman empire; in the eighth and ninth centuries the eastern part of the empire was disrupted by the iconoclast controversy, during which much church art in the East was destroyed. Once the Iconoclast Controversy was over, the use of icons, mosaics and frescoes in churches spread again throughout the Byzantine territories, and into the newly converted Slav lands. From the tenth century we find the Hospitality of Abraham represented in the Church of St John the Theologian on Naxos, and in Cappadocia at Goreme Chapel No. 22 (Carikli Kilise) and Goreme Chapel No. 7 (Tokali Kilise); from the eleventh century we have examples at Sta. Sophia in Kiev and at Sta. Sophia in Ochrid; examples from the twelfth century are more numerous, including the Mirozhsky Monastery in Pskov, the Church of the Saviour in Nereditsa, Samarina Church of the Life-Giving Spring, Messenia, St Cosmas and St Damian in Kastoria, St Saviour near Megara, and the Chapel of the Virgin at the Monastery of St John the Theologian on Patmos. All of these examples are either frescoes or mosaics. Clearly this theme was familiar throughout the whole Orthodox world, and the Hospitality of Abraham was a key element in the church programmes of iconography. From a later period we have evidence in the painted churches in the Troodos Mountains of Cyprus, and in the panel icons which survive in both the Byzantine and Russian traditions.

Sometimes the image is titled, 'The Holy Trinity', as in the examples mentioned at Naxos and on Patmos. In the period after the fall of Constantinople (1453) there was a considerable revival of the use of this title, particularly on Mount Athos. Whether the image was titled or not, its position in or near the bema (sanctuary) always gave it a close link with the Eucharist; even in small churches where there was little space for other Old Testament prefigurations of the Eucharist, space was found for this image. In the Chapel of the Mother of God in the Monastery of St John on Patmos this image is centrally placed in the apse above the altar, and so the Eucharistic associations are clear; the central figure is taller than the other two, and very much evokes the figure of the Pantocrator, being clad in a purple tunic and blue mantle, and holding a scroll in the left hand; this interpretation of the scene seems to be in the tradition exemplified in the quotation above from St John of Damascus.

Sometimes the central figure is named: 'Emmanuel' at St Saviour near Megara; 'IC XC' (the monogram for Jesus Christ) in other examples (including Goreme No. 22); the Greek *Ho On* ('The One Who Is') may be included within an inscribed cross in the halo. This raises the question of the interpretation of the identity of the three angels. As we saw in some of the patristic literature and in the mosaic panel at Sta. Maria Maggiore, sometimes the central angel is accorded greater significance than the other two; thus, the three angels can be seen as a type of the Trinity, or the outer two angels can be seen as angels attendant upon the Lord in an undifferentiated sense, or the central angel is seen as a manifestation of the as yet not-incarnate Word of God, whose incarnation will lead to the full disclosure of the triune nature of God. Sometimes the halo of the central angel is inscribed with a cross, the obvious symbol of

Jesus Christ, and therefore of the Person of the Son. Sometimes the haloes of each of the three angels are inscibed with the cross, as at Goreme No. 22 and at the Church of the Saviour at Palaeochorio in Cyprus (1510–1520). This practice is seen by some as very questionable, an example of icongraphic practice losing touch with theological discipline.

We find considerable variations in the way the attentant figures are placed in this image (Abraham, Sarah, and the servant killing the calf) and also in the variety of food and vessels placed on the table. Similarly there are variations in the way the house of Abraham, the tree and the mountain are shown. Sometimes the shape of the panel gives scope for a very wide representation, as in some post-Byzantine icons created to fit above the prothesis door of an iconostasis; other panel icons were made for the Church Feasts tier, or else to occupy a place in the lower part of the iconostasis – especially if the particular church is dedicated to the Holy Trinity.

◅ V ▻

THE HOLY TRINITY ICON
ST SERGIUS AND ST ANDREI RUBLEV

In view of all this information, the Holy Trinity icon painted by St Andrei Rublev represents the taking of a definite decision to embody the Trinitarian interpretation of the hospitality of Abraham. To appreciate this remarkable work we need to bear in mind the background to the theme which has already been given, but it is also important to know something about St Sergius of Radonezh and his contribution to the theological and spiritual developments of the fourteenth and fifteenth centuries in Russia. Andrei Rublev's Holy Trinity icon represents in many ways the blossoming of many elements in Orthodoxy that were an important part of the heritage of St Sergius and his disciples.

St Sergius (c. 1314–1392) lived during the time of the Tartar oppression of the Russian people – a time when Kiev had ceased to be the great centre of political and spiritual life; the Russian people were struggling under external attacks and internal disintegration as the various principalities vied with each other for prestige. Sergius and his brother Stephen felt called to live in isolation in the forest, dedicating themselves to a life of work, prayer and solitude; soon Sergius was left to face the rigours of this life alone. The chapel which the brothers erected in the forest was dedicated to the Holy Trinity; this was a rare dedication at that time, but so great was the influence of St Sergius that after his death dedications of churches to the Holy Trinity were almost as common throughout Muscovy as those to the Mother of God. Sergius yearned for a life of solitary prayer in the desert, but this longing was not to be fulfilled, for he was soon joined by others who wanted to share his life of prayer in the forest hermitage. The communal life of these monks was centred on the Divine Liturgy, and grew to become a large monastic institution with a library and icon painting workshops; many other communities were founded from the original one, and sometimes it was conflict that led to separation and new foundations. During the lifetime of St Sergius his disciples founded 50 new monasteries.

The Holy Trinity Monastery at Radonezh became powerful and influential; St Sergius had an influence on secular affairs as well as in spiritual matters. St Sergius helped the Russian people and their leaders to transcend their divisions and he helped the growth and prestige of the Muscovite principality; Moscow began to emerge as a new centre of unity, gradually increasing in political and religious prestige, and overshadowing Vladimir-Suzdal as the standard-bearer of the Orthodox faith in the Russian lands. In some respects St Sergius was used by the Muscovite leaders to strengthen their position, but he saw the vital importance of unity of faith, purpose and political organization if the Russian people was ever to free itself from the Tartar yoke and transcend its own tendency towards political fragmentation.

Epiphanius, a disciple and author of a Life of St Sergius, leaves his readers in no doubt as to the significance of the saint's devotion to the Trinity: 'St Sergius built the Church of the Holy Trinity as a mirror for his community, that through gazing at the divine Unity they might overcome the hateful divisions of the world'.[20] The bitterness and fragmented nature of Russian life could only be overcome in the power that derived from contemplation and worship of the Holy Trinity. St Sergius helped to accomplish a transformation of Russian life through the spiritual revival which emanated from his and similar monasteries. The sense of all areas of life being permeated by this spiritual force is well expressed by St Pavel Florenskii: 'St Sergius understood the azure-blue of the heavens [as the emblem] of the imperturbable world of eternal and perfect love. He understood that world of love as both the object of contemplation and the commandment to be realized in every life – as the foundation for the building of the Church and the person, of government, of society.'[21] It is not difficult to see why St Sergius continues to have such a powerful influence in the Russian Orthodox tradition, and to be such an attractive figure to those who come under his influence.

During the fourteenth century there was a great religious renaissance in Russia; St Sergius was not the only person to revive and revitalise the monastic life; others also sought out the solitary places in the forests of northern Russia and founded communities. Increasing links with Byzantium meant that spiritual influence spread from Constantinople and Mount Athos into Russia; spiritual texts were translated from Greek into Slavonic; the revival of hesychast spirituality in Byzantium had an influence in Russia; icon painters from Constantinople and elsewhere in Byzantium worked in Russia. The most notable of these in the late fourteenth and early fifteenth centuries was Theophanes the Greek; he worked in Novgorod, decorating the Cathedral of the Transfiguration in 1378, and the Holy Trinity is included among his frescoes there; he later worked in Moscow and there, as in Novgorod, he impressed people by his brilliance as a painter, a philosopher and a man of prayer.

The first mention we have of Andrei Rublev is in connection with Theophanes; Rublev and the Elder Prokhor of Gorodets worked with Theophanes on the decoration of the Annunciation Cathedral in Moscow in 1405. At this time Rublev was a monk of the Holy Trinity Monastery founded by St Sergius, and he had worked on the construction and decoration of the Church of the Saviour at the Andronikov Monastery in Moscow. In 1408 Rublev worked with the icon painter Daniil at the Cathedral of the Dormition in Vladimir, and they are recorded as working together decorating the Trinity-St Sergius Monastery in 1425–27. He died on 30th January 1430. The earliest suggested date for the painting of Rublev's Trinity icon is 1411; it is believed this icon was intended to occupy a place over the tomb of St Sergius. In 1423–24 the icon was placed on the lower tier of the iconostasis in the new church over the tomb, and some scholars have argued that the Trinity icon dates from 1425–27 when Rublev and Daniil were engaged in painting the frescoes of the church.

In the late fourteenth century there were controversies in Russia about the doctrine of the Trinity. One heretical group which did not recognize the doctrine of the Trinity, the Strigol'niks, had taken root in Novgorod and Pskov; another was influential in Rostov, and would not accept the veneration of icons. The theme of the Holy Trinity was not only a reconciling and unifying force in Russian religious life at this time, it was also a controversial issue, and it is possible that Rublev felt he had to stress the equality of the three Persons of the Trinity, or that he was asked by Abbot Nikon to paint an icon that expressed the fundamental truths of the Trinitarian revelation. Russian commentators remark how the icon expresses a profound Russian desire for liberation and harmony, the vision of beauty and the longing for freedom. A transcendent peace is given through the icon which brings healing and reconciliation to those caught up in 'the hateful divisions of the world'.

We end this section of the chapter with an extract from the writings of St Gregory of Sinai (c. 1265–1346); he was born on the western shores of Asia Minor, travelled to Cyprus, Sinai, Crete and Mount Athos, and then to the borders of Byzantium and Bulgaria where he had a large group of both Greek and Slav disciples. His teaching has much in common with that of St Gregory Palamas. Manuscripts of the writings of St Gregory of Sinai were present in the Holy Trinity Monastery of St Sergius during the fourteenth and fifteenth centuries. It is possible that they may have influenced Andrei Rublev, but even if that cannot be proved, the presence of these writings as part of the resources of the monastery is evidence of how spiritual influences spread throughout the Orthodox world during this period of great religious renaissance.

26. Orthodoxy may be defined as the clear perception and grasp of two dogmas of the faith, namely, the Trinity and the Duality. It is to know and contemplate the three Persons of the Trinity as distinctively and indivisibly constituting the one God, and the divine and human natures of Christ as united in His single Person.

29. The Trinity is simple unity, unqualified and uncompounded. It is three-in-one, for God is three-personed, each person wholly interpenetrating the others without any loss of distinct personal identity.

32. [The Fathers of the Church] bequeath to us the dogma of one God in three Persons as the hallmark of the true faith and the anchor of hope. For, according to Scripture, to apprehend the one God is the root of immortality, and to know the majesty of the three-personed Monad is complete righteousness (cf Wisdom 15:3). Again, we should read what is said in the Gospel in the same way: eternal life is to know Thee the only true God in three Persons, and Him Who Thou hast sent, Jesus Christ, in two natures and two wills (cf John 17:3).[22]

After looking at this background we may now consider Andrei Rublev's Trinity icon in detail (**Plate 22**). The size of the icon is 142 × 114 cm. It is a large panel which at one time formed part of the lower section of the iconostasis of the church where St Sergius is buried. Many reproductions of the icon trim the edge to make the print fit a standard size of paper; this often makes the icon look cramped. A full reproduction makes it clear that the figures are contained within the recessed surface of the icon, leaving a frame all round, and that the geometrical structures of the painting fit easily within the whole panel. In this composition the most obvious geometrical forms that are used are the circle, following the forms of the three angels (Ouspensky claims that traces of a circle are visible); the triangle (formed from the head and torso of the central angel and extending down to the lower corners); and the Cross (formed by the central axis of the icon – which includes the tree, the central angel, the chalice and the aperture in the front of the table – and the heads of the outer two angels). The circle may be associated with divinity and eternity; the triangle has obvious associations with the Trinity; and the Cross is at the centre of the Christian revelation. At the lower level of the icon Rublev uses a system sometimes known as inverse perspective in the depiction of the footstools and the seats; the lines which we would expect to converge as they recede in fact open out away from the front of the icon; this has the effect of drawing our attention up into the circle of the relationships between the three angels, inviting a certain participation by the viewer. The lines of the seats and footstools at the lower corners are balanced by the shape of the building and the mountain at the top corners; thus the four corners of the icon have been used in ways that enable us to discern an octagonal shape as well as a circle within the structure of the icon. The octagon, seven plus one sides, is seen as suggesting the eternal glory of the eighth day, the endless Sabbath of the heavenly kingdom. It is also suggested by some commentators that the table around which the angels are seated, being basically rectangular in form, may suggest the material, earthly realm in contrast to the heavenly circle and the octagon.

Whether or not one takes seriously the suggested interpretation of these geometrical forms, it must be recognized that Rublev uses them with great subtlety. This is particularly obvious when we look at the circular disposition of the figures of the angels: the circular form directs our attention to the relationships, to the communion of the three, to their coherent unity. Similarly when commentators point out the axial symmetry of this icon – a symmetry balanced around a dominant vertical line – it is important to see how broad and subtle is the central axis of the icon: it includes the tree, the central angel, the chalice and the rectangular opening in the front of the table; the strictly central line runs down from the left edge of the uppermost foliage on the tree to the right edge of the left footstool – which means that the head of the central angel is left of centre and the chalice is largely right of centre. Whatever forms Rublev may use he is the master of them, and they serve his artistic and theological purposes.

Within the icon many forms are echoed and repeated. This is clear in the case of the circular form of the haloes, the heads of the angels, and the rounded shape of the top of the wings; the sweeping curves of the wings reflect the same form which finds further echoes in the shapes of the bodies and the curved surfaces of the mountain. In contrast with the circular and rounded forms are the strong linear features in the icon. The horizontal lines of the footstools and the table provide levels of ascent into the heart of the icon. There is an almost fan-like array of linear details progressing across the composition which seem to take our attention from left to right: at the lower level these include the diagonals of the footstools and seats, but above these are the radiating linear forms within the garments of the angels; each of the angels holds a slender staff, and the angles at which these are held fall further from the vertical as we move from left to right. Moreover the tips of the staffs take our attention up towards the three major symbols in the top section of the icon, but not slavishly as direct pointers, for each one ends well to the right of the house, the tree and the mountain. Rublev uses these details to counterbalance the powerful right to left inclination of the angels in the centre and on the right, and a similar right to left direction in the presentation of the tree and the mountain. Thus the powerful gestures which take us towards the still figure of the angel on the left are balanced by an opposite movement of linear forms. The linear structure of the building in the top-left corner of the icon creates a stable element above the angel on the left.

Part of the effect of these subtle techniques is to create a situation where the eye is unable to rest simply on any one significant detail, for each stands in relation to the whole composition. For example, the strength of the central vertical axis (especially in prints where the outer edges have been trimmed off) and the elevated position of the head of the central angel may appear so great as to anchor our attention on the central figure, the tree and the chalice; but the inclination of the central head moves our attention away from the central axis, and towards the left; but that also is not a final resting-point for the eyes, for the whole posture of the body on the left moves us down and across to pick up the circular movement back through the centre, and yet again to the angel on the left.

Another form evident within the icon is created by the inner edges of the outline of the angels on the left and right; this conforms with the shape of the chalice – the ultimate vessel of sacrificial love and communion. This downward sweep of the inner line of the outer angels is reinforced by the gesture of the central angel's hand. Amid the circular movement within the icon this powerful downward thrust counterbalances the upward movement of the lines of the footstools and seats, and focuses our attention on the central symbol of sacrifice. The chalice contains the head of the calf, which not only recalls the calf killed by Abraham for his visitors, but represents a type for the Lamb of God in Christ.

The figures of the angels are designed on a rhomboid principle frequently used by Rublev; the proportions of the body are elongated, calculated to be fourteen times the diameter of the heads compared with the usual seven times. They are represented as youthful figures of great tenderness, clothed in freely falling garments. The eyes are much smaller than those usual in Byzantine icons, and their gaze is inward and contemplative rather than directed at the beholder. There is no heaviness about the pose of the angels; the bowed heads and faces express compassion and attentiveness. Neither is there any hint of rigorous asceticism; we meet a sense of harmony in the integration of the spiritual and the material, and the communion of love suggested in the communion of the three figures.

At this point we should take stock of what Rublev has omitted and what he has retained from the traditional heritage of the Hospitality of Abraham images. Abraham and Sarah are not represented, and in this Rublev was not entirely an innovator. In many icons of the Hospitality Abraham and Sarah had an almost liturgical role, as their offering suggests a prefiguration of the Eucharist; but here they are omitted as part of the process of enhancing the Trinitarian character of the composition. In some icons we can sense the busy-ness and speed with which Abraham and Sarah set about providing refreshment for their visitors; there is no sense of busy-ness or speed in Rublev's icon; a calm, tranquil, undisturbed communion exists between the three figures. The servant killing the calf is also omitted, but the head of the calf is retained within the one vessel on the table (according to some commentators the head of the calf has been replaced with the head of a lamb – the symbolism of which is obvious); the lavish fare which we see in some icons has been reduced to the one vessel, and the one symbol of food and sacrifice; all extraneous, interesting but potentially distracting detail has been omitted. Likewise, the building, the tree and the mountain cease to be phenomena which have an interest in their own right; they are there as symbols, signs which have their roots in the story and in the earlier iconographic tradition, but which point us beyond the incident in Genesis 18.

The mountain has associations with Mount Moriah and Mount Sinai, and also with Mount Tabor, the Transfiguration of Christ and the presence of the Holy Spirit. The tree has associations which take us from the oak of Mamre to the wood of the Cross, and to the Tree of Life in Genesis 3 and Revelation 22. The tent/house of Abraham and Sarah has associations which lead us from the community of the Old Covenant, to the Church and the Heavenly Kingdom, and the Father's house to which we now have access.

Rublev has selected key elements of the tradition to be used in the creation of an icon which expresses the Trinitarian nature of the Godhead, especially that Orthodox understanding of the nature of the Divine life which was assimilated and expressed in the life and work of St Sergius and his disciples. It is an icon which both offers and invites communion. The lines of inverse perspective converge on those who behold the icon and draw them into the mystery expressed in the icon. The communion of the three Persons of the Godhead is not detached from the troubles of the world and the Church, but has been opened up to humanity by the Incarnation of the Son; his sacrificial living and dying has opened the way to the Kingdom; his presence is celebrated in each offering of the Divine Liturgy, and at Baptism and Marriage: 'Blessed is the kingdom of the Father and of the Son and of the Holy Spirit.'

A question that is inevitably raised by this icon is the identification of the three angels with the Persons of the Holy Trinity. It must be remembered that the Persons of the Trinity cannot properly all be depicted, and so any identity suggested with the particular angels in the icon is valid at a symbolic level. The revelation of God the Holy Trinity which is given through Jesus Christ is expressed in the icon in a symbolic way; the angels do not represent the persons of the Trinity in the way that an icon of Christ represents Christ himself. The two main schools of interpretation of this icon are agreed that the angel on the right is to be seen as representing the Holy Spirit, but there is deep disagreement over the interpretation of the other two angels. One school of thought sees that central angel as representing the Father, who reveals himself through his two arms, the Son on his right and the Spirit on his left. The other school argues that we should look at the icon in terms of the doxology, 'Glory be to the Father, and to the Son, and to the Holy Spirit', working from left to right. Both schools agree that the central angel is clad in a manner that is associated with the incarnate Christ; the first school says that this is in keeping with Christ's words, 'I and the Father are one', and 'He who has seen me has seen the Father'; the second school says that the use of the clothing and colours that are associated with Christ, especially the marked *clavis* on his right shoulder, is a deliberate way of indicating the identity of the second Person of the Trinity. The first school base much of their argument on the existence of a similar icon which it is claimed was used by St Stephen of Perm (a friend of St Sergius) in his missionary work among the Zyrians in the north of Russia; this icon has the appropriate inscription for 'Son', 'Father' and 'Spirit', from left to right. However, Leonid Ouspensky argues strongly that this icon is an exception and provides no adequate basis from which to interpret the work of Andrei Rublev. Ouspensky argues strongly in support of the second school. It is worth noting that this suggested interpretation of the figures receives a certain support from the three angels' hands. The figure on the left which may represent the Father puts no hand on the table ('No man has ever seen God', 1 John 4:12), but holds his staff in both hands. The central angel who may represent the Son places his hand above the chalice on the table in a clear gesture of benediction. The third angel who may represent the Spirit has his hand over the table but in a less deliberate and more gentle gesture which would seem to reflect the action of the Spirit in the world.

It has been said that Rublev painted not with colours but with lights. This icon emanates light. There is no hint of an external source of light which would create shadows in the icon; the whole icon is luminous in a way that can hardly be conveyed in prints of the icon. Some colour may have been lost in the process of restoration, but many commentators are eloquent about the colours that remain. 'His delicate blues, transparent golden yellows, light greens and deep purple are luminous with an interior radiance and what is so striking in this unique icon is their interplay, forming a harmonious whole as of a musical symphony. The pale gold, much of which is unfortunately lost, makes the icon glimmer with a light that no reproduction can give.'[23] Rublev's use of colour and form has prompted many writers to speak of harmony, rhythm, musicality, complementarity, melody, and sonority in relation to this icon. It truly is a masterpiece in terms of art, theology and spirituality.

⪻ VI ⪼

THE ICON OF THE DESCENT OF THE HOLY SPIRIT

In the final section of this chapter we consider the icon associated with the Descent of the Spirit and Pentecost Monday. The sixteenth-century Cretan icon in **Plate 23** represents the events of the Day of Pentecost (Acts 2:1–4) not in a literalistic manner, but in a way which expresses the theology of the Church and its mission.

There is a movement from the upper edge of the icon down to the lower areas which corresponds with the divine activity on, in and through the Church. At the top we see the segment of a circle representing the divine realm (the outer ring a pale cobalt blue, and the inner section black); from this gold rays of light emerge and twelve rays spread out over the assembled group of the apostles. In many icons the tongues of fire are shown above the heads of the apostles. The building in the background draped with vermilion cloths represents the Upper Room, and the apostles are seated there in a raised semi-circle; the posture and gestures of each figure suggest a liveliness and even speech, but the apostles form a harmonious company. The size of each figure is almost identical; this detail and the absence of familiar Western styles of perspective give the impression that St Peter and St Paul at the head of the group are larger in size than the others. The inclusion of St Paul does not represent historical accuracy, since St Paul was, of course, not present on the Day of Pentecost; the important point that Paul does form part of the apostolic group is clearly stated. In the same way St Luke (third from the top left) and St Mark (third from the top right) are included with the others to show the importance of the Gospel in the apostolic group. Five of the figures whose written work is important for the Church are shown in the icon holding books (the four Evangelists and St Paul), while the others hold scrolls as a sign of their teaching authority. Given that St Luke is remembered as an icon painter as well as an evangelist, this icon sets the two traditions of icon painting and Gospel writing together within the heritage that stems from the outpouring of the Holy Spirit at Pentecost: word and sacrament and image are the means by which the revelation is transmitted and appropriated through the work of the Holy Spirit within the Church.

The sense of unity and diversity within the apostolic group is enhanced by the vibrant colours and highlights that are used for the clothing. Undergarments are in a greyish-blue violet, raw sienna, pale burnt sienna and vermilion, while the outer garments are in a subdued chrome-green, raw umber, vermilion and raw sienna. This varied group of apostles and evangelists, is presented as possessing inner unity and cohesion, the unity and harmony that the Spirit creates within the Church.

In the centre of the lower part of the icon, beneath the seated apostles, we see a royal figure against a dark background: this is a symbolic figure, Cosmos, representing the people of the world living in darkness and sin, and involved in pagan worship; yet in his hands he carries the scrolls representing the teaching of the twelve apostles who were believed to have preached in all parts of the world. The fact that the darkness in this part of the icon is surrounded by the assembly of the apostles is significant, for as God so loved the world that he gave his only-begotten Son, so the indwelling Holy Spirit enables the Church to enfold the world in love and to fulfil its mission. We may perhaps compare a feature of the Nativity icon, where the darkness of the cave receives the Word made flesh; so here the darkness of the world receives the apostolic teaching. The dark centre of the segment of the divine realm represented at the top of the scene, from which light and fire descend, is balanced by a different darkness at the base of the picture, suggesting the darkness of sin and ignorance to which the Spirit and the Church bring the divine revelation.

The formal structure of this composition is reminiscent of the Mid-Pentecost icon (see **Plate 20**). There Christ the teacher is in the centre among the teachers of the law; here after the fulfilment of the promise of the Holy Spirit we see the assembled apostles who will teach the nations in obedience to Christ's command. This icon may also have some conceptual relationship with the Trinity icon. Just as the Trinity icon embodies certain truths about the relationship of the Three Persons within the one Godhead, so this icon embodies certain truths about the life and unity of the Church: the relationships between the Persons of the Holy Trinity form the source of the ecclesial relationships; the Church is sustained in unity and truth by the indwelling of the Holy Spirit; its mission to the world is prompted and guided by the Spirit; its cohesion and growth in truth and love are the fruit of the indwelling presence of the Spirit within the Body of Christ and all its members.

> Once, when He descended and confounded the tongues, the Most High divided the nations; and when He divided the tongues of fire, He called all men into unity; and with one accord we glorify the All-holy Spirit. (Kontakion for Pentecost)[24]

★   ★   ★

The main biblical readings during the Feast of Pentecost are as follows:

At Great Vespers: Numbers 11:16–17, 24–29; Joel 2:23–32; Ezekiel 36:24–28.
At Mattins: John 20:19–23.
At Pentecost Sunday Divine Liturgy: Acts 2:1–11; John 7:37–52, 8:12.
At Pentecost Monday Divine Liturgy: Ephesians 5: 8–19; Matthew 18:10–20.

⊰ 16 ⊱

The Ark of God Goes to Her Rest

THE DORMITION OF OUR MOST HOLY LADY
THE THEOTOKOS AND EVER-VIRGIN MARY (15TH AUGUST)

Neither the tomb nor death had power over the Theotokos, who is ever watchful in her prayers and in whose intercession lies unfailing hope. For as the Mother of Life she has been transported into life by Him who dwelt within her ever-virgin womb. (Kontakion).[1]

⊰ I ⊱

In the cycle of the Church Feasts the Dormition of the Mother of God in some ways takes us full circle: we come back again to the Mother of God, with whom this consideration of the Feasts began; we come back again to the reality of the Incarnation and its consequences, particularly the truth affirmed by many of the Church Fathers that 'God became man that man might become God'; and we come back again to the Resurrection and Ascension of Christ as we consider the Mother of God raised into the glory of heaven. She who said 'Be it unto me according to thy word', and made possible the Incarnation, is now honoured in her Dormition or 'Falling asleep' as the Church marks the end of her earthly life. As in the second chapter of this book when we considered the Birth of the Mother of God and her Entry into the Temple, so now in this chapter we are dealing with traditions about the end of the earthly life of the Lord's Mother which are not given in the canonical Scriptures of the New Testament, but have been preserved within the Church's consciousness and sacred Tradition. Christian apocryphal literature contains a variety of accounts about Mary's death and her entry into the heavenly life, but the earliest extant manuscripts of these accounts are relatively late; they transmit traditions about the end of Mary's life, often in an exotic and legendary form.[2]

The Church's celebration of the end of the earthly life of the Mother of God probably began in Jerusalem, where the Tomb of Mary in the Gethsemane area is still a place of pilgrimage; by the sixth century the Feast was widely observed, and by about 600 AD the date had been fixed as 15th August. In current Orthodox practice the Feast is preceded by a fast from 1st August to the one day of Forefeast on 14th August; eight days of Afterfeast complete the festival. Two separate strands in the celebration can be seen: first, the death and burial of the Mother of God, and second, her Resurrection/Ascension/Assumption into heaven. In the West the Feast has long been known as the Assumption of the Blessed Virgin Mary. In the East it is generally known as the Dormition of the Mother of God. (The Greek word *koimesis*, 'falling asleep', has the same root as *koimeteria*, 'sleeping place' or cemetery.) In the Catholic Church a formal doctrinal statement by Pope Pius XII in 1950 made explicit the long-held tradition that Mary was taken up soul and body into the glory of heaven. In the Orthodox Churches the teaching about the final destiny of the Mother of God is transmitted rather through the liturgical texts and the homilies of the Church Fathers (especially of St John of Damascus).

⤜ II ⤐

The Orthodox texts develop the tradition that the apostles and disciples were mysteriously gathered together from the ends of the earth to be present in Jerusalem at the death of the Theotokos, and that they buried her body in the Garden of Gethsemane; according to one tradition certain Jews tried to disrupt the funeral procession. The apostle Thomas had not been among those present, and when he arrived three days after the burial and wanted to see the body of the Lord's Mother, it was discovered that the tomb was empty. As with most of the liturgical texts quoted in this book, so with this Feast there is a wonderful sense of the inter-relation of different aspects of the history of redemption, and a sense of awe at the work of God being accomplished. The Church glorifies God for what he has done, and is in no doubt about the significance of her who is 'the origin of Life and the holder of God'.[3] The following quotations are concerned with the traditional events that are celebrated and represented in the icons: the assembly of the apostles at the death bed of the Theotokos, her Dormition and Translation, and her continuing communion with the Church. Images and paradoxes form an integral part of the way in which we celebrate the Feast and view the prospect of our own death.

1. The gathering of the disciples to prepare for the death and burial of the Mother of God has a conspicuous place in the hymns for the Feast.

> At thy departing, O Virgin Theotokos, to Him who was ineffably born of thee, James the first bishop and brother of the Lord was there, and so was Peter, the honoured leader and chief of the disciples (literally, 'the theologians'), and the whole sacred fellowship of the apostles. In discourses that showed forth heavenly

161

things they sang the praises of the divine and amazing mystery of the dispensation of Christ our God; and they rejoiced, O far-famed Virgin, as they buried thy body, the origin of Life and holder of God. On high the most holy and venerable of the angelic powers bowed in wonder before this marvel, and said to one another: 'Open wide your gates and receive her who bore the Creator of heaven and earth. With songs of praise let us glorify her precious and holy body, dwelling-place of the Lord on whom we may not gaze.'[4]

At thy deathless Dormition, O Theotokos, Mother of the Life, clouds caught the apostles up into the air: though dispersed throughout the world, they were brought together to form a single choir before thy most pure body. And burying thee with reverence, they sang aloud the words of Gabriel: 'Hail, thou who art full of grace . . .'[5]

2. The imagery from the Old Testament that is used in the celebration of Christ's Ascension is also used here to speak of Mary's entry into glory. Mary 'commends her most pure soul into the hands of her Son', who has made her 'dwell in the Holy of Holies as a bright candlestick'.[6] Such language is reminiscent of the Feast of the Entry of the Mother of God into the Temple (cf Chapter 2).

What songs filled with awe did all the apostles of the Word then offer thee, O Virgin, as they stood around thy deathbed and cried aloud in wonder: 'The Palace of the King withdraws: the Ark of holiness is raised on high' (cf Psalm 132:8 [131]). Let the gates be opened wide that the Gate of God may enter into abundant joy, she who asks without ceasing for great mercy on the world.'[7]

Thy Son, O Virgin, has truly made thee dwell in the Holy of Holies as a bright candlestick, flaming with immaterial fire, as a golden censer burning with divine coal, as the vessel of manna, the rod of Aaron, and the tablet written by God, as a holy ark and table of the bread of life.[8]

She who is higher than the heavens and more glorious than the cherubim . . . today commends her most pure soul into the hands of her Son. With her all things are filled with joy and she bestows great mercy upon us.[9]

3. The gathering of those who keep the feasts of the Church is an expression of the Communion of Saints; the Church's communion with God embraces the 'ties of kinship' that bind Christ, the Christian and the Church into a unity of love. Within this Communion the Mother of God has a place of honour, and is an ever-flowing fount of healing grace for those in need, for she has followed her risen and ascended Son into the glory of heaven.

Come, O gathering of those who love to keep the feasts, come and let us form a choir. Come, let us crown the Church with songs, as the Ark of God goes to her rest. (cf Psalm 132:8 [131]). For today is heaven opened wide as it receives the Mother of Him who cannot be contained. The earth, as it yields up the Source of life, is robed in blessing and majesty. The hosts of angels, present with the fellowship of the apostles, gaze in great fear at her who bore the Cause of life, now that she is translated from life to life. Let us all venerate and implore: Forget not, O Lady, thy ties of kinship with those who commemorate the feast of thine all-holy Dormition.[10]

Come, O ye faithful, let us approach the tomb of the Mother of God, and let us embrace it, touching it sincerely with the lips and eyes and foreheads of the heart. Let us draw abundant gifts of healing grace from this ever-flowing fount. O Mother of the living God, accept from us this burial hymn, and cover us with the shadow of thy light-giving and divine grace.[11]

4. 'The source of life is laid in the tomb, and the tomb itself becomes a ladder to heaven.'[12] This is one of the central paradoxes that we celebrate in this Feast, and it derives from the death and Resurrection of Christ himself; Christ is the Pass-over, the One in and through whom we pass from death into life. The Dormition of the Mother of God reaffirms the destiny which Christ has gone ahead and prepared for us, and allows the grave to be seen as the gateway to Paradise. The Dormition of her who is 'the Holy Place of God', 'shining with grace in divine brightness'[13] is a source of hope and confidence for those who celebrate this Feast.

O marvellous wonder! The source of life is laid in the tomb, and the tomb itself becomes a ladder to heaven. Make glad, O Gethsemane, thou sacred abode of the Mother of God. Come, O ye faithful, and with Gabriel to lead us let us cry: 'Hail, thou who art full of grace: the Lord is with thee, granting the world through thee great mercy.'[14]

⋘ III ⋙

The traditional iconography for the Dormition of the Mother of God is well developed by the time it appears in tenth-century ivories from Constantinople: the Mother of God is shown lying on a bier with the apostles grouped around her; Christ stands behind the bier holding her soul in his arms. The image became a popular one for devotional purposes. By the twelfth century additional details include buildings, the cloud-borne apostles arriving at the scene, bishops and mourning women; we also see the incident where the Jew Jephonias, having attempted to upset the bier during the funeral procession, has his hands cut off by an angel, and restored on his conversion to Christianity. A later development is the depiction of the open gates of heaven, ready to receive the Virgin's body.

In **Plate 24** we have a sixteenth-century Russian icon of the Dormition. The body of the Mother of God lies on her deathbed, which is covered with a brown drape; she is clothed in a deep crimson outer garment over a grey tunic, and her body stands out against the white mattress of the bier; her head is slightly raised, and her folded hands rest on her breast. On the left St Peter censes the body of the Theotokos, and behind him are four other apostles, two bishops and a group of three women; on the right, St Paul with veiled hands bends low at the foot of the bier; behind him are six more apostles, two bishops and three more women. The bishops traditionally represented are St James the brother of the Lord and first Bishop of Jerusalem, together with Timothy, Heirotheus, and Dionysius the Areopagite; they are shown with haloes and wearing episcopal vestments. The women represent other members of the Church in Jerusalem. Buildings frame the upper section of the icon on both sides.

In the centre behind the Mother of God stands the figure of Christ; his gold halo is Cross-marked and bears the inscription *Ho On*; he is clothed in gold ochre robes shaded with crimson, and lines of gold radiate from him. A lozenge-shaped triple green mandorla surrounds him, decorated with stars on the inner area, and with radiating gold lines and stars on the middle two sections; angels can be seen in the outer section, and at the top, above Christ, a large six-winged seraph extends the image into the upper border of the icon. In his covered hands Christ holds 'the most pure soul' of his Mother, represented as a small child clad in brilliant white garments. This calls to mind images of the Mother of God holding Christ in her arms, particularly the Hodegitria icon; now the imagery is reversed, and the Son of God, who had been held in his Mother's arms as a child, receives the soul of his Mother as she 'commends her most pure soul into the hands of her Son'.

The posture of the assembled apostles, bishops and women draws our attention towards the body of the Theotokos in the lower half of the icon, while the upward movement of the lines of the mandorla takes our attention up to the glorious figure of Christ who has come to receive his Mother into the glory of heaven. The censer held by Peter and the candle placed on the ground in front of the bed to the left of the central axis of the icon are balanced by the brilliance of the soul of Mary to the right of centre in the upper part of the panel, and echoes the imagery of one of the hymns already quoted: 'Thy Son, O Virgin, has truly made thee dwell in the Holy of Holies as a bright candlestick, flaming with immaterial fire, as a golden censer burning with divine coal.'

The iconography of the Dormition of the Mother of God is a profound statement of truths about the Mother of God, and also of a Christian attitude towards death. In Orthodox churches which have been decorated with the iconographic cycle of the feasts, the image of the Dormition is often placed on the west wall of the nave, above the door through which one leaves the church. On leaving the place of the Divine Liturgy one passes under an image of death which is a statement about entering into new life; one can also picture a funeral procession leaving the church beneath the same image, and see the theological and linguistic links involved in passing under a representation of the *koimesis* of the Mother of God in order to proceed to the *koimeteria* for a Christian burial. The faith expressed in the Dormition icon is a faith which transforms our view of death from one of unmitigated loss into one of commendation and hope. Like the apostles gathering around the body of the Mother of God, we gather around the bodies of those we love as we take part in their funeral rites. Like the Mother of God herself, we commend our souls into the hands of her Son. Like millions of Christians before us we pray that the ties of kinship which bind us together within the Body of Christ and the Communion of Saints will sustain us both as we pray for those who have passed through the gates of death, and as we ourselves prepare to tread that same path. Like the soul of Mary in the arms of her Son we hope to be born again into the new life of the Age to Come, of which we have already had a foretaste in this life.

These chapters on the Church Feasts and their icons began with the birth of the Mother of God; we have ended with the Dormition of the Mother of God. It would seem to be entirely appropriate to end this chapter with the prospect of our own death, and the light that is shed on it by the Dormition of the Mother of God, and by some texts from the Byzantine Funeral Rite. The extracts that follow are from the translation used by English-speaking Christians of the Melkite–Greek Catholic Patriarchate, a translation which was warmly welcomed by the Ecumenical Patriarch Athenagoras in 1968, as a sign of participation 'in the work of the Church as it strives towards the promotion of the oneness of Christians'.[15]

Two petitions from the Litany of the Resurrection in the funeral rite are reminiscent of some of the imagery developed in the hymns for the Dormition:

> That we may deserve the grace of entering into the chamber of his divine wedding-feast, and rejoice beyond words, together with his heavenly attendants and the hosts of the saints glorified through Him in the Church Triumphant in heaven, let us pray to the Lord.

> Let us remember the all-holy, spotless, most highly blessed and glorious Lady, the Mother of God and ever-virgin Mary, and all the saints, and commend ourselves and one another and our whole life to Christ our God.[16]

Three of the Troparia of the Dead recall the themes we have seen recurring throughout the feasts: repentance as the way back to God in response to the Saviour's call; human beings created to bear the image and likeness of God, and restored to the original beauty of God's creation; and the role of the Mother of God in enabling us to find Paradise.

The choirs of saints have discovered the Fountain of Life and the Gate of Paradise; may I also, through repentance find the way back to You, O Lord. I am a lost sheep: O Saviour, call me back to your fold and save me.

O Lord, who with your own hand have fashioned me from nothingness, and adorned me with your divine image, and who, when I transgressed your commandment, did cast me down into the dust whereof I had been made: deign, O Lord, to restore me to your likeness, that my original beauty may be renewed in me.

Hail, immaculate Mother of God, who, for the restoration of mankind, have brought forth God in the flesh. Through this same God, the human race has found salvation, blessed Mother of God; may we also through you find paradise.[17]

Finally, two eloquent prayers for the salvation of the soul of the person whose funeral is being celebrated, one to the Mother of God and one to Christ:

O Mother of the Sun without setting, O Mother of God, we pray to you: save those who put their trust in you. We beseech you to intercede with your Son that he may grant to the soul of the departed one to rest with the souls of the just in heaven. O immaculate Mother of God, grant him (her) also that he (she) may enjoy the eternal inheritance of heaven in the courts where the just repose.[18]

Christ our true God who have dominion over the living and the dead, deign, through the intercession of your all-immaculate Mother, of our venerable and God-fearing Fathers, and of all your saints, to establish in the mansions of the just the soul of your departed servant N, and to number him (her) among the saints, and to have mercy on us, for You are gracious and the Lover of Mankind.[19]

★   ★   ★

The main biblical readings for the Feast are:

At Great Vespers: Genesis 28:10–17; Ezekiel 43:27–44:4; Proverbs 9:1–11.
At Mattins: Luke 1:39–49, 56.
At the Divine Liturgy: Philippians 2:5–11; Luke 10:38–42; 11:27–28.

Notes

Chapter 1

1. St Gregory of Nyssa, *The Song of Songs*. Translated with an Introduction by Casimir McCambley OCSO (1987) Brookline, Massachusetts: Hellenic College Press.
2. Trubetskoi, Prince E. N., translated by Gertrude Vakar (1973) *Icons: Theology in Colour*. New York: St Vladimir's Seminary Press, pp. 41–2.
   a. More recently scholars have concluded that the development of the oklad may go back as far as the fourteenth century.
   b. The 'dark spots' in this translation seem to refer to the dark surface of the icon seen through openings in the oklad.
3. Quoted in *Anglican-Orthodox Dialogue: The Dublin Agreed Statement 1984* (1984) London: SPCK, p. 38.
4. Zander, V. (1975) *St Seraphim of Sarov*. Translated by Father Boris Bobrinskoy, London: SPCK, p. 16.

Chapter 2

1. *The Festal Menaion*. Translated from the original Greek by Mother Mary and Archimandrite Kallistos Ware (1969) London: Faber and Faber, p. 100. First sticheron at Great Vespers of the Birth of the Theotokos.
2. M. R. James, *The Apocryphal New Testament* (1924) Oxford: Oxford University Press, p. 39.
3. Ibid., p. 40.
4. *The Lenten Triodion*. Translated from the original Greek by Mother Mary and Archimandrite Kallistos Ware (1978) London: Faber and Faber, pp. 423–4. Ikos One of the Akathistos Hymn.
5. Ibid., p. 428. Canticle Three of the Akathistos Hymn.
6. Ibid., p. 435. Ikos Eleven of the Akathistos Hymn.
7. *The Festal Menaion*, p. 99. Second sticheron at Small Vespers of the Birth of the Theotokos.
8. Ibid., p. 101. Fifth sticheron at Small Vespers.
9. Ibid., p. 106. From the Aposticha at Great Vespers.
10. Ibid., p. 106. From the same Aposticha.
11. Ibid., p. 111. From the First Canon in Canticle One at Mattins.

12. Ibid., p. 121. From the First Canon of Canticle Eight at Mattins.
13. *The Apocryphal New Testament*, p. 41.
14. *The Festal Menaion*, p.185. Kontakion of the Entry of the Theotokos.
15. Ibid., p. 164. First sticheron at Small Vespers.
16. Ibid., p. 178. From the Second Canon of Canticle Three at Mattins.
17. Ibid., p. 184. From the Second Canon of Canticle Six at Mattins.
18. Ibid., p. 165. Aposticha at Small Vespers.
19. Cf Ware, Bishop Kallistos (August/September 1989) 'The Feast of Mary's Silence: The Entry into the Temple', *The Month*, 114 Mount Street, London.

Chapter 3

1. *The Festal Menaion*, p. 438. From the first sticheron at Small Vespers of the Annunciation.
2. Ibid., p. 452. From Canticle Five at Mattins.
3. Ibid., pp. 439–40. From the first sticheron at Great Vespers.
4. Ibid., p. 459. From the Exapostilarion at Mattins.
5. Ibid., p. 437. From the first sticheron at Small Vespers.
6. Ibid., p. 456. From Canticle Eight at Mattins.
7. Ibid., p. 460. Final sticheron at Mattins.
8. Ibid., p. 445. Aposticha at the Lity in the Vigil Service.
9. Cf Maguire, H. (1981) *Art and Eloquence in Byantium*. Princeton, New Jersey: Princeton University Press.
10. Cf Lazarev, V. N. (1976) *Novgorod Icon Painting*. Moscow: Iskusstvo Publishers; and *Novgorod Icons 12th–17th Century* (1980), Oxford: Phaidon and Leningrad: Aurora Art Publishers.
11. *The Festal Menaion*, p. 456. From Canticle Eight at Mattins.
12. *The Apocryphal New Testament*, p. 43.
13. *The Festal Menaion*, p. 443. From the Lity in the Vigil Service.
14. Ibid., p. 443. From the same Lity.

15. *The Lenten Triodion*, p. 620. From Canticle Seven of Small Compline for Good Friday.

16. *The Festal Menaion*, p. 92. From the Magnificat.

Chapter 4

1. *The Festal Menaion*, p. 278. Ikos after Canticle Six and the Kontakion for the Nativity.

2. Ibid., p. 212. From Canticle Four of Mattins for the Forefeast.

3. Ibid., p. 218. From the second sticheron at the end of Mattins for the Forefeast.

4. Ibid., p. 205. From Canticle Four at Compline of the Forefeast.

5. Ibid., p. 201. Aposticha in the Greek use at Vespers for the Forefeast.

6. Ibid., p. 270. From the Second Canon of Canticle Two at Mattins of the Nativity.

7. Ibid., p. 214. Ikos of the Forefeast (in the Slav use only).

8. Ibid., p. 254. Sticheron from Vespers of the Nativity.

9. *The Apocryphal New Testament*, p. 46.

10. *The Festal Menaion*, p. 213. From Canticle Five at Mattins of the Nativity.

11. Ibid., p. 259. Troparion, at Vespers of the Nativity.

12. Ibid., p. 254. Sticheron from Vespers of the Nativity.

13. *Nicene and Post Nicene Fathers*, Vol. XIII (1976) Ephraim Syrus, Homily *On our Lord*, para. 3, p. 306. Grand Rapids, Michigan: Wm B. Eerdmans Publishing Company.

14. *The Festal Menaion*, pp. 438. From sticheron at Small Vespers of the Annunciation; and p. 455, from Canticle Seven at Mattins of the Annunciation.

15. Ibid., p. 225. Sticheron from the First Hour on Christmas Eve.

16. Ibid., p. 245. Sticheron from the Ninth Hour on Christmas Eve.

17. Ibid., p. 253. Sticheron from Vespers of the Nativity.

18. Ibid., p. 277. Kontakion for the Nativity.

Chapter 5

1. *The Festal Menaion*, p. 421. From Canticle Four at Mattins of the Meeting of the Lords.

2. Cf Maguire, H. (1981) *Art and Eloquence in Byzantium*. Princeton, New Jersey: Princeton University Press, pp. 85–86.

3. Ibid., pp. 85–86.

4. *The Festal Menaion*, p. 415. From the Lity at Great Vespers.

5. Ibid., p. 416. Aposticha at the end of Great Vespers.

6. Ibid., p. 427. From Canticle Nine of Mattins.

7. Ibid., p. 428. From sticheron at the end of Mattins.

8. Ibid., p. 407. Aposticha at Small Vespers.

9. Ibid., p. 422. From Canticle Five at Mattins.

10. Ibid., p. 427. From Canticle Nine at Mattins.

11. Ibid., p. 413. From the Lity at Great Vespers.

12. Ibid., pp. 413–414. From the same Lity.

13. Ibid., p. 414. From the same Lity.

14. Ibid., p. 413. From the same Lity.

15. Ibid., p. 420. From Canticle One at Mattins.

16. Ibid., p. 428. Expostilarion at Mattins.

17. Ibid., p. 406. From the first sticheron at Small Vespers.

18. Ibid., p. 416. From the end of the Lity at Great Vespers.

19. Ibid., p. 406. From the first sticheron at Small Vespers.

20. Ibid., p. 424. From Canticle Seven at Mattins.

21. Ibid., p. 426. From Canticle Nine at Mattins.

22. Ibid., p. 429. From the sticheron at the end of Mattins.

23. Ibid., p. 424. From Canticle Seven at Mattins.

Chapter 6

1. *The Festal Menaion*, p. 299. From Canticle Five at Compline of the Forefeast of The Theophany.

2. Discourse 37, *On the Baptism of our Lord and Epiphany*. Quoted in Ouspensky, L. and Lossky, V. (1982) *The Meaning of Icons*. Crestwood, New York: St Vladimir's Seminary Press, p. 164.

3. *The Festal Menaion*, p. 308. From the Kontakion of the Forefeast.

4. Ibid., p. 308. Ikos, after the Kontakion at the end of Canticle Six at Mattins of the Forefeast of The Theophany.

5. Ibid., p. 327. Sticheron at the Sixth Hour on the Eve of The Theophany.

6. Ibid., p. 338. Sticheron at Vespers of The Theophany.

7. Ibid., p. 295. Aposticha at Vespers of the Forefeast.

8. Ibid., p. 304. From Canticle One at Mattins of the Forefeast.

9. Ibid., p. 307. From Canticle Six at Mattins of the Forefeast.

10. Ibid., p. 355. From the prayer of Sophronios, Patriarch of Jerusalem, at the Great Blessing of the Waters.

11. Ibid., p. 367. From the First Canon of Canticle One at Mattins of The Theophany.

12. Ibid., p. 381. From the Second Canon of Canticle Nine at Mattins of The Theophany.

13. Ibid., p. 361. From the Lity at the Vigil Service for The Theophany.

14. Ibid., p. 297. From Canticle One at Compline for the Forefeast.

15. Ibid., p. 303. Second sessional hymn at Mattins of the Forefeast.

16. Ibid., pp. 307–8. Kontakion of the Forefeast.

17. Ibid., p. 311. Sticheron at Mattins of the Forefeast.

18. Ibid., pp. 372–3. From the Second Canon of Canticle Five at Mattins of The Theophany.

19. Ibid., p. 300. From Canticle Six at Compline of the Forefeast.

20. Ibid., p. 306. From Canticle Five at Mattins of the Forefeast.

21. Ibid., p. 301. From Canticle Eight at Compline of the Forefeast.

22. Ibid., p. 322. Sticheron at the Third Hour on the Eve of The Theophany.

23. Ibid., p. 359. From the Troparion of the Feast, at the Great Blessing of the Waters.

24. Ibid., p. 296. Aposticha at Vespers of the Forefeast.

25. Ibid., p. 362. From the Lity at the Vigil Service for The Theophany.

26. Ibid., p. 301. From Canticle Eight at Compline of the Forefeast.
27. Ibid., p. 301. From Canticle Seven at Compline of the Forefeast.
28. Ibid., p. 354. From the prayer of Sophronios, Patriarch of Jerusalem, at the Great Blessing of the Waters.
29. Ibid., p. 303. Second sessional hymn at Mattins of the Forefeast.
30. Ibid., p. 332. Sticheron at the Ninth Hour on the Eve of The Theophany.
31. Ibid., p. 356. From the prayer of Sophronios, Patriarch of Jerusalem, at the Great Blessing of the Waters.

Chapter 7

1. *The Festal Menaion*, p. 495. Sticheron at the end of Mattins of the Transfiguration.
2. Ramsey, A. M. (1949) *The Glory of God and the Transfiguration of Christ*. London: Longmans, Green & Co, p. 144.
3. 'Pseudo-Chrysostom', quoted in *The Oxford Dictionary of Byzantium* (1991) Oxford: Oxford University Press, p. 2104.
4. *The Festal Menaion*, p. 489. Kontakion of the Transfiguration.
5. Cf St Gregory of Nyssa, *The Life of Moses*. Translation, introduction and notes by Malherbe, A. J. and Ferguson, E. (1978) New York: Paulist Press.
6. *The New Testament of our Lord and Saviour Jesus Christ*. Newly translated from the Latin Vulgate and authorized by the Archbishops and Bishops of England and Wales. London: Burns Oates and Washbourne Ltd (1945).
7. Quoted in Ware, K. (1979) *The Orthodox Way*. London & Oxford: Mowbray, p. 27.
8. A translation by Clifton Wolters is published in the Penguin Classics series.
9. Quoted in Ouspensky, L. and Lossky, V., *The Meaning of Icons*, p. 211.
10. *The Festal Menaion*, p. 477. Apolytikion at Great Vespers of the Transfiguration.
11. Ibid., p. 479. Sessional hymn at Mattins in the Slav use.
12. Ibid., p. 476. From the Lity at Great Vespers.
13. Ibid., p. 476. Aposticha at Great Vespers.
14. Ibid., p. 484. From the Second Canon of Canticle Three at Mattins.
15. Ibid., pp. 493–4. From the First Canon of Canticle Nine at Mattins.
16. Ibid., p. 470. First sticheron at Great Vespers.
17. Ibid., p. 487. Katavasia of Canticle Five at Mattins.
18. Ibid., p. 494. Katavasia of Canticle Nine at Mattins.
19. Ibid., p. 471. Sticheron at Great Vespers.
20. Ibid., p. 478. From the first sessional hymn at Mattins.
21. Ibid., p. 495. Exapostilarion at Mattins.
22. Ibid., p. 469. Sticheron at Small Vespers.
23. Ibid., p. 469. Aposticha at Small Vespers.
24. Ibid., p. 478. From the first sessional hymn at Mattins.
25. Ibid., p. 477. Aposticha at Great Vespers.
26. Ibid., p. 474. From the Lity at Great Vespers.
27. Ibid., p. 487. From the Second Canon of Canticle Five

at Mattins.
28. Ibid., p. 469. Aposticha at Small Vespers.
29. Ibid., p. 469. Aposticha at Great Vespers.

Chapter 8

1. *The Lenten Triodion*. Translated from the original Greek by Mother Mary and Archimandrite Kallistos Ware (1978), London: Faber and Faber, p. 497. From Canticle Three at Mattins of Palm Sunday.
2. Cf Schmemann, A. (1990) *Great Lent*. New York: St Vladimir's Seminary Press, p. 11.
3. *The Lenten Triodion*, p. 101. From sticheron before the Canon at Mattins of the Sunday of the Publican and the Pharisee.
4. Ibid., p. 99. Sticheron from Vespers of Saturday for the same Sunday.
5. Ibid., p. 107. From Canticle Seven at Mattins of the same Sunday.
6. Ibid., p. 107. From the same Canticle.
7. Ibid., p. 113. From the Lity at Saturday Vespers for the Sunday of the Prodigal Son.
8. Ibid., p. 116. From Canticle Three at Mattins for the same Sunday.
9. Ibid., p. 117. From Canticle Five at Mattins for the same Sunday.
10. Ibid., p. 138. From the Expostilarion at Mattins of Saturday of the Dead.
11. Ibid., p. 139. Sticheron at the end of Mattins for the same Saturday.
12. Ibid., p. 151. From the Lity at Saturday Vespers for the Sunday of the Last Judgement.
13. Ibid., p. 166. Aposticha at the end of Vespers on the Sunday of the Last Judgement.
14. Ibid., p. 168. From the stichera at Saturday Vespers for the Sunday of Forgiveness.
15. Ibid., p. 175. From Canticle Seven at Mattins for the same Sunday.
16. Ibid., p. 497. From Canticle Three at Mattins of Palm Sunday.
17. Ibid., p. 169. Stichera at Saturday Vespers for the Sunday of Forgiveness.
18. Ibid., p. 177. From Canticle Nine at Mattins of the same Sunday.
19. Ibid., p. 181. Sticheron from Vespers of the same Sunday.
20. Ibid., p. 191. From the First Canon of Canticle One at Mattins on Monday in the first week of Lent.
21. Ibid., p. 232. From Canticle Nine at Mattins on Wednesday of the same week.
22. Ibid., p. 254. Sticheron at Vespers on Thursday of the same week.
23. Ibid., p. 284. From the first canon of Canticle One at Mattins on Saturday of the same week.
24. Ibid., p. 290. Kontakion, at Mattins of the same day.
25. Ibid., p. 286. From sessional hymn in Canticle Three at the same Mattins.
26. Ibid., p. 306. Kontakion for the Sunday of Orthodoxy.
27. Ibid., p. 300. Sticheron at Saturday Vespers for the

Sunday of Orthodoxy.

28. Ibid., p. 300. Sticheron at the same Vespers.

29. Ibid., p. 304. Sessional hymn in Canticle Three at Mattins for the same Sunday.

30. Cf Buckton, D. (ed.) (1994) *Byzantium – Treasures of Byzantine Art and Culture from British Collections*. London: The British Museum, pp. 129–31.
Cormack, R. (1997) *Painting the Soul – Icons, Death Masks and Shrouds*. London: Reaktion Books, pp. 46–8, 61–3.
Petsopoulos, Y. (ed.) (1987) *East Christian Art*. London: AXIA Byzantine and Islamic Art Consultants, pp. 49–50.

31. Majeska, G. (1984) *Russian Travellers in Constantinople in the 14th and 15th Centuries*. Washington, p. 362.

32. *The Lenten Triodion*, p. 314. Sticheron at Saturday Vespers of the Second Sunday in Lent.

33. Ibid., p. 317. From the First Canon of Canticle One at Mattins of the same Sunday.

34. Ibid., p. 320. From Canticle Four of the same Mattins.

35. Ibid., p. 337. From Canticle One at Mattins of the Sunday of the Cross.

36. Ibid., p. 342. Kontakion of the Sunday of the Cross.

37. Ibid., p. 345. From Canticle Nine at Mattins of the same Sunday.

38. St John Climacus, *The Ladder of Divine Ascent*. Translated by Luibheid, C. and Russell, N. (1982) New York: Paulist Press, and London: SPCK.

39. Published in Weitzmann, K. (1978) *The Icon: Holy Images, Sixth to Fourteenth Century*. London: Chatto and Windus.

40. *The Lenten Triodion*, p. 358. Second Canon of Canticle Three at Mattins of the Fourth Sunday in Lent.

41. Ibid., p. 360. From the Second Canon of Canticle Four at the same Mattins.

42. Ibid., p. 358. From Canticle Three at the same Mattins.

43. Ibid., p. 369. Aposticha at Vespers of the same Sunday.

44. Ibid., p. 419. Sticheron at Friday Vespers in the Fifth Week of Lent.

45. Ibid., p. 390. From Canticle Four of the Great Canon.

46. Ibid., p. 392. From the same Canticle.

47. Ibid., p. 452. From the Second Canon of Canticle Three at Mattins of the Fifth Sunday in Lent.

48. Ibid., p. 455. From the Second Canon of Canticle Five at the same Mattins.

49. Ibid., p. 451. From Canticle Three of the same Mattins.

50. Ibid., p. 454. From Canticle Five of the same Mattins.

51. Ibid., p. 462. Sticheron from Sunday Vespers of the same Sunday.

Chapter 9

1. *The Lenten Triodion*, p. 469. From Canticle Four at Great Compline on the Saturday of Lazarus.

2. Ibid., p. 483. The Kontakion of the Saturday of Lazarus.

3. Ibid., p. 465. Sticheron at Friday Vespers for the same Saturday.

4. Ibid., p. 486. Sticheron at Mattins.

5. Ibid., p. 470. From Canticle Five at Great Compline.

6. Ibid., p. 472. From Canticle Six at Great Compline.

7. Ibid., p. 469. From Canticle Four at Great Compline.

8. Ibid., p. 486. Sticheron at the end of Mattins.

9. Ibid., p. 487. Sticheron at Mattins.

10. Ibid., p. 484. From the Second Canon of Canticle Seven at Mattins.

11. Ibid., p. 483. From the same Canon.

12. Ibid., p. 471. From Canticle Five at Great Compline.

13. Ibid., p. 472. From Canticle Six at Great Compline.

14. Grabar, A. (1969) *Christian Iconography – A Study of its Origins*. London: Routledge & Kegan Paul Ltd, p. 8.

Chapter 10

1. *The Lenten Triodion*, p. 489. From sticheron at Saturday Great Vespers of Palm Sunday.

2. Ibid., p. 488. Sung in place of the Trisagion at the Divine Liturgy on the Saturday of Lazarus.

3. Ibid., pp. 491–2. Aposticha after the Lity at Saturday Great Vespers of Palm Sunday.

4. Ibid., p. 493. First sessional hymn at Mattins.

5. Ibid., p. 492. Apolytikion of the feast, at Saturday Great Vespers.

6. Ibid., p. 493. Troparion after the Apolytikion at Great Vespers.

7. Ibid., p. 505. Aposticha at Palm Sunday Vespers.

8. Ibid., pp. 501–2. From a sticheron at Mattins.

9. Ibid., p. 497. From Canticle Three at Mattins.

10. Ibid., p. 500. From Canticle Eight at Mattins.

11. Ibid., p. 494. Sessional hymn at Mattins.

12. Ibid., p. 499. Kontakion of Palm Sunday.

13. Ibid., p. 501. A sticheron at Mattins.

14. Ibid., p. 492. Aposticha at Saturday Great Vespers.

15. Ibid., p. 491. From the Lity at Saturday Great Vespers.

16. Ibid., p. 499. Kontakion of Palm Sunday.

17. Extract printed in *The Divine Office – The Liturgy of the Hours according to the Roman Rite*, Volume II (1974) London: Collins, p. 254.

Chapter 11

1. *The Lenten Triodion*, p. 507. From Canticle One at Small Compline of Palm Sunday.

2. *The Festal Menaion*, p. 140. From the Lity at Great Vespers of the Exaltation of the Cross.

3. *The New Testament of Our Lord and Saviour Jesus Christ*. Newly translated from the Latin Vulgate and authorized by the Archbishops and Bishops of England and Wales. London: Burns Oates and Washbourne Ltd, 1945.

4. *The Lenten Triodion*, p. 590. From the stichera after the sixth Gospel in the Service of the Twelve Gospels.

5. Ibid., p. 590. From the same stichera.

6. Ibid., p. 612. From the stichera after the Great Litany at Vespers.

7. Ibid., p. 609. From the stichera at the Ninth Hour.

8. Ibid., p. 586. Antiphon Fourteen from the Service of the Twelve Gospels.

9. Ibid., p. 589. From the stichera after the Sixth Gospel in the same service.

10. Ibid., p. 614. From the Aposticha at Vespers.

11. Ibid., p. 615. From the same Aposticha.
12. Ibid., p. 618. From Canticle Three at Compline.
13. Ibid., pp. 618–20. From Canticles Five, Six and Seven at Compline.
14. See Grabar, A. (1969) *Christian Iconography: A Study of its Origins*. London: Routledge & Kegan Paul Ltd, p. 132.
15. See Belting, H. (1990) *The Image and its Public in the Middle Ages*. Translated by Mark Bartusis and Raymond Meyer. New Rochelle, New York: Aristide D. Caratzas.
16. Extract printed in *The Divine Office – The Liturgy of the Hours according to the Roman Rite*, Volume II (1974) London: Collins, pp. 522–4.
17. *The Festal Menaion*, p. 141. Apolytikion for the Exaltation of the Cross.
18. Ibid., p. 148. Kontakion of the feast.
19. Ibid., p. 140. From the Lity at Great Vespers.
20. Ibid., p. 152. Exapostilarion at Mattins.
21. Ibid., p. 131. From the stichera at Small Vespers.
22. Ibid., p. 131. From the same stichera.
23. Ibid., p. 137. From the Lity at Great Vespers.
24. Ibid., p. 157. Sung during the veneration of the Cross at Mattins.
25. Ibid., p. 139. From the Lity at Great Vespers.
26. Ibid., p. 151. From the Canon after Canticle Nine at Mattins.
27. Ibid., p. 146. From Canticle Four at Mattins.
28. Ibid., p. 145. From Canticle One at Mattins.
29. Ibid., p. 137. From the Lity at Great Vespers.
30. Ibid., p. 139. From the same Lity.
31. Ibid., p. 147. From Canticle Five at Mattins.
32. Ibid., p. 148. Kontakion of the feast.

Chapter 12

1. Hapgood, Isabel Florence (1906) *Service Book of the Holy Orthodox-Catholic Apostolic (Greco-Russian) Church*, Boston & New York: Houghton, Mifflin and Company, p. 228. Troparion from the Canon of Easter.
2. St Gregory Nazianzen, *The Second Oration on Easter*. In *Nicene and Post-Nicene Fathers* Volume VII (1983) Grand Rapids, Michigan: Wm B. Eerdmans Publishing Company, p. 423.
3. *The Pentecostarion* (1990) Translated from the Greek by the Holy Transfiguration Monastery, Boston, Massachusetts, p. 32. From Ode Eight at Mattins, Easter Sunday.
4. Cf Hapgood, *op cit.*, p. 226. Paschal Troparion.
5. *The Pentecostarion*, p. 30. Kontakion of Easter Sunday.
6. Ibid., p. 29. The Hypakoe, after Ode Three at Mattins.
7. Ibid., p. 30. From Ode Six at Mattins.
8. Ibid., p. 30. From the same Ode.
9. Ibid., p. 41. Sticheron at Vespers.
10. Ibid., p. 34. From the Ninth Ode at Mattins.
11. Ibid., p. 30. From Ode Five at Mattins.
12. Ibid., p. 36. A sticheron of Pascha at Mattins.
13. Ibid., p. 33. From Ode Nine at Mattins.
14. Ibid., p. 38. Sticheron used at the Hours, Compline and Nocturns throughout Renewal (Easter) Week.
15. *Byzantine Daily Worship*. Translated and compiled by the Most Revd Joseph Raya and Baron José de Vinck (1969) Allendale NJ: Alleluia Press, p. 860.
16. Grabar, A. (1969) *Christian Iconography – A Study of Its Origins*. London and Henley: Routledge & Kegan Paul, p. 124.
17. A full study of the origins and development of the Anastasis image can be found in: Kartsonis, Anna D. (1986) *Anastasis – The Making of an Image*. Princeton, New Jersey: Princeton University Press.
18. Cf James, M. R., *Apocryphal Gospels*, p. 94ff.
19. In *Nicene and Post-Nicene Fathers*, Volume IX (1983) Grand Rapids, Michigan: Wm B. Eerdmans Publishing Company, pp. 72–73.
20. Jill Storer, M. Litt. thesis (1986) *The Anastasis in Byzantine Iconography*, Vol. I. Birmingham University Faculty of Arts, p. 48.
21. St Ephraim the Syrian. Homily 'On our Lord'. In *Nicene and Post Nicene Fathers*, Volume XIII, Grand Rapids, Michigan: Wm B. Eerdmans Publishing Company, p. 306.
22. See Tregubov, A. (1990) *The Light of Christ – Iconography of Gregory Kroug*. Crestwood, New York: St Vladimir's Seminary Press.
23. *The Services for Holy Week and Easter Sunday from the Triodion and Pentecostarion according to the use of the Orthodox Greek Church in London* (1915) London: Williams and Norgate, p. 305.
24. From Symeon Metaphastis's Paraphrase of the Homily of St Makarios of Egypt, *The Freedom of the Intellect*. In *The Philokalia*, Volume III (1984) Translated by G. E. H. Palmer, Philip Sherrard and Kallistos Ware, London: Faber and Faber, p. 337.

These homilies which have long been attributed to St Makarios of Egypt (c. 300–390) are more likely to have their origin in late fifth or early sixth century Syria.

Chapter 13

1. *The Pentecostarion* (1990) Translated from the Greek by the Holy Transfiguration Monastery, Boston, Massachusetts, p. 193. From a sessional hymn at Mattins of the Wednesday of Mid-Pentecost.
2. Vladimir Lossky. In Ouspensky, L. and Lossky, V. *The Meaning of Icons* (1982) New York: St Vladimir's Seminary Press, p. 193.
3. Brown, Raymond, E. (1971) *The Gospel According to St John I-XII*. London: Geoffrey Chapman, p. 326 ff.
4. Ibid., p. 328.
5. *The Pentecostarion*, p. 195. From Ode Six at Mattins of Wednesday of Mid-Pentecost.
6. Ibid., p. 202. From a sticheron at Vespers.
7. Ibid., p. 193. From a sessional hymn at Mattins.
8. Ibid., p. 197. From the Second Canon of Ode Seven at Mattins.
9. Ibid., p. 196. Kontakion of the feast.
10. Ibid., p. 193. From a sessional hymn at Mattins.
11. Ibid., p. 193. From a sessional hymn at Mattins.
12. Ibid., p. 193. From a sticheron at the end of Mattins.
13. Ibid., p. 192. From Ode Three at Mattins.

14. Ibid., p. 201. From the Second Canon of Ode Nine at Mattins.
15. Ibid., pp. 202–3. From a sticheron at Vespers.
16. Ibid., pp. 196–7. Oikos at Mattins.
17. Ibid., p. 203. From a sticheron at Vespers.

Chapter 14
1. *The Pentecostarion*, p. 326. From the Entreaty at Great Vespers of the Ascension.
2. *The Ferial Menaion or Book of Services for the Twelve Great Festivals and the New Year's Day*, translated by Professor N. Orloff (1900), London: J. Dent & Sons, p. 260.
3. *The Pentecostarion*, p. 334. From Ode Six of Mattins of Ascension Thursday.
4. Ibid., p. 328. Sessional hymn at Mattins.
5. Ibid., p. 335. From Ode Seven at Mattins.
6. Ibid., pp. 327–8. Dismissal hymn at Great Vespers.
7. Ibid., p. 334. Kontakion of the feast.
8. Ibid., p. 331. Sessional hymn at Mattins.
9. Ibid., p. 327. From the Entreaty at Great Vespers.
10. Evdokimov, P. (1990) *The Art of the Icon: A Theology of Beauty*. Translated by Fr Steven Bigham, California: Oakwood Publications, p. 300.
11. *The Lenten Triodion*, pp. 424 and 426. From Ikos Two and Ikos Six of the Akathistos Hymn.
12. *The Pentecostarion*, p. 334. From the Oikos at Mattins.
13. *The Ferial Menaion*, p. 261.
14. *The Pentecostarion*, p. 331. From the Second Canon of Ode Three at Mattins.

Chapter 15
1. *The Pentecostarion*, p. 404. Sticheron at Saturday Great Vespers for Pentecost Sunday.
2. Ibid., p. 407. From first sessional hymn at Mattins.
3. Ibid., p. 415. From Ode Nine at Mattins.
4. Ibid., p. 407. Aposticha at Saturday Great Vespers.
5. *Byzantine Daily Worship*, p. 891. Translated and compiled by the Most Revd Joseph Raya and Baron Jose de Vinck (1969). Allendale, NJ: Alleluia Press, p. 891. A sticheron at Saturday Great Vespers.
6. *The Pentecostarion*, p.408. From Ode One at Mattins.
7. Ibid., p. 409. From Ode Three at Mattins.
8. Ibid., p. 416. A sticheron at Mattins.
9. *Byzantine Daily Worship*, p. 893. At the Lete (Lity) at Saturday Great Vespers.
10. *The Pentecostarion*, p. 413. From Ode Seven at Mattins.
11. Ibid., pp. 410–11. From Ode Four at Mattins.
12. *Byzantine Daily Worship*, p. 894. Aposticha at Saturday Great Vespers.
13. *The Pentecostarion*, p. 407. Second sessional hymn at Mattins.
14. Ibid., p. 416. Exapostilarion at Mattins.
15. Ouspensky, L. (1992) *The Theology of the Icon*, Volume II. Crestwood, New York: St Vladimir's Seminary Press,

pp. 398–9. It is worth mentioning that in the Byzantine tradition there is evidence of the depiction of the three angels by themselves as early as 1370–1375, in the upper register of a miniature of the Emperor John VI Cantacuzene. See Beckwith, J., *The Art of Constantinople*, p. 149.
16. Origen, *Homilies on Genesis and Exodus*, translated by Ronald E. Heine (1982) Washington DC: The Catholic University of America Press, p. 103 ff.
17. Ibid., p. 111.
18. St Ambrose, *On the Death of his Brother Satyrus*, Book II, para. 96. In *Nicene and Post Nicene Fathers*, Volume X (1979) Grand Rapids, Michigan: Wm B. Eerdmans Publishing Company, pp. 189–90.
19. St John of Damascus, *On the Divine Images*. Translated by David Anderson (1980) Crestwood, New York: St Vladimir's Seminary Press, p. 94.
20. *Epiphanius the Wise, The Life of St Sergius*.
21. Archpriest Pavel Florenskii, *On the Icon*, translated by John Lindsay Opie, in *Eastern Churches Review*, Volume VIII, Number 1, Oxford: The Clarendon Press, p. 24.
22. St Gregory of Sinai, 'On Commandments and Doctrines . . .'. In *The Philokalia*, Volume IV (1995) translated by G. E. H. Palmer, Philip Sherrard and Kallistos Ware, London: Faber and Faber, pp. 217–18.
23. Militza Zernov (1899–1994). I have been unable to trace the source of this quotation.
24. *The Pentecostarion*, p. 412. Kontakion of Pentecost.

Chapter 16
1. *The Festal Menaion*, p. 520. Kontakion of the Dormition.
2. Cf James, M. R. *The Apocryphal New Testament*.
3. *The Festal Menaion*, p. 511. Aposticha at Great Vespers.
4. Ibid., p. 511. The same Aposticha.
5. Ibid., pp. 525–6. Sticheron at the end of Mattins.
6. Ibid., pp. 505 and 519. From a sticheron at Small Vespers, and the First Canon of Canticle Six at Mattins.
7. Ibid., p. 504. Sticheron at Small Vespers.
8. Ibid., p. 519. From the First Canon of Canticle Mattins.
9. Ibid., p. 505. Sticheron at Small Vespers.
10. Ibid., p. 509. From the Lity at Great Vespers.
11. Ibid., p. 525. From the Second Canon of Canticle Nine at Mattins.
12. Ibid., p. 511. From a sticheron at Great Vespers.
13. Ibid., pp. 504 and 506. From a sticheron at Small Vespers and another at Great Vespers.
14. Ibid., p. 506. Sticheron at Great Vespers.
15. From a letter printed in the early pages of *Byzantine Daily Worship*.
16. *Byzantine Daily Worship*, p. 989. From the Litany of the Resurrection.
17. Ibid., pp. 992–3. Troparia of the Dead.
18. Ibid., p. 1010. Hymn to the Mother of God.
19. Ibid., p. 1008. Apolysis.

Further Reading

Aslanoff, Catherine (ed.) (1995) *The Incarnate God – The Feasts of Jesus Christ and the Virgin Mary* (two volumes), trans. Paul Meyendorff. New York: St Vladimir's Seminary Press.

Bryer, Anthony and Herrin, Judith (eds) (1977) *Iconoclasm*: papers given at the Ninth Spring Symposium of Byzantine Studies, University of Birmingham, 1975. Birmingham: University of Birmingham.

Cormack, Robin (1985) *Writing in Gold – Byzantine Society and its Icons*. London: George Philip.

Cormack, Robin (1997) *Painting the Soul – Icons, Death Masks and Shrouds*. London: Reaktion Books Ltd.

Kazhdan, Alexander (Editor-in-Chief) (1991) *The Oxford Dictionary of Byzantium* (three volumes). New York and Oxford: Oxford University Press.

Kitzinger, Ernst (1988) 'Reflections on the Feast Cycle in Byzantine Art.' *Cahiers Archeologiques*, 36, pp. 51–73.

Lossky, Vladimir (1957) *The Mystical Theology of the Eastern Church*. London: James Clark & Co. Ltd.

Ouspensky, Leonid and Lossky, Vladimir (1982) *The Meaning of Icons*. New York: St Vladimir's Seminary Press.

Ouspensky, Leonid (1978 and 1992) *Theology of the Icon* (two volumes). New York: St Vladimir's Seminary Press.

Sendler, Egon, SJ (1988) *The Icon – Image of the Invisible*. California: Oakwood Publications.

Stuart, John (1975) *Ikons*. London: Faber and Faber.

Talley, Thomas J. (1986) *The Origins of the Liturgical Year*. New York: Pueblo Publishing Company Inc.

Ware, Timothy (1963) *The Orthodox Church*. Penguin.

Weitzmann, Kurt (1978) *The Icon – Holy Images, Sixth to Fourteenth Century*. London: Chatto & Windus.

Weitzmann, Kart *et al.* (1982) *The Icon*. London: Bracken Books.

Wybrew, Hugh (1989) *The Orthodox Liturgy*. London: SPCK.

The Festal Menaion (1969), translated from the original Greek by Mother Mary and Archimandrite Kallistos Ware. London: Faber and Faber.

The Lenten Triodion (1978), translated from the original Greek by Mother Mary and Archimandrite Kallistos Ware. London: Faber and Faber.

Glossary

The AKATHISTOS HYMN. An anonymous Kontakion in honour of the Mother of God during the singing of which the congregation stands (the title *Akathistos* means, literally, non-seated). The hymn was probably composed in the sixth century, and the pro-oimion or initial verse, referring to the lifting of the siege of Constantinople in 626, added in the seventh century.

The First COUNCIL OF NICAEA. The Council of the Church convened in 325 by the Emperor Constantine to resolve the conflict within the Church known as the Arian controversy. The Council, among other matters, condemned the teaching of Arius and affirmed the Incarnate Logos to be consubstantial with the Father. The Emperor's desire to see religious and political unity within the Empire was not fully realized, as the Arian controversy continued to be a problem in the East until the Council of Constantinople in 381; after that date Arianism still remained strong in the West.

HESYCHASM, HESYCHAST. From the Greek *hesychia*, stillness, *hesychasm* refers to an Orthodox tradition of prayer which is exemplified in the writings gathered together in *The Philokalia*; *hesychast*, as an adjective, describes this tradition, and as a noun refers to someone who practises this spiritual discipline. Stillness, attentiveness, guarding the heart, and an attitude of listening to God are used to gather up the whole of a person's life in response to God.

HODEGITRIA. The type of icon of the Mother of God in which Christ is seated on his Mother's left arm, while her right hand points towards Christ; she is 'the one who points the way'. Christ is shown not as an infant but as the pre-eternal God who has taken our humanity and come into the world for our salvation. He holds a scroll in his left hand and raises his right hand in blessing. Christ looks straight out of the icon at the beholder, as does the Mother of God in most examples; she is also shown with an inward contemplative gaze. The original Hodegitria icon was believed to have been painted by St Luke, and was kept from the twelfth to the fifteenth century in the Hodegon Monastery in Constantinople.

ICONOCLASM, ICONOCLAST CONTROVERSY. From 726 to 843 the Byzantine Empire was deeply divided over the question of the making and veneration of icons; during the period there was a respite between 787 and 815. The Seventh Ecumenical Council in 787 defined the theology of the icon and posited for it an essential role in the life of the Church; these formulations were re-affirmed when the conflict was brought to a close in 843. Those who sought to destroy the icons are known as *iconoclasts*, those who defended them are known as *iconodules* or *iconophiles*. The movement of iconoclasm had political as well as theological aspects.

ICONOSTASIS. The screen which marks the boundary between the nave and the sanctuary in an Orthodox church. It developed from the more modest templon or chancel screen that had become common by the fifth century; icons were placed within the frame of the screen, and gradually the whole screen became an icon-filled frame with doors which allow passage between the sanctuary and the nave for the priests and other liturgical ministers. The most elaborate developments took place in Russia, where some examples reach from the ground almost up to the vaults of the church.

In the centre are the Royal Doors, bearing depictions of the Annunciation and the four Evangelists, or St Basil and St John Chrysostom, traditionally authors of the two forms of the Divine Liturgy; above the doors there is often an icon of the Last Supper, and on either side large icons of Christ and the Mother of God, followed by Archangels, sometimes Deacons, and an icon of the titular saint or festival of the particular church. The next row above is the Deesis tier, with saints and archangels turned in intercession towards a central icon of Christ Pantocrator. Above this range comes the Church Feasts tier, and above that may be a row of Prophets centred on an icon of the Mother of God of the Sign. The tallest screens may culminate in a row of Old Testament Patriarchs. In descending sequence the onlooker views the history of salvation, through the Patriarchs, the Prophets, the Incarnation to the life of the Church and the Communion of Saints.

Non-Orthodox may regard the iconostasis as a barrier. For the Orthodox it presents a powerful visual statement of the unity of the Church in heaven and on earth, and the unity of past, present and future within the purposes of God.

INTELLECT. In the spiritual terminology of Orthodoxy, the Greek word *nous*, translated as 'intellect', does not refer to the ability to reason and engage in what is commonly called intellectual activity, but to the faculty of the soul which, when purified, enables us to know God. It is sometimes referred to as 'the eye of the heart'.

KENOSIS. In Philippians 2:7 St Paul quotes a Christological hymn which says that Christ 'emptied himself' in taking the form of a servant, being born in human likeness and in humility accepting death on the Cross. The imagery of this text recurs in many Orthodox hymns, expressing the condescension of the Son of God in taking our humanity and enduring death in order to gain our salvation. Theories and theologies of kenosis face problems when the imagery of this hymn is taken literally, for they imply a change in the eternal God; and if Christ literally emptied himself of his divinity there could be no union of divinity and humanity in the person of Christ. Kenosis needs to be interpreted as the humility of God in elevating humanity to himself. Christ's humility changes us, not God.

KONTAKION. Originally a chanted sermon in verse, in which each stanza ends with the same refrain; it was a common feature of Mattins in Byzantine worship from the fifth to the seventh centuries, but was gradually replaced by other forms in the eighth century. Among the present liturgical texts the Kontakion still forms part of Mattins as a single stanza from a much longer work, and provides a helpful summary of the significance of the Feast.

The PEACE OF THE CHURCH: the major change in the place of the Church within the Roman Empire after the granting of religious freedom and toleration of the Church early in the fourth century. The key date has generally been seen as 313 with the so-called Edict of Milan, but toleration had been granted by edicts in 306 and 311. These early years of the fourth century mark a major shift from circumstances where the Church was liable to face opposition and persecution to a state of affairs where the Church acquired considerable power within the Byzantine Empire. The change had a marked effect on church building, on the way in which Baptism was administered, and on the development of penitential discipline. The monastic movement became influential as the fourth century developed and the era of the martyrs seemed to draw to a close. It is worth noting that Pope Sylvester I (314–335) was the first Bishop of Rome not to die a martyr's death.

THEOPHANY. This term is used to describe a manifestation of God to man. Examples in the Old Testament include the appearance of God to Moses at the Burning Bush and to Elijah on Mount Horeb. In the Orthodox tradition the Feast of the Baptism of Christ is known as *The Theophany*; the Transfiguration of Christ and the Feast of Pentecost are also celebrated as theophanies; in the events commemorated at these three Feasts there is a manifestation of the Holy Trinity.

THEOSIS or *deification* indicates the goal of human life as union with God. The distinction between the Creator and his creature remains, but by participation in the energies of God man can be brought to union with him, even though the essence of God remains hidden and unknowable. The Incarnation opens up the possibility for this goal to be fulfilled: 'In his unbounded love, God became what we are, that he might make us what he is' (St Irenaeus). We are baptized into Christ, and in Christ we share in the union that has been established through the Incarnation. Theosis implies the fulfilment of the goal for which we were created, and for which the Incarnation took place: that the human person be brought to a union of love with the God who is the source of our existence (cf 2 Peter 1:3–4).

THEOTOKOS. A title used to refer to the Virgin Mary as, literally, *God-bearing*, or Mother of God. The title is first found in the third century; it was used by St Athanasius in his opposition to Arianism, and by St Gregory Nazianzen to defend the truth of the Incarnation: 'If anyone does not confess that the Virgin Mary is Theotokos, he is found to be far from God.' The appropriateness of the title was formally recognized at the Council of Ephesus in 431, and it is used frequently in Orthodox liturgical texts.

TROPARION. The earliest and basic form of hymn in the Byzantine tradition; a short prayer sung between the verses of a psalm. The Troparion of a Feast sums up the significance of the celebration, and is sung three times at the end of Vespers and at the beginning of Mattins, once at the end of Mattins; it is sung at the Divine Liturgy, Great Compline, and at all the Hours.

TYPE, TYPOLOGY. New Testament writers saw events of the past as *patterns* of God's activity and revelation; such events foreshadowed a greater revelation that came later in time. Thus, the exodus of the Israelites from slavery in Egypt under the leadership of Moses was seen to prefigure the deliverance of the new people of God from the slavery of sin through Christ. The past event is described as the *type*, and this kind of theological thinking is termed *typology*. Many details of the Old Testament have been related to the Christian dispensation, each throwing light upon the other, and the method can be seen in many of the texts cited in this book.

Where to See Icons

In Orthodox Churches throughout the world one can expect to see icons in their original settings. Many icons of historic importance are now in museums and art galleries, but ancient icons can still be seen in the churches and monasteries for which they were intended. The following list may be of assistance to readers who want to pursue their interest further.

In the British Isles
London: The British Museum has a small collection.
Blackburn: a small collection in Museum and Art Gallery.
Brighton: Art Gallery and Museum.
Dublin: The Lane Collection in The National Gallery.

Icons can also be seen in London at Christie's and Sotheby's when auctions are being prepared. The premises of icon dealers in London are frequently worth visiting.

Greece and the Greek Islands
The Benaki Museum and the Byzantine Museum in Athens.
The Monasteries of Mount Athos.
The Monasteries of the Meteora.
The Churches in Kastoria and Thessalonika.
Local Ecclesiastical and Municipal Museums.

Cyprus
The Icon Museum in Nicosia, and churches throughout the island.

Egypt
St Katherine's Monastery in Sinai.

Italy
Rome: early Christian churches.
Venice: the Museum next to the Orthodox Church of San Giorgio dei Greci.

The Former Yugoslav Republic of Macedonia
Museum collections in Skopje and Ohrid.

Turkey
The Ecumenical Patriarchate and other churches in Istanbul.
The Aya Sofia Museum in Istanbul.

Russia
Moscow: The Tretyakov Gallery and the Andronikov Monastery; the Kremlin churches.
St Petersburg: The Russian Museum.
Churches and museums in Novgorod, Pskov, Vladimir-Suzdal, Kiev, etc.

Index